The Springs

By

Bruce E. Norris

Published By Hemingway Publishers
Cover Design By Hemingway Publishers
Isbn: Printed In The United States

Dedicated to the real Captain Virgil and Jeanne, Chuck, Bill and Ian. All of whom will live forever in the adventures between these pages.

Table of content

1

The campfire crackled, and the glowing ambers drifted forebodingly into the night like fireflies. Although it was mid-August and the heat was virtually unbearable, the six campers laughed and joked as they drank an endless supply of beer and celebrated what was deemed the last weekend of catching up before the girls returned to their busy lives.

Angie Carr, Amanda Tipper and Gina Martin grew up together in the same neighborhood and had known each other since kindergarten. It was not planned, but when they reached high school, life took over, and they headed down separate paths. It was Angie who called out of the blue and thought it would be fun to get together and camp near Clearview State Park.

While Angie still lived in South Florida with her boyfriend Ned, Amanda moved out to California and found a boyfriend. Within the year, he asked for her hand in marriage. Gina lived the life of a vagabond, roaming around the country to her heart's content. If not for her sister being able to contact her, Angie and Amanda may have never seen her again.

After a full day of tubing down the Springs, they were lounging by the fire, dressed in long pants, jeans and long-sleeved t-shirts to help keep the mosquitos from biting, reminiscing over the events of the day and making plans for the following days.

"Tomorrow, we should go snorkeling with the guys. The water in the Springs is so clear that you don't need a mask," Amanda said.

Angie looked at her and laughed, "Sure you do. It's nice and clear, but you still need a mask."

"I don't. I'm like a mermaid," replied Gina, sipping a beer.

Angie looked at her with raised eyebrows, "Ok then."

"When this little camping trip is over, I'm going back home to tell my parents that I'm going to Haiti for a year or so to help out," Gina stated, changing the subject, lounging in a beach chair.

Angie and Amanda looked at each other and asked, "Who are you helping out?"

"Oh, you know. This and that. I always hear there's something going on down there," she replied nonchalantly.

"Good for you," Amanda said, rolling her eyes.

"Yeah, let me know what your dad says about that," Angie snickered, lounging on the ground with her head propped on a rock.

She turned her head slightly to see the guys stirring and gathering their fishing poles.

"Come on ladies, we're going across the road and sneak into the park," said Ned, stuffing beer into his backpack. "Jay and I are going to see what we can catch fishing tonight."

Ned Fisher and Angie had been dating for nearly five years, and he felt somewhat responsible for taking her away from her friends, although Angie insisted it wasn't true. Even so, he felt the urge to invite his friend along so they could fish while the girls did their thing.

His buddy Jay Ward thought differently at first but later figured it wouldn't hurt to come along so Ned wouldn't be bored out of his mind. He knew that Ned wasn't much for tubing with the ladies all day, so he figured that while they went tubing, he and Ned could find a secluded spot and do some serious fishing.

Jay also planned to take his neighbor along. Tommy Mills lived in the same apartment complex as him and considered himself a ladies' man, reflecting his good looks and boyish charm. Jay thought it would be the perfect distraction so he and Ned could fish in peace.

"Go for it. We're not getting caught over there," replied Angie.

"Yeah, you know what will happen if we get caught breaking into Clearview Springs at this hour?" Gina jeered.

"No."

"Well, neither do we, but it can't be good," she jeered.

4

"Fine, have it your way, we'll be back in a while, so keep the fire burning and fingers crossed that we catch something good," Ned said, trotting off with his fishing gear. Jay and a drunken Tommy followed behind, laughing about something Tommy said about the girls that they couldn't hear.

"He's such a goofball," Amanda snickered.

"He's my little goofball," Angie smiled, grabbing a log and throwing it on the fire.

"Little? There's nothing little about that guy," Gina added.

"What is he, about six-five?"

"Yup," Angie smiled.

"Let's follow them after they cross the road," Amanda suggested, looking over her shoulder and watching them trot away. She giggled out loud when Tommy fell, splattering the contents of his beer can on the road.

Clearview Springs State Park is located in Northern Florida. The park sits on ,000 acres of marshlands with a canopy of shaded hammocks throughout. The Ichetucknee River flows through it for several miles before meeting with the Santa Fe River. Like many other rivers in Northern Florida, Ichetucknee River is fed by natural Springs.

The year-round temperature of the Springs is a cool seventy-two degrees, making it a popular destination for the locals and tourists to escape from the heat.

Tubing and snorkeling are the most popular activities besides swimming around the crystal-clear water, and experienced divers can also explore the caves if they've got the nerve.

Ned, Jay and Tommy crossed the road and cautiously climbed the six-foot chain link fence on the outskirts of the park. Jay cursed as the tip of his fishing pole slid through a hole in the fence when Tommy bumped it with his knee, "Damn it! Almost broke the bait caster."

"Wait until I'm over, and you can toss me the gear," replied Ned, placing a foot halfway up the fence before leaping over.

Jay tossed his gear over to Ned and climbed over while Tommy looked confused.

"Come on, Tommy, just climb over," said Ned.

"Hmm, I don't know. Maybe I think I should go back to the camp and make sure the ladies are safe. I'm not really into climbing fences when I've been drinking," he slurred.

"Great idea, see ya," Ned and Jay said in unison, turning to walk away.

"Hold on, wait a second. I change my mind."

Ned and Jay stopped and turned to see him scaling the fence. He looked like the fat guy in the boot camp movies, only he was slim and drunk.

"Come on, buddy, you can do it," Jay pretended to care.

"I believe in you. You got this," Ned laughed.

He finally crossed a leg over the top of the fence and sat in discomfort, riding the fence pole. The look on his face caused Ned and Jay to burst out laughing before they quickly recovered and looked around, somehow neglecting that they should be quiet since they were breaking into a closed park.

"Ok, ol' pal, just flip the other leg over and come on down," Jay tried to say without a snicker.

Tommy took a deep breath, flipped his other leg over the fence, snagged the crotch area of his shorts and crashed down the fence, all in one swift motion.

Ned and Jay burst out laughing as Tommy stood with a dumbfounded expression and a crotchless pair of shorts.

"Jeez, Tommy, I remember the first time I climbed a fence," Ned said, resuming his walk down the path.

"What the fu...I have to go back and change my pants," he snapped.

"Parks closed. Nobody's going to see your undies," Jay replied, shaking his head and following Ned.

Angie, Amanda and Gina were laughing as they watched Tommy blunder over the fence. They quietly followed across the road when the guys disappeared in the darkness. They walked around the fenced area, hoping for an opening or area to crawl under before deciding to climb over.

"Oh man, this is creepy," Amanda said, "I hope we don't get lost.

"How can we? Just follow the sound of the drunks," Angie replied.

"Hey, we're not all drunks, ya know," said Gina, trying to finish off the warm Corona that she'd been sucking on since the sun went down.

Angie and Amanda did all they could not to break out in laughter at the thought of their friend thinking she was in the same league as Tommy.

"Just don't fall over the fence like Tommy did," Angie said.

"Hope not, I'm not wearing underwear."

"TMI Gina, TMI," replied Amanda, rolling her eyes.

Angie and Amanda tended to stay away from the drinking part of parties because they were athletes. Angie was a softball pitcher on a travel team, and Amanda was shooting for a spot on the women's Olympic swim team. To the best of their knowledge, they've never seen Gina sip a beer, let alone hold her own bottle.

They stopped when they spotted Tommy sitting near the water of what was called the Headspring. The water was smooth and pristine as the moonlight reflected off the surface. They spotted Ned and Jay searching the area with their little cell phone flashlights for what turned out to be a makeshift selfie stick.

"Oh my, oh my, now I've seen it all," Angie cracked, putting her hands over her mouth to keep from laughing.

"Let's jump out and surprise them just before they take the picture," Amanda wheezed, trying to keep herself together.

They watched as Jay untied a shoestring and wrapped the phone to the end of the stick. When finished, they walked into the water until they were knee-deep, then turned and posed together with the river and moon behind them and smiled for the picture.

"Ok, let's do this," Gina whispered, preparing to burst out of the foliage and scare the group before the picture was taken. They got down on their haunches as Angie counted, "One...Two...

Before she got to the count of three, they were startled by the sight of what looked like a giant trunk of an oak tree and, over thirty-foot-long, cruising past Ned and Jay. Only the back portion swayed left and right as if it were... swimming.

They stood straight up and screamed for their friends to get away from the water, "Get out of there! There's something huge swimming behind you!" they screeched.

Jay panicked and unwittingly dropped the phone in the water as he sprinted away.

Angie and Amanda sprang from their spot and ran into the shallows to pull Ned out of the water while he stood there, looking behind and trying to see what they were talking about. They quickly grabbed him by the arms and dragged him out, keeping watch for whatever it was that swam past.

"I...I think there's a huge alligator swimming out there!" Angie shouted, her heart pounding like a hammer in her chest.

"Good one, you scared the shit out of Jay!" he replied, trying to catch his breath. "Paybacks are a bitch."

"What the hell?" Jay finally said, catching his breath. "I dropped my damn phone."

"Come here and look for yourselves," Angie said, walking back to the water's edge and pointing at the large wake moving upriver.

Everybody stopped talking and merged closer to the water, where they witnessed the small ripple of the wake lap at their feet.

"It was big, whatever it was," said Ned, walking ankle-deep in the water, splashing his feet around and hoping it would come back.

"I'm going back to the camp," Gina announced, "This is too much. Oh, I changed my mind. I'm not going snorkeling tomorrow."

They watched as she helped herself off the sand and stumbled off through the sandy trail.

"I think we should all go back," replied Amanda, taking a final look at the water. It was eerily calm; the reflection of the moon showed a bluish flicker of light across the Springs that seemed to glow in the darkness.

"Go on ahead. I'll catch up in a minute," Tommy said, walking down the shoreline and disappearing behind a tree.

"Are you nuts! Let's get out of here," replied Angie, taking Ned by the hand and walking him away from the water.

"Go on, I'll be there in a minute," Tommy countered from behind the tree.

"Well, hurry up, they think there's something in the water."

"If it comes up near me, I'll pee on it!" he hissed, becoming irritated.

Ned didn't say another word. If Tommy wanted to risk it and prove how brave he was to stay behind, let him. He took a couple of steps back and checked the water one last time before turning to catch up with Jay to collect the fishing gear. When they arrived at the fence, Angie and Amanda were helping Gina as she climbed.

"Everybody, get down!" Ned blurted from behind. Gina was straddling the top of the fence when a police car cruised past the road between the park and the campground. Amanda was on the verge of panicking as she stooped behind some foliage while Angie and Ned hit the ground and lay flat. Jay was caught off-guard and elected to freeze where he stood. They thought they were in the clear until the police car's break lights came on, and it stopped and pulled off the road. Gina scurried to the ground outside of the park as the car backed up.

Before she could get up and blatantly try to make a getaway to the campground, a spotlight clicked on and blinded her, "Stop right where you are, young lady!" the officer's voice boomed over a loudspeaker.

Gina froze and watched as the officer exited the car and walked over with a hand resting on his holstered gun, scanning the area with a flashlight.

"And what are we doing out here tonight?" he questioned.

He was no idiot; the police officer kept scanning the area as he relaxed to some extent when he noticed she had been drinking. "Well, I know pretty darn well that drunken ladies don't stroll around in the middle of the night trying to break into the park by themselves. So...I'm only going to say this once...Everybody out with your hands where I can see them, or I'm going to haul your friend off to jail!" he shouted into the darkness.

In the blink of an eye, Angie, Ned, Jay and Amanda rose from the damp ground inside the park and rested their hands on the fence. The officer smirked and waved Gina over to join them as he started walking in their direction.

"Well, well, well, what have we here?"

Ned was about to reply, but the officer held out his hand, "Save it, son. I was a kid once. I don't want to hear your stories. I'll ask the questions, and you just give me a simple answer," he ordered, taking a small pocket notepad out of his shirt pocket.

"Where are you kids staying tonight?"

Angie had never been in trouble her entire life, and the anxiety made her quiver, "We are camping across the street, sir."

"Why did you break into the park? You kids can be in serious trouble."

"We just wanted to get a group picture by the Headspring with the moon shining in the water behind us," Gina smiled, looking like she didn't have a care in the world.

The officer wrote down their names and information before closing his notepad and giving them all a stern look, "Like I said, I was a kid once and understand you kids had a few beers. I'm going to suggest that you all get back to your camp and stay there for the rest of the night. If I see any of you out here again tonight, I will arrest all of you. Are we clear?"

"Yes sir," they replied like a drunken choir. Angie and Amanda easily hopped over the fence as Ned followed, wandering where Tommy was. Jay rested against the fence for an extra minute as his legs refused to move.

"Thank you, ossifer," Gina said, waving goodbye as she crossed the street.

"Ossifer? It's officer...police o-f-f-i-c-er," Angie whispered.

The police officer watched with amusement as they walked back to their campground. He smiled and shook his head as he climbed into his patrol car and drove away, remembering back to when he and his high school buddies did the exact same thing.

The campfire was out, but the ambers were still glowing as Ned placed two more logs on the ashes and squirted lighter fluid over them. The ladies scrambled to their tents, gathering their toiletries and headed off to take hot showers.

Ned and Jay retrieved sodas from the cooler and stood watching the area across the street where Tommy should have returned twenty minutes ago.

Angie was the first to return and took a soda from the cooler before sitting next to Ned and Jay. "We sure got lucky," she said, plopping down beside the rising flames and drying her wet hair with a towel.

"Yeah, that cop could have really ruined our weekend."

"It's your fault, you know," she teased.

"What? I think Jay is the one who suggested it."

"Oh no, it was you that brought it up. Jay just carried it out," she smirked, poking Jay on the shoulder with her elbow. "Oh, and let's not forget about your drunken friend Tommy," she continued.

"Not my friend, Jay's friend."

"Oh, I wouldn't go that far. I'd say he is an acquaintance. That's what he is," Jay replied, switching to a beer after gulping the soda.

"So, where is the drunken acquaintance? Passed out in the tent?

"Hell, if I know, he didn't come back yet."

Amanda and Gina returned from the showers and noticed the concerned look on their friend's faces, "What's going on? Gina asked.

"Tommy didn't come back yet," replied Angie.

"Should we look for him?" said Amanda, drying her short hair.

"I didn't see him come out of the park," replied Ned, beginning to feel uneasy.

"I thought he was behind us after that cop busted us," said Gina, scratching her head and looking around the campground.

"Did you see him?

"Nope."

"Did anybody see him hop over the fence?" Angie questioned.

"I thought he was with you," said Gina, pointing her long, skinny finger toward Jay.

"What if he got attacked by the huge alligator?" Amanda asked.

They gave Tommy another ten minutes to return before they decided they would set out looking for him, retracing their steps across the road.

"Do you think something happened to him?" Gina nervously asked.

"I'll let you know," Ned replied, leaping onto the fence and climbing over.

"Whoa, wait a second. If that cop comes back and finds us in that park again, he'll arrest us," Amanda said, looking down the road nervously.

"You guys go back and search around the campground. Maybe he got sick and didn't want anybody to see him. I'll be back in a few minutes," Ned replied, poking his lips through the fence to give Angie a peck goodbye.

"Wait for me," said Angie, kicking off her flip-flops as she prepared to climb over the fence. "Two eyes are better than one."

Ned helped her as she slid down the fence and waited for Amanda to toss over her flip-flops.

"You guys check the bathrooms again, and we'll be right back."

Amanda rolled her eyes and slowly shook her head as she watched the two scurry off toward the Springs. When they were gone, she hissed something under her breath and turned to head back to the camp.

"What was that?"

"Nothing, Gina. I just know that police officer is going to show up again."

16

"You think he'll bust us twice?"

"He didn't bust us. Why don't you two head toward the pool area while I check out the walking trail," Jay suggested.

"You can look for him. I'm going to get some sleep," Gina yawned. "I'm sure he's alright. When we drink too much, the only way we'll make it the next day is to get some sleep."

"Jeez! What is wrong with you?" Amanda blurted, disappointment in her tone.

"I've been drinking beer all day, I got busted for breaking out of a park at night, and Tommy is probably too embarrassed to come back to camp with his crotch hanging out. Trust me, he'll be here when we wake up in the morning," she casually replied, walking back to the camp.

"Hope you're right."

2

Angie and Ned stumbled across roots and overgrowth as they followed the path with their cellphone flashlights and finally made their way back to the area where Jay tried to take the picture.

They scanned the crystal-clear water prudently for anything out of the ordinary and found nothing. They quietly moved on to the tree where Tommy was last seen and still found no trace of their friend.

Angie was suddenly startled when her bare feet felt the wet sand between the spring and the tree.

"Hey! The ground's wet!"

"Huh?"

"Come here and feel this...the ground's wet!" she replied, squatting down and investigating the ground around her with the flashlight beam.

Ned knelt beside her and felt around; the hair stood on the back of their necks as they looked at each other. Angie stood and surveyed the surroundings, "Look at the ground! Look how it dips...It looks like something real heavy came ashore...something big and heavy to make this indent!"

"Yeah, but it's too big to be an animal. It looks about eight-feet wide...I think somebody landed a boat here. They probably pulled up on shore, got something and, pushed the boat back in the water and continued up stream.

"What about that big wake we saw?"

"They were probably rowing...or maybe they have an electric motor. They make those things pretty quiet these days."

"So, where's Tommy? It sure didn't look like a boat to me."

"Wish I knew. You know how he knows everybody. Maybe he knows the people in the boat, and they decided to find a fishing spot."

They stood with their hands on their hips and a sigh of relief as they felt they had come to a respectable conclusion. Ned thought it strange that Tommy wouldn't tell them, but on second thought, he'd probably do the same thing if he wasn't camping with his girlfriend. They casually stepped closer to the water, their toes dipping in the cool Springs as they searched for the boat.

The crisp, clear air and the sparkle of the moon on the water were all he needed to sidle closer to Angie as he slid his hand around her waist, "Did you really think you saw a big ass gator?"

"Well, its dark, but I sure thought I saw a huge tail swimming behind that thing. But it would have to really be a big gator...I'm talking over twenty-foot."

Ned smiled and squeezed her hand, "I think it was a boat."

19

They walked back through the thicket and followed the footpath to the surrounding fence, reaffirming their story that Tommy had gone for a boat ride with other friends he met up with. Although Angie didn't know Tommy all that well, Ned admitted that it was like him to always run into people he knew in the oddest places.

When they got back to the camp, Amanda was sitting by herself around the campfire.

"Did you guys find him?"

"There's no sign of him. But we did find what looks like a boat landing on shore. We figure he knows the people and went fishing," Angie stated, looking around for Gina.

"If it was a boat, it sure was pretty low in the water, though," Angie continued, suddenly having second thoughts.

"What do you mean?" she asked, eating a well-cooked marshmallow.

"Because what I saw looked more like a submarine."

"Whew! Imaginations sure run wild in the dark," Amanda smiled.

Angie shot her a contentious look and sat by the fire.

"What do you think you saw?"

Amanda ignored the question and spoke, "What now? Are we just going to wait around for him?"

"Forget about him. Let him cruise around with his other friends. He'll be back in the morning," said Ned, popping open a cold IPA beer. Angie noticed the first signs of him sulking, probably because he got left behind while Tommy went fishing.

"By the way, where's Gina?"

"Sleeping," replied Amanda.

"Sleeping? How can she sleep when one of us is missing."

"Easy for her. She doesn't know him."

Minutes later, Jay returned and let them know he searched the entire campground and didn't find Tommy. He sat and joined them by the fire as they tried to keep their minds off Tommy by playing charades. Nobody was willing to admit it, but they were worried. Angie watched as each of them craned their neck every now and then, expecting to see Tommy walking back. At a little past two-thirty, they crawled off to sleep.

The sun rose with little fanfare as a slight drizzle cascaded down onto the somnolent campground. The sound of a few early morning birds bit into the sultry air as if they were questioning if it were time to wake up or not.

Angie lifted an eyelid, not feeling that it was time to rise, but her eyes opened to the sound of the chirping birds and the water dripping on her forehead. She actually woke up a couple of hours earlier and heard the rain. Her mistake was that she didn't believe what she thought was a myth and pressed a finger into the tent, causing it to leak.

As she lay on her sleeping bag yawning and preparing to hike toward the bathrooms, she suddenly remembered that Tommy was missing in action when they went off to sleep.

She looked over to Gina, who was still sound asleep with a smile on her face no less, then turned to Amanda and nearly peed her pants.

"What the heck are you doing?" she asked feebly.

Amanda was already dressed in a one-piece bathing suit with shorts, sitting cross-legged on her sleeping bag, staring at Angie.

"Been up for an hour watching the rain drip on you. I peeked outside and it looks like it's going to be a rainy day," she replied, amused that it took Angie so long to wake up with water dripping on her forehead.

"Do you know if Tommy has returned yet?"

"I don't have a clue."

Angie opened her sleeping bag and quickly got dressed in shorts and a bikini top while Amanda unzipped the tent opening and crawled out. A minute later, Angie joined her for a quick stop at the restrooms.

Gina, Jay and Ned wore bathing suits with raincoats and were sitting at the picnic table under a screen tent when they returned, and there was no need to ask about Tommy as the disquieted look on their faces answered Angie's question without inquiring.

"He didn't come back yet," Jay said, stretching and wiping sleep out of his eyes.

"What should we do? Want to split up and try to find him?" Angie queried.

"I already looked," replied Ned, sitting on top of the table with his head down in his hands.

"Maybe we should go back to the Springs again and get a better look at that indentation in the sand that we saw last night," said Angie.

"Why should we do that," Gina protested.

Angie and Ned gave her a dour look, and he replied, "It was dark, and we could barely see the hands in front of our faces. Let's check it again since it's daylight."

Clearview Springs State Park opened daily at eight o'clock, and as they crossed the road with ten minutes to spare, there was already a line of people in cars with inner tubes and kayaks waiting to get in. The line for walk-ins was relatively short, and within minutes, they paid their two-dollar fee and strolled in.

"I think we should have called the police," Amanda said, breaking the quiet walk toward the headspring.

"He would have busted us again," replied Gina.

"We weren't busted!" all three shot back.

"Tommy will probably be sleeping like a baby when we return. He can sleep all day in this balmy weather," Jay suddenly said, sensing Angie and Amanda's eyes piercing through him like laser beams. "That's what he does," he continued. "When he fishes all night, he sleeps all day."

They reached the headspring and stood by the water's edge, looking around. Even though it was a grey morning and the light rain looked like it would continue for hours, the water was crystal clear and looked inviting. Visitors began jumping in and splashing around as the campers followed the path and walked over to the area with the indentation in the sand.

They surveyed the surroundings like detectives while Gina, believing they were wasting their time, leaned on the tree where they had last seen Tommy. As she was about to tell her friends how they reminded her of Scooby-Doo and the meddling kids looking for a mystery, a sharp object embedded in the tree scratched her elbow.

With a pained look on her face, she looked at the tree and bent lower to get a better look, "Uh…guys, come here and check this out."

Without a word, they rushed over and looked closely at the object sticking out of the tree where Gina was pointing.

"Is that what I think it is?" Angie asked with a concerned look.

"It looks like a tooth...a broken piece of a tooth," Ned replied, retrieving a pocketknife from his pocket and trying to dig it out.

They stood staring at the tree as Ned pried it out, each one thinking the same thing. How big was the conical tooth if the broken piece in Ned's hand was well over two inches long?

Finally, Amanda spoke, "We should tell the park rangers or somebody."

Stacy and her husband, Rich Thomas, were standing knee-deep in water at a more secluded area of the park called Anahita's Landing. After months of pleading with him to come to the Springs and enjoy the great outdoors, she finally got him off the couch.

The cool, refreshing water beckoned them after their leisure walk through the wooded path along the bank of the Springs. With their paddle boards in tow, they were happy to see they were probably the first visitors of the day to launch from this site.

"What luck! I think we're the first ones here today," Stacy said eagerly. "The place is ours. The time we reach the end, it should be about noon."

"Fantastic, lunch 'o clock."

"We just finished breakfast, and you're already thinking about lunch?" Stacy replied, applying suntan lotion on her arms and legs.

"It's not like we're going to reach the end soon. It should take at least a couple hours. Figure in the bugs and mosquito bites, and that should wrap up your outdoor fun for the month."

Stacy smiled and rolled her eyes as she hopped onto the board and stood up, her bright red one-piece bathing suit reflected off the water like a beacon.Rich adjusted his baggy dockers, rolled the long pants up to his calves, and followed, but only made it to his knees before splashing face down on the other side of the board and into the cold water. His long-sleeved shirt slid over his beer belly and covered his head, making him gasp for air.

The laughter seemed to echo through the park as Stacy burst. The look on Rich's face when he surfaced from the cold water was priceless.

"Maybe we should have practiced a little before we came here," she laughed, standing on her board like a pro.

"I just slipped," he retorted, diligently climbing back on his inflatable board.

It took a couple of minutes for them to get familiarized with their new boards before Stacy paddled off with Rich, trying hard to keep his balance and bringing up the rear. As they cruised downstream, the implausible clear water was hypnotizing, while a creepy mist seemed to hover on top. Stacy couldn't keep the smile off her face while she pointed out the purple and yellow flowers just off the banks in the glistening wet woods.

At one point, Rich got down on his knees and tried to grab the curious brim that swam under his board. Playfully running his hand around the fish as they gracefully dodged his touch, he marveled at how beautiful the crystal-clear water was and how lucky he was to be there. Perhaps this was a good idea after all, he thought.

Suddenly, a large, dark object came into view. His heart sank, and he felt the blood drain from his head as he watched the massive anomaly drift in the opposite direction of the current... or was it crawling?

All at once, he jumped up and paddled through the marsh until he hit shore, "Stacy! Don't panic, but get to shore...quick!" he blurted fearfully.

"What's wrong?" she replied, her smile gone as she turned her head.

"There's something big down there! Hurry up!"

"Big baby," she said under her breath while turning her board toward the bank. She looked down and saw the outline of her board reflecting off the bottom and smiled.

Rich grabbed her arm when she was in reach and quickly pulled her up, losing traction with his left foot and sliding into the water. Stacy watched suspiciously as he turned and climbed out faster than she had ever seen him move.

"What the hell did you see?" she said as they stood safely on a sandy trail.

Rich took a minute to catch his breath and wipe the misty rain off his face before replying, "I don't know what it was…but it was big, real big. I know you won't believe me, but I'm sure it was a huge alligator."

"There are people in here all the time. Nobody's ever seen a real huge gator in these Springs?" she snickered as she relaxed and was pretty sure he saw the shadow of his board.

"It was huge, and I mean huge."

He crouched down and held his head in his hands as he tried to relax his breathing. Stacy didn't bother prodding him. Instead, she got down beside him and put an arm around his neck, "I know what you probably saw was the reflection of your board on the bottom."

Rich exhaled a deep breath and stood up. With hands on his hips, he turned to his wife and replied, "The bottom is about thirty feet in this spot. What I saw was not a reflection of my board because it was heading in the opposite direction, and I'm telling you, it's the size of about three of these paddle boards."

She looked at him as though he'd finally lost his mind. Looking him dead in the eye and wondering why he was making up such a story, she finally threw her hands in the air and replied, "Okay…Fine, I get it. You don't want to continue downriver. Let's get these boards out of the water and walk all the way back," she said, with an assiduous tone, walking closer to the water to retrieve her board.

"Stay away from the water. Leave the boards there!" he barked, grabbing her arm and pulling her back.

Stacy was beyond words. She gave him a dirty look as she pulled her arm away and walked up to the sandy path. Before she could recover and dig into a full-fledged argument, they both turned to see a group of eight to ten people splashing around the bend on inner tubes.

"Are you going to tell them to get out of the water as well?" she asked sarcastically.

Instead of answering, Stacy saw her husband break out in a sprint along the path as he headed toward the tubers, shouting for them to get out of the river. The tubers stopped splashing around and watched Rich with detached fascination. A couple of middle-aged women heeded his warning and pulled off to the side as the group shouted back obscenities and continued downriver.

Rich ran over to the women and explained what he saw. When they seemed reluctant to believe him, he whipped out his wallet and showed them his old policeman's union card, hoping they'd believe he wasn't some drunken maniac trying to stir trouble.

Stacy watched from a distance and figured whatever he showed them worked because they both scattered up to the path and shouted for their friends to get out.

As the tubers passed Stacy, they continued shouting vulgarities toward her and shouted to their two lady friends that they'd meet them at the end of their ride.

A few minutes later, when the river was once again quiet, Rich came walking over with the confused ladies, "Did you two really see a giant alligator? Is he really a cop?" one of them asked.

"Retired, he's a retired Hollywood Police officer," Stacy replied, beginning to take him a little more seriously now.

"Oh good, at first we thought he was some crackpot running around in these woods, trying to spoil our day," the other lady replied, sipping from a Bush beer bottle.

"Well, he might be a crackpot, but if he says he saw something scary down there, I'd believe him," Stacy replied, already not liking the two.

"Ok, dear, thanks for the warning. We'll just walk up a little and put our inner tubes in further downstream," the first woman said, with a back-woods accent.

"There are gators in these waters, but they leave people alone. I been comin' 'round here for years. Thanks for the warning, but the gators are more afraid of us than we are of them," said the other.

Stacy and Rich watched them walk away and couldn't believe their eyes as the one lady finished her beer bottle and threw it in the bushes before setting her tube back in the water and directing her large bottom into the inner tube.

"Well, super cop, I guess you did your good deed for the day," Stacy chided.

"They have no idea what I saw. It is definitely not a gator," he replied, pondering if he should run over and just pull them out of the water.

"I thought you said it was?" Stacy replied with an irritated tone.

"It looked like a gator, only bigger...much bigger."

"I know what you're thinking, you can't demand they get out, they will sue your ass. And don't forget that you're not a cop anymore," she reminded him as she poked a finger on his stomach.

They walked separately without a word as they headed back to the headspring. Stacy looked up at him every now and then, noticing he was deep in thought. Finally, after they stopped to watch a group of kayakers go by, Stacy broke the silence, "So...was it a gator? Of course, they've been known to swim here from time to time."

"Like I said, it looked like one…a big one."

"Should we tell a park ranger?"

He didn't reply. His mind was far away, and his thoughts were definitely not on his wife's questions. Suddenly, he stopped and faced her, "Remember that marine officer in Fort Lauderdale…His name is Randy Taylor?"

She stopped and thought for a moment before rolling her eyes and replying, "Don't even go there. Are you talking about that officer who hunted and killed a giant alligator a few years ago?"

"That's the one."

"Jeez, you've got some imagination," she gestured, letting go of his hand as she continued walking.

"It's not my imagination. What I saw swimming down there was huge," he retorted.

"Okay, fine. Look him up and give him a call. Just don't let me catch you hunting for a gator. Whatever you saw is no threat to anybody. There has never been any word about somebody getting bit in this park."

3

The massive reptile swam undetected up the Ichetucknee River. It was the last of three hybrid species that had escaped from a compound in the Everglades years ago and headed north. Within a couple of months after its escape, it found comfort nearly two hundred miles north in Myakka State Park.

It became aware that it was being hunted after the remains of a family were found in a secluded area of the park. The thirty-eight-foot monster avoided detection by staying hidden in the saw grass and only moving in the dark, quiet night.

The elusive reptile swam miles upriver and entered an isolated Creek, where it feasted on a young man fishing near the banks, causing yet another hunt for the immediate demise of a large creature.

Its newfound taste for humans was repulsive, as it learned their scent became overpoweringly appetizing the more fear it conveyed before being eaten.

Days later, the reptile swam through the Venice Jetty and out to open water, where it swam unobserved for miles further north until entering the Chassahowitzka National Wildlife Refuge.

In this area, the colossal reptile found a home for nearly two years without being detected. The Refuge sat on thirty-one-thousand acres of saltwater bays, estuaries and desolate marshes. It fed with a ferocious appetite on more than twenty different types of mammals, including the endangered West Indian Manatee.

When it appeared to be hunted again, the reptile reluctantly escaped and entered the mouth of the Suwannee River, where it eventually found its way to Clearview Springs.

After a quick lunch at the park's restaurant, Gina elected to go back to the camp and take a nap. Ned and Jay stayed in the park to look for Tommy or anything that would relate to his disappearance while Angie and Amanda sauntered into the park ranger's office to report him missing.

The morning gloom and misty rain gave way to the heat of the sun as it cleared the mist off the waters of the Springs. Clearview State Park was in full swing as kayakers, divers, and sunbathers cooled off in the clearing weather.

Two female rangers sat behind a counter by the door and greeted Angie and Amanda when they entered.

"Good afternoon, ladies. How can I help you," one said.

"Well, I think we'd like to report a missing person," Angie replied.

"Okay…male or female?"

"Male."

"Where and when was he last seen?"

Angie and Amanda looked at each other and decided just to come out and tell the truth…most of it. "We are camping in the campground across the street. There are six of us. Last night, after the park was closed, Tommy wanted to take a picture at the headspring with the moon shining on the water," Amanda explained, with a hint of uneasiness.

"Hmmm, all by himself, eh?" the ranger asked suspiciously, eyeing the girl through the top of her reading glasses.

"He never returned. We searched the campsite, and when the park opened this morning, we checked the area he was supposed to be at," Angie continued, ignoring the question.

"What's this fella's full name?"

"Tommy Mills."

The two rangers looked at each other before the one asking questions took a deep breath and exhaled, "It's very rare that people become missing in this park. Are you sure he didn't meet up with anybody else and just decided not to return to your campsite?"

"Well, when we went back to the spot he was in, we noticed an indentation in the sand where it looked like maybe a boat came ashore. We thought maybe he did find some people to hang out with…but we also found this stuck in the tree," Angela replied, pulling a napkin out of her pocket and revealing the content.

The two park rangers tipped their heads to look at the tooth in the napkin. It was broken near the root, and there was no doubt that the creature who lost it was large…very large. Their easy-going expression quickly switched to investigative mode as they took the girls more seriously and sat them down to get a full report.

Amanda was staring out of the front window, admiring a giant spider web on the frame, when a local police car drove up and stopped. She swallowed hard and smacked Angie's leg to get her attention when she saw the towering form of the same officer who had stopped them the previous night stepping out.

"Tommy wasn't the only one that snuck into the park last night," Angie suddenly blurted, knowing the police officer would rebuke their story of Tommy going solo.

"You don't say," replied the ranger, shaking her head with a slight smile.

The police officer walked inside the office and took off his hat, "My, my…hello ladies. Hope you're enjoying our beautiful park…during operational hours, of course."

Like the park rangers, he also took their story with a grain of salt until they showed him the tooth. He then proceeded to fill out a missing person's report and called for backup.

Within the hour, several police officers, along with park rangers, followed the two girls to where Tommy was last seen. As they looked for anything out of the ordinary, Ned appeared with a fishing pole.

"Are you with these two ladies?" a ranger inquired.

"Yes, he is," replied the officer who stopped them the night before, not forgetting the tall six-foot-five man he saw climbing the fence.

"I have something I want to show you," said Ned, pulling his cell phone out. "I took this picture about twenty yards over there," he pointed.

The officers passed the phone to one another as Ned watched the same astonished look on their faces.

"Is this a joke son?" the officer asked with a firm tone.

Ned looked him in the eye and fired back equally, "I wish it was."

The photo revealed the sandy imprint of a claw that looked like it could have belonged to an alligator, only about three times larger.

"Where did you take this picture?"

"Like I said, right over there," he pointed again. "About twenty yards from where Tommy was last seen," replied Ned, swallowing hard.

"It looks to be about the same size as these imprints on the sides of where I presume a boat landed," an officer looked down, pointing.

"They may be from oars, hard to tell since the high tide erased any detail," said another.

"Oars? You think those are from oars?" Ned questioned.

"It's hard to tell since the water messed up the imprint."

"I've never seen oars look like that," replied Ned, walking into the water until it reached his knees.

"I don't think you should go in the water," the police officer said, watching Ned searching for something.

"Are you going to chase everybody in the park out?" Ned replied hastily.

"Not right now," the police officer replied.

Ned stopped walking around in the knee-deep water and dropped down, reaching for something in the sand.

"Hey, you found it!" Angie smiled. "You found Jay's cellphone!"

"Yeah, but it's a goner," replied Ned, walking out with the dripping phone.

After the police and park rangers did a thorough search around the area and took Angie and Ned's statements, the campers were free to go and promised they would let the authorities know if Tommy returned while they camped for the next few days. A copy of the photo was sent to all the officers as they waited for the campers to leave so that they could plan the next step they would take to see what they were dealing with.

4

Sergeant Randy Taylor sat inside his new office located in Port Everglades, one of the busiest ports in Florida. The office was in a new sub-station that Randy had fought to open for the last couple of years since becoming Sergeant and team leader of SWAT's Waterbourne Entry Team [WET].

The undersized station sat beside a canal on the north end of the Port, only one-hundred yards from the inlet, where he and his team had easy access to get wherever needed with their patrol boats.

Although a good officer, it was a mystery how he made it up the ranks so fast. Close associates knew differently how it took little time to climb the ladder.

It was rumored but never confirmed how he and a group of men hunted and finally killed a monstrous reptile mutation that escaped confinement in the Everglades. After a fatal accident that took the lives of the mayor and his family, the new mayor, whose daughter had lost a leg to the mutant reptile, felt there was no better way to repay Taylor.

Before becoming Sergeant, Randy had spent a number of years patrolling the waterways in and around the port. Standing six-foot tall and weighing one-hundred and eighty pounds, he was rarely intimidated by the many unruly characters he'd met.

His wavy blond hair and dark-tanned skin gave him the appearance of a local surfer who rarely strayed indoors. A confirmed bachelor, his family and friends had become increasingly concerned at his callousness since returning from the reptile hunt, where it was said there had been plenty of bloodshed.

It was just after noon on a slow Tuesday as he sat completing reports when the phone rang, "Sergeant Taylor, how can I help you?"

"Hello, Sergeant, my name is Rick Thomas. I'm a retired Hollywood police officer."

"Congratulations, Mr. Thomas. I hope retirement is treating you well. How can I help you?" he replied cheerfully, biting into a ham and cheese sandwich.

"Well, before I tell you this, I want you to know that I followed your story a few years ago when you and a group of men hunted and eventually killed that enormous reptile."

"Oh yes, I see. Yeah, that was certainly an enormous croc," replied Randy, sitting back in his chair and taking another bite.

He was used to the fact that other officers from around the state would call him from time to time and want to talk about the infamous battle with the monster.

"Well, sir, I also know that it was no ordinary croc. As a matter of fact, I know it was a thirty-five-foot hybrid reptile, half alligator and half crocodile."

Randy stopped chewing his sandwich and sat straight in his chair, cursing his luck. After the reptile was killed, he saw no point in elaborating with the press about the actual size and ferociousness of the creature. The reason was that it was unimaginable to believe such a monster could really exist, and most importantly was that he didn't want the media circus to continue the story and scare the public. The monster was dead and gone, and he wanted to leave it like that.

"What are you getting at?" he stopped chewing and stood up.

"My wife and I were paddle boarding up here at Clearview State Park this past weekend, and I swear I saw a reptile over thirty-foot long swim under my board."

Randy choked on his sandwich and coughed as he reached for the water bottle and took a long swig, "Are you sure? How deep was the water?"

"The water was deep but crystal clear; I have no doubt what I saw. I was wondering if maybe there's another monster out there like the one you confronted."

Randy's first impulsive thought was how badly he wanted to kill Don Henderson, the man responsible for creating the hybrid reptiles that the Indians in the Everglades referred to as AlliCrocs.

Years ago, Don met up with a couple of scientists experimenting with genetically altered catfish. They were part of some secret research where they somehow made them grow faster and bigger, so their fish farms could make more money in less time.

They created a super breed that grew relentlessly large. For a while, all seemed good until they became extremely aggressive and territorial. Soon, they began attacking everything in their path, including each other.

Finally, they saw no choice but to destroy the project for fear of the fish escaping one day and wreaking havoc on the entire ecosystem.

Don had this bright idea that maybe his new friends could somehow make a transgenic reptile, splicing genes from the biggest alligator with a twenty-two-foot saltwater crocodile. The result was the creation of the most dangerous reptiles on the planet. Not only were the mutant reptiles large and aggressive, but they were nearly indestructible.

Where alligators have little whisker-like stubble on their head area, and crocodiles have them everywhere, called integument sense organs, the mutant reptiles had them all over their body and were twice the size, meaning the AlliCrocs could sense a pressure drop in the water nearly a mile away.

The skin on the reptile is an inch thick and practically bullet-proof because what looked like armored plates called scutes on their back were comparable to steel.

Three of the eggs hatched, and the reptiles were raised in a sanctuary located in the Everglades. When they grew too large and powerful for containment, they escaped, and one was quickly killed by hunters. The second reptile swam east and wreaked havoc before Randy and a crew of seven hunted and finally killed it.

Unfortunately, the third reptile got away and went north where it was believed would never be a danger to people, but now appears to have been spotted inside Clearview State Park.

The first thing Randy did when the phone conversation was terminated was look up the name and number of the mayor of Fort White, Florida. He dialed the number and was courteously patched through to the mayor, where he sat on the phone for over an hour, explaining in great detail about the horrors of his ordeal with the pervasive reptile. Before he was through, he gave the email address to the only man crazy enough to go after the monster, and his name was Captain Bloodfoot, the world renown hunter.

When finished listening on the other end of the line, Mayor Clarence Simon drew a heavy sigh and asked, "Why did this fella, Don Henderson, want to mess with Mother Nature like that?"

Randy sat quiet for a moment before replying, "He wanted to create a monster greater than King Kong. He thought people would come from all over to see his creation, *"Nature said it couldn't be done…Man-made it happen"*, is how he billed it," then hung up. Something about the mayor irked him. The condescending tone of his voice or maybe the feeling the man wasn't going to do anything about it. Whatever it was, Randy said his piece and hung up the phone. There was no way possible that he was going to get involved with AlliCroc again.

Mayor Simon sat back in his chair and rested his head on the backing, pondering the story he'd just heard. He scoffed at the idea of hiring the guy named Bloodfoot for such a high cost of one million dollars, even after Sergeant Taylor's plea, when he could hire a local trapper for less than five grand.

Jack Morgan lived on the outskirts of Fort White in a small wooden house along the Santa Fe River, not five miles away from Clearview State Park.

His love affair with hunting alligators began in his early teens when he would skip school to hunt in his small boat. He would mercilessly shoot the reptiles in the head and hack off their tail, selling the meat to nearby country kitchens with no questions asked.

Now, in his late thirties, he was a trapper with a legitimate business called *Morgan's Gator Meat,* which he sold to local restaurants.

Jack was outside on the dock when a local police officer pulled his squad car onto the gravel drive out front. The officer sat in his car for a few moments, surveying the area before realizing that he had better call in to dispatch and let them know he had arrived, just in case there were some backwoods folks waiting behind a tree like in the scary movies.

Drawing his gun from the holster, he checked to make sure it was ready before he slowly slid it back and buckled the holster strap. Looking at the dilapidated old house and the overrun flora, he wondered if Jack had maybe died in the house weeks or months ago, which would be the reason he didn't answer his phone.

It would make perfect sense since nobody in town had seen him in a while. He wiped the sweat off his forehead with his shirt sleeve before getting out and making his way to the tattered front door of the wooden shack that Jack called a house.

After a few minutes of fruitlessly knocking at the door, the officer searched around the decrepit yard and spotted Jack on the dock, repairing a crab trap.

"Good morning, Mr. Morgan," the officer said as he walked over, glad to see he was alive.

Jack ignored the pleasantries and continued working, "What can I do for ya?"

"The mayor's office called this morning, but nobody answered, so I was sent out here to see if you're interested in hunting a big alligator?"

"How big?"

"Some lunatic tourist claims he saw a thirty-footer in Clearview Springs this past weekend," the officer scoffed, walking onto the dock.

"Don't come out here!" he shouted.

"What the hell? I'm just walking closer so we don't have to shout," the officer replied, taking a step back.

"These old boards are rotted out. You have to be careful to step on the good ones so you don't fall through."

Jack stopped what he was doing, stood up, and turned to face the officer, "I've seen big ones from time to time, but they don't come that big. I once saw a fifteen-footer, and the damn thing almost ate my boat...before I shot it right between the eyes with my trusty 12-gauge."

The officer chuckled and leaned back on a piling with his arms folded across his chest, "Well, somebody put a bug in the mayor's ear, and he seems to disagree. You want the job or not?"

Jack stood quietly, thinking about the situation, before spitting a juicy chunk of tobacco into the water. "I'll do it. I want two-hundred dollars a day for up to a full week. If at the end of the week I don't deliver the head, I will refund half the money."

"Whew! That's a lot of green, you think you can catch that thing in a week?"

"I'll catch it."

"Ok, you've got a deal," the officer replied, reaching out to shake Jack's hand. "Here's four-hundred dollars to get you started," he gave him an envelope with cash. "Start tomorrow. The mayor wants this done quickly and quietly.

The Devil's Hole spring is located in a more secluded area of the park. A nature trail would take you from the more popular Springs as you walk through a wooded area for less than a mile.

One of seven Springs leading to the Ichetucknee river, divers and swimmers alike tended to stay away because of the unyielding current. The round pool of crystal-clear water is so vibrant that you can see the hole in the middle of the Springs while standing on the boardwalk.

Nathan Miller was a former navy seal with a lifelong passion for exploring underwater caves. His wife, Jamie, had recently completed a scuba-diving course that she figured she had no choice in taking after months of prodding and pleading from Nathan. She finally did it in hopes of spending more time together.

Although she wasn't yet an experienced cave diver like her husband, she hauled her own gear on a little cart as they trekked through the woods and finally reached the platform at the end of the boardwalk.

Placing her gear down on the wood planks, she stretched her back and looked around, "The crystal blue water sure looks inviting, but this place kind of gives me the creeps."

Nathan smiled as he ambled up beside her, "That's because it's early, and we're the only ones here. Give it an hour, and this place will be hopping."

"I'm not so sure of that," she replied. "I've done a bit of research on this hole. Do you know why they call it the Devil's hole?"

"No, but I'm sure you're going to tell me."

"They call it the Devil's hole because three divers have drowned in it. There's an old saga that says some divers have gone down so far; their dive suits started burning."

"Three inexperienced divers died in what...the last ten years?

"Twenty years," she replied self-consciously.

Nathan laughed and gave her a discreditable look, "Three divers in twenty years? That sounds like pretty good odds to me."

"What about the burning dive suits"?

"Well...I guess when you're running out of air and starting to panic because you were dumb enough to go cave diving without a guideline, your body might heat up as you're trying to get back to the surface," he replied with a comforting smile.

"Ok, I know you're always right. Let's go have some fun."

He smacked her on the bottom and prepared his gear, grinning from ear to ear as he spotted the hole entrance to the cave, "Once you get your gear on and jump in to see what you've been missing, you'll thank me for begging you to join me in these little excursions."

As he took his time while bragging about his exploits, Jamie sat down and slid into her inflatable tank harness and slipped into the cool water with her fins in each hand. After the temperature shock that made her lips turn instantly blue, she slipped the fins on and put the air regulator in her mouth. She took one last look at Nathan, who was now attaching his new three-hundred-foot, mm polypropylene lifeline to his weight belt. Adjusting her mask, she dove under and swam toward the bottom.

Irritated at the fact that her ears had a hard time popping at the forty-foot depth, she began to smile at the lively fish that swam around and hid in the grassy patches.

Jamie leisurely swam to the center of the spring and grabbed onto the side of the hole to prevent the strong current from sweeping her away. As she sat watching the fish, she mentally went through the drill.

Nathan, if he ever got his act together, would clamp the lifeline to his weight belt, and the other end with the reel would be held by her, and then he would go down the hole and enter the cave. Since she was not cave-certified, she'd stay at the entrance and make sure he was safe while feeding out the line.

She turned as something bumped her leg and laughed to see Nathan burning up his air supply as he fought the current. Looking through his mask and seeing the maddened look on his face, Jamie smiled nicely and patted his shoulder.

She watched as he swam headfirst inside the fifteen-foot opening while the current pushed him to the sidewall, where his tank scraped the wall. She nearly burst out laughing until she suddenly noticed something deeper near the bottom move into the cave.

Jamie froze and grabbed Nathan's fin as she peered toward the entrance. Whatever she saw, or thought she saw, was big. Sediment near the opening whirled lightly before settling back on the bottom. Nathan spun around until he was facing her and saw that she was pointing up. He returned a baffled look before she ran a finger across her throat and pointed at the cave entrance. With that, he had no choice but to follow her up to the surface.

"What's the matter?" he asked as their heads broke the surface and they pulled off their regulators.

"There's something down there," she replied with a skeptical look.

"What did you see? People go down there every day; it's perfectly safe if you know what you're doing".

"It happened so fast. I thought I saw something big retract back inside the cave."

"Oh really," he mused, "Sure it wasn't one of those long-nosed fish that look a little like a barracuda?" he queried, wishing he knew a little more about freshwater fish.

Becoming frustrated, she replied insidiously, "Look, I don't know what I saw; it moved quickly out of the corner of my eye, but it seemed big."

"Seemed big? Hmm, this water's so clear. Maybe it was the shadow of a cloud in the sky."

"Clouds don't kick up sand from the bottom," she persisted.

While they were arguing about what Jamie might have seen, the current carried them to the banks, where their tanks skidded in the sediment. Nathan stood and walked up the embankment and waited for Jamie to follow, "C'mon up, we'll sit out a while and decide what we want to do," he said, with disappointment in his tone.

Jamie sat watching him as she slipped her fins off. The last thing she wanted was to ruin his weekend excursion because of something she thought she saw.

They walked over to the wooden platform and sat with their feet dangling in the water. After a while, he calmed down and decided to take it easy on his wife. After all, she was new to the sport, and he wanted to make it a pleasant weekend for the two of them.

Not twenty minutes later, a family of snorkelers jumped in the Springs and splashed around. The father took one of his two sons to the center of the spring where the hole was and disappeared below. Ten seconds later, they breached the surface and tried to blow water out of their snorkels to no avail.

"Rookies," Nathan snickered, wrapping his arm around Jamie as they watched.

Jamie was now relaxed and smiled as a good-sized turtle leisurely cruised about two feet down below her feet. She realized that maybe what she saw was a big turtle, and as Nathan said, nobody's ever been hurt diving these Springs if they knew what they were doing.

They relaxed and watched the family get out of the water and walk off to explore the nature trail. Looking back, she felt silly for causing a fuss. After all, there were lots of fish swimming around, and even that big turtle seemed peaceful in the surroundings.

"C'mon, big guy, let's go check out that cave."

Nathan smiled and squeezed her shoulder, "Are you sure you want to?"

"Sure, let's go!" she giggled, standing up and reaching for her gear.

This time, they both slipped their tanks on and jumped into the spring together with fins in hand. Nathan was the first to put his fins on and waited for Jamie as she shivered and adjusted her mask over her face. When they were ready, they swam against the strong current until they were hovering over the hole.

"Ok, you ready? No sea monsters down there?" he jibed, noticing Jamie fervently checking below.

They let the air out of their BC vests and slowly descended. They reached the bottom at the forty-foot depth, according to the depth gauge dangling from Nathans's vest, and Jamie felt more relaxed this time because her ears easily popped, and the pressure didn't make her eyes feel like they were about to burst.

Nathan pressed a button enabling his safety line to spool freely and attached the free end to his waist while Jamie held the spool. When they gave each other the ok sign, Nathan hovered over the hole, turned to face the bottom and dove down against the current. She watched with detached amusement as he dove effortlessly through the fifteen-foot-wide hole and disappeared into the cave.

Time seemed to stand still as she planted her dive fins against a boulder to help fight off the strong current. Jamie watched the safety line as it played out at about ten feet at a time before stopping and becoming slack. There was no doubt that Nathan was having a hard time with a strong current inside the cave as well.

A turtle in the distance was swimming straight for her as she smiled to herself and pondered how close it would get before flinching away. It was one of the biggest turtles she'd ever seen outside of a zoo. The circumference of the shell was no more than thirty inches round. She watched in awe as it turned away and swam down the hole and into the cave. She smiled to herself as she watched the line gently slide between her fingers and thought of the surprise Nathan would have when the turtle swims past him.

Seconds later, she laughed and accidentally swallowed water when she saw the turtle come out of the hole at twice the speed it went in.

Suddenly, the line jerked forward with brutal force, pulling her into the hole before going slack. Her heart sank as she thought the line had snapped. She quickly reached for the spool and unhooked it from her vest. She felt her heartbeat pounding in her chest as she began to panic while reeling more than twenty-foot of slack line.

The line finally tightened but stayed still, Nathan wasn't going further in the cave nor coming out. She waited patiently for a full minute until the line slowly withdrew from the cave. With a sigh of relief, she slowly reeled the line, watching the cave opening and waited for Nathan to swim out.

A dumbfounded look creased her masked face when one black dive fin shot out of the cave and began floating up with the current. She probably would have smiled and thought her ex-Navy Seal husband must have really had a tough time fighting the current if not for the red-colored trail following behind it.

Jamie reached out and grabbed the fin as it gently passed by and nearly lost her mind when she saw his foot inside, torn off just below the ankle. The bile in her stomach surged up through her throat like a raging volcano, exploding in her air regulator.

Choking and trying not to scream, she kicked hard and clawed her way up the forty-foot swim toward the surface as quickly as possible. Still halfway to go, her lungs burned for oxygen, but she was too panicked to find her regulator and put it in her mouth. The black veil of unconsciousness nearly overcame her as her head shot through the surface. Inhaling lungs full of fresh air, she screamed out for help only to find there was nobody around.

Shaking uncontrollably, she stuck her head back under water and looked for the cave entrance but couldn't find it. When her eyes focused on where the hole should have been, she screamed out in horror and disbelief at the sight of the enormous alligator head glaring straight up at her as it looked enraged at being stuck at a forty-five-degree angle where the hole met the cave entrance. Never in her lifetime had she ever seen such a huge reptile. Its entire head covered the hole.

The thirty-eight-foot reptile quivered with menacing bliss as it watched its prey try to escape. With an insatiable appetite and unrelenting strength, it leisurely positioned its hind legs and sprang up towards the surface.

With only twenty yards to swim before reaching the ladder connected to the boardwalk, Jamie screamed out in horror when she felt a strong current swoosh under her.

Shaking hysterically, she began to doubt if she would be able to climb the ladder, but when she found the strength and prepared to grab the step, the giant reptilian head slowly emerged and nudged her away. The sight of the dull-green, lifeless eyes looked like pure evil as Jamie screamed and kicked to get away.

The pervasive reptile seemed content, terrorizing its quarry as it continued to prod her toward the middle of the Springs with its snout.

Jamie was so overwhelmed with fear but found herself screaming obscenities at the reptile while it swam unhurried around her as if taunting its prey.

Struggling to get her wits back, she slipped the regulator back in her mouth and figured her chances were better if she dove to the bottom. She kept a sharp eye on the menacing reptile as she sank deeper and deeper, finally standing at the bottom.

Thoughts of surviving the ordeal entered her mind as she took a couple of deep breaths in the regulator and watched the monster slowly swim away, still on the surface. She looked around and tried to blend in with the rocky bottom while carefully swimming toward the shoreline. Trying to breathe lightly so her air bubbles wouldn't give away her position, she began to think that if she could keep her wits together and stay clear of danger, she might be able to swim through the foliage, then ditch the tank and peel off the fins and sprint up the embankment.

With only yards to go, the rocky bottom was now only eighteen feet deep. Fear engulfed her entire body as she looked to her right and saw a big submarine shaped object headed her way. The blue water was so clear she could see it coming from the opposite side of the spring. She watched in frozen terror as the shape grew bigger and bigger the closer it came. The gigantic tail swept from left to right in an unhurried motion.

Again, she couldn't grasp the way the creature seemed to swim so leisurely, knowing there was no escape for its prey, bathing in its fear. Her body felt completely numb as she relinquished the fight for survival, only managing to scream out until her lungs burst.

She watched through bloodshot eyes as the unsightly jaws opened wide and chomped down on her with alarming force, adjusting its kill in its bear trap jaws until it was able to gulp down every piece of its prey.

Soon after, a little girl, the age of five ran down the path and stopped at the end of the boardwalk, "Oooh, that's pretty," she said, pointing at the beautiful colors of crimson and blue as they dispersed with the current.

Her older brother ran up behind her and grabbed her by the arm without looking at the water, "Bad girl, you're not supposed to run over here by yourself," he lectured, taking her by the hand and walking away.

5

After a long night of hunting the elusive reptile, Jack woke from a wrestles nap and drew lines on a map where he figured he'd hunt next. With the advance money sitting in his pocket, itching to escape the envelope, Jack Morgan decided to go to the Tucknee Well, the local watering hole where he could be found nightly.

The patrons knew him and called him Morgan, while most of the waitresses called him Jack the Creeper for never failing to creep them out. It wasn't for his knack for trying to date them as for the stories he would tell about his alligator jaunts. The bar was no more than a glorified wood shack off a main road called Highway 7.

He was drinking his fourth Jim Beam on the rocks when he spotted a couple of young men enter and take up stools on the opposite side of the bar from where he sat.

He smirked to himself, thinking they couldn't be a day over twenty-one if they were old enough to be in his favorite establishment at all.

He watched, fascinated at the polite way they ordered their draft beers, and looked around the smoke-filled room. The tall guy had a thick beard, so now he figured they were in their early twenties. A slight smile creased his unshaven face as he tried to remember his younger days, slapping a flat hand on the bar when he couldn't.

His attention drifted from them when the front door creaked open, and more tourists entered, their faces wrinkling at the impervious environment. The three ladies made a U-turn and exited as the two young men seated at the bar stood up and watched as if deciding if they should follow them out or let them go back to the camp while they had a drink with the locals.

Jack shook his head and focused on the two across the bar once again. He couldn't help but hear them discussing the whereabouts of a friend; one thought he met up with other friends while the other, gulping his beer, was sure he was taken by a big alligator. Jack drank the last drop from his glass and ordered another before sliding off the stool and walking over.

"Hello, fellas. I couldn't help hearing you talking about a big gator. My name's Jack, Jack Morgan," he said, holding out his hand for them to shake.

"Jay," the gulper replied, shaking Jack's hand.

"Ned," the other replied, agitated.

"What makes you think your friend was attacked?"

"Why do you want to know?" Ned shot back.

"I'm a trapper, and believe it or not, I've been hired to catch a large alligator. Ya, fellas, mind if we grab a table so I can ask some questions?" Jack said, spreading an arm out toward a table.

Ned and Jay looked at each other and decided it wouldn't hurt to tell their story. They stood up and followed Jack to a corner table where they could talk in private.

Jack ordered a round of draft beers and listened ardently to the two young men. Although he now believed there was most likely a good-sized alligator roaming around in the park, he doubted their friend was eaten alive by the vicious monster they invigorated in their conversation.

The front door opened, and two lovely young ladies entered with an air of good times written on their faces. Jack, already bored with the conversation with Ned and Jay, promised he'd check out the area where their friend was last seen and excused himself, following the two ladies to the bar.

"So, he's the guy they hired to try and catch the alligator," Ned shrugged, watching the wretched man as he stumbled behind the two ladies.

"What a redneck," replied Jay, shaking his head and watching Jack make a fool out of himself.

Ned ordered an IPA while Jay switched to a local beer from the tap and tried to figure out what they were going to do about finding Tommy.

It was now a quarter to midnight, and the later it got, the more customers strolled in. As they sat watching the patrons, they were amazed to see Jack kicking back and actually getting somewhere with the ladies.

"Look at him. He must know every one of these rednecks in here," Ned said, sipping his beer and watching people strolling by and patting Jack on the back.

"What can they possibly see in him," added Jay.

Before he could complete his sentence, Jack turned his head in their direction and gave them a piercing look that took them by surprise. He no longer looked like a drunk redneck in a honky-tonk bar picking up chicks. Something they must have said changed his entire demeanor.

Before they could laugh it off, Jack scooped three more beers from the bar and headed back to their table.

"Hello, Jack, what brings you back here? It looks like you're doing really well with those ladies," said Ned.

"Yeah, well, guess what?" he said with a disturbed tone. "Those chicks said they're looking for their sister. It seems the sister and her husband never returned from a diving trip at the Devil's Hole."

"Where the hell is the Devil's hole?"

"It's in the Clearview Springs Park. Same place your buddy's missing from, only in a more isolated area."

"Did they notify the park rangers? Ned asked. I mean, "Maybe they were attacked by the gator too."

"Yeah, well, I didn't ask them," Jack responded, his hands flaring up animatedly."I'm not a cop. I don't ask questions. But yes, they contacted a ranger. Turns out they came here to surprise them and wanted to take them to lunch after the dive. They cruised through the park, found their car and waited. When the park closed, and they still didn't show up, they got hold of a park ranger. All he said was that he would keep an eye out for them."

Ned and Jay looked at each other and replied, "We're going to check out the Devil's Hole."

"Now, wait a second. The Park's closed, and it's pitch black out there."

They sat in silence, staring at each other, knowing they were all thinking the same thing.

"So now what?" Jay blurted.

"You two go back to the Springs tomorrow and try to find a quiet area along the banks and sit there, watching the ripples in the water and any sudden change of motion in the water. Here's my card. Call me if you see anything unusual."

"Why don't we join you tomorrow and help you hunt," Ned asked.

"I hunt alone… just me…nature…and my twelve-gauge shotgun that I like to call Betsy," he scolded as he excused himself and headed out the door.

"He's a strange man. He's going to get himself killed," Jay said, watching Jack stumble out the door.

"I hope not. Let's get back to camp and tell the others. When the sun comes up, maybe they will join us and keep an eye out for that gator," Ned replied, drinking the last drop in his bottle and standing up to leave.

Angie and Amanda were not in the tent when Ned and Jay returned. Instead of sitting in the smoky bar with them, they decided to go back to the camp and drop off their drunken friend. It seemed that their little friend was hell-bent on proving she was a drinker, so they wound up putting a blanket around a drunk, passed-out Gina and headed out in search of the alligator.

It was now past the midnight hour as they both sat on a tree limb stretching twenty feet over the water with flashlights in their hand. Every few minutes, they would both flash their lights on in different areas, hoping to see the eerie green eyes of an alligator.

Earlier, Amanda had cut her bare foot as they scaled the fence while sneaking into the park. As usual, prepared for anything,

Angie happened to bring a pocketful of bandages and gave one to her friend to stop the bleeding.

Now, as Amanda sat in the tree feeling bored out of her mind, she looked down at her foot and began to peel back the band-aid.

"Ew, what are you doing?" Angie whispered.

Amanda snickered and replied, "I'm taking this off and throwing it in the water."

"Why?"

"The blood might attract the gator."

Angie wrinkled her nose and decided not to reply. She sat quietly while her mind recalled a picture she'd seen in a wildlife magazine where a man held a chicken over the water until a huge alligator seemed to slither straight up out of the water, leaving only his back legs and tail in the water and snatched the chicken.

She glanced down and was relieved to know they were nearly twenty feet above the water, which would make it nearly impossible for an alligator to reach them, she thought.

As the night wore on and a light-dewy fog began to seep into their bones, Angie checked the time on her iPhone and called over to Amanda, who was now sitting on the thick tree branch sloping slightly higher and almost to the middle of the spring, "Hey crazy, it's two-fifteen, and I'm colder than an ice cube, let's get back to camp."

"Let's give it a few more minutes. I'm dripping some more blood from my foot," Amanda replied, sitting on the branch like a monkey and squeezing her foot.

"It's still bleeding?" Angie stood up with concern.

"Just a little bit, she replied, squeezing her foot harder."

Angie turned on her flashlight and pointed it beneath her friend to see if she could see blood dripping. Instead, she witnessed the outline of what looked like a submarine a split second before it shot straight out of the water and clamped down on the tree branch where Amanda sat.

"Nooo!" Angie screamed as she watched Amanda curl up and grasp the branch with all her might. She ran the beam of her light up and down the creature with dismay at the way the ubiquitous reptile clung onto the branch with Amanda in its mouth.

The horror of seeing how big the mammoth was made Angie think she was having a nightmare. But there it was, hanging from a branch at least twenty feet high, and its back legs didn't even breach the surface of the water.

Too shocked to move, Angie stopped screaming and watched as the reptile seemed to take pleasure in not moving. She marveled how such a gigantic creature with irrefutable weight didn't snap the tree, until she took a closer look and saw the tail swishing from side to side.

A cold chill streaked up her spine as she realized the reptile was consciously keeping its full weight from snapping the tree. To make matters worse, her heart sank to the pit of her stomach when the demonic reptile rolled its eyes and fixated on her.

Angie felt the full force of malice as they locked eyes on each other. Never in her wildest nightmares would she have thought she would see a creature that appeared to take great pleasure in tormenting its prey.

Suddenly, Angie snapped out of her thoughts when she heard Amanda give out a high-pitched scream.

"Amanda! Where are you?"

Without a word, Amanda poked her head out of the colossal jaws and screamed out, "I'm alive! It couldn't shut its mouth because the branch is in the way!" she screamed hysterically while trying to escape through the two-foot gap of the gaping jaws and razor-sharp teeth.

Angie couldn't do anything but watch as her friend began to crawl past the serrated teeth. Her arms, legs and torso bled as if cut by scalpels. To her horror, she saw the reptile's tail stop swimming and heard a loud crack in the branch.

Amanda let out a blood-curdling scream as she cleared the six-inch conical teeth and reached out to grab onto the cracked branch. In one swift motion of the creature's body, the branch snapped off, hurtling Amanda and the creature down into the water.

Paralyzed with fear, Angie could only watch as Amanda breached the surface in a split second and swam for her life to the embankment. She just made it to dry land when the reptile charged out of the water like a raging bull and gave chase.

Without looking back, Amanda knew it was following and ran as fast as she could. She took a sharp right turn, hoping the large predator would slow its speed. When it seemed to work, she took a turn to her left and sprinted to the fence, hopping over it like it was hardly there.

Angie cringed her teeth as she watched the reptile smash through the foliage in hot pursuit. Numb with fear, she hugged the tree branch as tight as she could and listened, trying to be confident that Amanda had made it to safety.

Now, she was alone. She looked down and saw the water had returned to calm, and the only ripples were from the large branch floating downstream. She held tight to the tree branch and thought it best if she could climb a little higher. All was quiet as she sat looking around the area; only crickets and the occasional frog could be heard.

Too frightened to move a muscle, Angie sat hugging the tree, hoping and praying her friend would make it and the insidious reptile wouldn't come back for her.

When Amanda and the hideous reptile splashed into the water in a heap, fear gripped her entire body when she found that she had landed directly on the monster's head. Before she could find her bearings, she bolted to the surface and swam with everything she had. Too scared to think about how lucky she was to make it to shore, she sprang out of the water and ran for safety.

To her horror, she detected the predator was giving chase and was close behind. The lactic acid pumping through her veins and adrenaline racing through her heart helped her not to overthink her situation and to keep running.

She reached the six-foot fence bordering the park and nearly leaped over it, tumbling to the ground on the other side. It was only then that she turned her head to see if the reptile was still chasing.

In the darkness, she could barely make out the silhouette of what looked like a low-rider school bus careening through the brush. Only when it slammed into the cyclone fence did she begin to scream hysterically.

The mammoth's head pierced through the six-gauge chain link fencing at a ferocious speed, bending the steel poles on either side before coming to a stop when its front legs became entangled. Snapping its jaws only feet away from its prey, it let out a horrifying hiss as Amanda rolled into the street.

Amanda sat shaking uncontrollably, watching the raging reptile continue a slow crawl toward her, the fence poles bending as if made of rubber. She tried to get up and run but expended every drop of energy.

When she resided in defeat, dropping her head and waiting for the inevitable, the bright lights of an eighteen-wheeler rounded a corner as the big rig truck came into view.

Amanda lifted her head and barely had the strength to lift an arm to wave down the driver. She looked back at the reptile and was shocked to see it stopped and looked through hellish eyes at the oncoming truck.

It sat as if pondering its options before retreating from the fence and disappearing in the dark.

The big-rig truck slowed and passed Amanda before coming to a complete stop and reversing. She watched as the truck driver got out and ran towards her with a flashlight beaming in her direction.

"What on earth happened to you?" he said, squatting beside her and running his flashlight up and down her bloodied body.

In an inaudible tone, he thought he heard that she was chased by a monster gator.He took his jacket off and bundled it up, placing it under her head like a makeshift pillow. He stood and focused the beam of the flashlight on the gaping hole in the fence before running back to his truck to radio for help.

Within minutes, he returned with a blanket and draped it over Amanda, "It's okay. I called paramedics, and they're on their way. You may be going in shock so I'm covering you with this blanket until help arrives."

Amanda was tired and weak but managed to hear what he said and tried to tell him about her trapped friend in the tree before passing out. Looking at the lacerations all over her extremities caused him to fight off the urge to vomit as he tried to make her comfortable. His thoughts were racing while he waited for help and fought to confirm what he thought he'd seen when he rounded the bend.

It was dark and hard to make out what was poking through the fence, but he imagined it must have been some sort of ATV. Tired from too many hours on the road, he concluded that the crazy kid must have been tearing through the park on some sort of off-road buggy when she hit the fence, sending her through to the other side. The bleeding cuts would have been from scraping through the fence. It was the only thing that made sense.

When she looked comfortable enough, he stood and started to walk over to the fence to check out the wreckage. It was gone.

He couldn't fathom what kind of person would leave the scene with the young lady lying in the street. He flashed his light around the wrecked fence and inside the park. All was quiet.

He shook his head and went over to sit with the young lady until help arrived.

6

Amanda woke up in the hospital with a nurse attempting to take her temperature. Feeling groggy, she lay there for a moment to collect her thoughts. Glancing over to the clock on the wall, she saw it read eight-thirty and thought it was funny how she never sleeps so late.

All at once, it dawned on her about what happened a few hours earlier. Her heart skipped a beat when she thought about Angie. Did she make it? Is she still in the tree?

She sprang up, yelling for her friend, and tried pulling the intravenous line out of her arm as she struggled to get out of the bed. The startled nurse made an effort to calm her down and finally pressed a help button on the wall. Within seconds, two more nurses entered the room along with a police officer.

"Calm down, honey!" the first nurse said with a soothing tone, carefully grabbing Amanda by the elbow, one of the few places not bandaged.

"Angie! I have to find Angie!"

"Who is Angie?" the officer shouted, putting himself between Amanda and the door.

"The monster, the monster was after us!" she gasped frantically.

The nurses held her down as one quickly administered a shot in her arm to calm her down. Amanda relaxed and sat back on the bed when the door opened, and a ragged-looking, red-headed young lady entered the room. She staggered over to a visitor's chair and plopped down, drained and completely exhausted.

"Who are you? The officer asked as all heads turned toward the visitor.

"I'm Angie."

"Oh my goodness, what happened to you?" a nurse asked with surprise, rushing over to help the poor girl.

Angie leaned forward in the chair and held her head in her hands. A few deep breaths later, she replied, "There's a very large alligator in the Springs. My friend and I were attacked last night. Amanda was sitting on a thick tree branch, and it leaped out of the water and grabbed the branch with her in its mouth."

The police officer squinted and shook his head, "You ladies should no better than to be hanging on a branch, dangling your feet in the water in the middle of the night."

Angie looked up and faced the officer, "The branch was about twenty feet over the water."

"Sure it was a kid? That would make the gator to be about...oh, let's say about twenty feet long?"

"Bigger, its back half was still in the water," Angie replied, understanding how hard it was for the officer to believe.

Angie and Amanda sat for the next hour, giving the officer their statement. Every time they mentioned the size and wickedness of the predator, the officer would shake his head and give them a skeptical look. But they didn't care; they told their story straight and to the point and hoped damn well something would be done about it because they still had a missing friend out there.

Ned and Jay were at wit's end. After returning to the campground and finding Angie and Amanda missing, the thought crossed their mind that they would go back to the park to search for the alligator. The only thing they could do now was to sneak back into the park and find them.

As they walked outside the entrance to the campground, they saw the semi-truck make an abrupt stop. They watched as it backed and turned on its emergency flashers before coming to a complete stop. If the truck hadn't blocked their view, they would have seen Amanda lying near the road next to the gaping hole in the fence.

Realizing they wouldn't be able to jump the fence and sneak into the park, they turned and headed back to the campsite until the truck was gone. Hopefully by then, Angie and Amanda would be back.

If they knew they'd be sneaking back into the park, they would never have spent the time drinking in the local bar. They tried to stay awake but fell asleep in their camping chairs as they waited for the truck to leave. Now, it was early morning, and the sun was baking them where they sat.

Ned was the first to rise and noticed the girls hadn't returned.

"Hey Jay, wake up," he said, holding his head from the slight hangover.

"Ugh, what time is it?"

"Time to get up. Angie and Amanda didn't come back last night."

Jay jumped up and opened their tent. He peeked inside, hoping to see Angie and Amanda, but only noticed their sleepy friend.

Gina sat on top of her sleeping bag, staring at Jay, "Peek-a-boo to you too," she said, looking like she should have gotten more sleep.

"Where's Angie?" asked Jay.

Gina replied with a slight shrug.

"C'mon, let's get moving," Ned said to Jay, with increasing concern in his tone.

"I'll stay here in case they come back," said Gina, yawning as she spoke.

They quickly changed into a pair of long-sleeved tee-shirts and headed across the street. A police car was spotted on the side of the road where the truck was parked earlier, and then they spotted a gaping hole in the fence and hurried over to see what was going on.

"Excuse me, officer, what the heck happened here?" asked Ned, choosing not to say the F word.

"Looks like somebody went through the fence last night," the officer replied, looking at the two young men. "Where are you two coming from?" he continued, squinting his eyes and thinking that maybe they were the culprits.

"The campground across the street," replied Jay, grabbing the fence where he spotted a blood stain.

"I need you guys to back away; this may be a crime scene."

"A crime scene?" they both asked.

The officer turned and pointed toward the police car, and they walked to it. Leaning on the front fender, the officer answered, "Long story short, a trucker found a young lady lying here last night with cuts all over her body. She said she was chased by some kind of monstrous reptile before blacking out. The truck driver called 9-1-1, and four officers showed up. All in all, it looks like some crazy kids lost control of their vehicle and went through the fence. Now you two arrive and I'm thinking maybe you know a little more."

Ned turned his head and looked at the metal fence polls. They were bent outward, not inward, although the fence area around the hole was definitely pulled inward.

"Do you believe that? I mean, look at the poles; they're bent out toward the street."

"You're right. Something doesn't add up, and that's why I'm here, trying to figure this out."

"Well, what do you think?"

The officer casually focused his attention, "What do you think?"

"What about the girl? Where is she?" Ned blurted, sounding anxious.

"She's at the hospital about five miles up the road. Why? Do you think you might know her?"

Ned and Jay were already running across the road, "We might. We have two friends that didn't return to the campsite last night," Ned shouted over his shoulder.

The officer wanted to question them more, but they had already gone inside the campground. He called ahead to the officer at the hospital and told him to hold them when they arrived.

They tore off in Jay's pickup truck and were at the hospital in minutes. When they entered the room, Amanda was squinting in pain as she was just finishing tying her shoes and Angie was seated talking to an officer.

"You're both here! Whew, what a relief. What the fuck happened?" Ned gasped with a surprised look as he held the door open for Jay.

"Please watch your language, sir," a nurse said, looking stern.

The officer turned, said something on his radio, then requested all four to come to the police station to answer some questions.

Angie could barely keep her eyes open when she told the officer she had already given a statement earlier. It fell on deaf ears as the officer instructed them to stop by anyway.

The clock on the wall in the police station read 10:45 as Angie, Amanda, Ned and Jay sat in a small, stuffy office, giving the skeptical officers their account of what had happened. When they were finished, the officers walked out of the room scratching their heads and they waited another half-hour before what must have been the police chief entered and closed the door behind him.

His black slacks were perfectly creased, and the starched white shirt was neatly trimmed to hug his muscular biceps. The neatly trimmed salt and pepper-colored hair parted to the side looked like it came straight out of GQ magazine.

Letting out a deep sigh, he took a seat at the head of the table and stared into each of their eyes, trying to decide if they were being truthful.

All the while, Ned and Jay returned the stare and were repulsed at the thought of another figure of authority trying the act of intimidation.

"Do you all really believe you saw an alligator over thirty-foot long? My name is Chief Clark, and I want to be damned sure you kids are telling the truth."

"It's true, it's all true," Angie spoke up.

To their surprise, the Chief answered with a sudden reassuring expression, "I believe you. The fact is…there appear to be other victims as well. I do, however, find it hard to believe the size is as big as you say."

"It's huge! I should know. I was inside its mouth!" blurted Amanda defensively.

The Chief locked eyes with her for a long minute and replied, "Unfortunately, I believe that too. While you were sleeping at the hospital, they took samples of your cuts. I was expecting the slices all over your body would be from being thrown through the hole in the fence, but as it turns out, they're infected by the nasty bacteria of a reptile…a large one."

"Am I going to be okay?" she stammered wearily.

"You'll be fine. The nurses gave you some shots for the bacteria and whatnot," he smiled for the first time.

As the conversation with the Chief wound down, Angie became startled and looked around the room as if she had seen a ghost, "Where's Gina?"

"She's at the camp, lounging around without a care in the world," replied Jay.

Trapper Jack Morgan was awake, sipping a mug of coffee and standing on his dock as the sun rose through the covert river in his backyard. Dressed in camouflage pants and a long-sleeve shirt, he sat on the dock and wrestled with the boot laces of his waterproof-design hunting boots after guiding them over his size-eleven feet.

All said and done, the man was an early riser, no matter how drunk he had gotten the night before or how late he crashed his bed.

He loaded the last of ten wooden fence poles onto his boat that he would use to stake on the banks of the river and hang chicken quarters just touching the water on heavy duty tarred twine.

Stepping into his fourteen-foot camouflage skiff, he took a quick sweep of his checklist and cursed out loud as he stepped back onto the dock to retrieve a pack of stainless-steel fishing clips that he would use to clamp the twine to a nail on the poles. When the alligator takes the bait, the clip will snap, allowing the gator to run off with the bait before the thirty-foot twine would tighten, setting the hook.

Aware that alligators usually feed at night, his early start would allow him to scan the area of the supposed attack and find the best spots to set his traps.

Cruising down the Ichetucknee River with his trusty twenty-five horsepower Johnson outboard humming along, he slowed and put the motor in neutral as he turned into the Springs and drifted with the current. A pair of fishermen were floating in a small canoe with fishing poles in the water gave him a shifty look as he slowly cruised nearer.

"Mornin' fellas, how's the fishin'? He shouted.

"Good until you showed up, now find your own damn spot!" a red-faced fisherman replied, not holding back his anger.

The first thing Jack wanted to do was start a pissing match, but he took a deep breath and smiled, "I'm not fishing. I just wanted to know if you two asses saw a big gator," he responded, turning off the motor and dropping the shaft of his electric motor on the bow into the water.

The startled fishermen looked at each other and quickly changed their tone, "Is there a big gator around here?"

"You'll find out when it swims up and bites you in the ass!" replied Jack, cherishing the alarmed look on their faces.

He quietly cruised up the springs, passing the sign that forbade powerboats from entering the springs, where divers, swimmers and kayakers frequented.

By mid-morning, he prepared to set his traps along a quarter-mile area where the young man named Tommy was reportedly missing. He spotted the yellow police tape forming a perimeter around a tree and decided to come ashore and have a look.

Jack spotted the area where Ned and Jay said there was an indentation in the sand of a large boat.The depression was still visible, and he whistled out loud, thinking that if an alligator made that, it would really have to be a big one. He looked around the area before stepping closer, grabbed his measuring tape and stood in the middle to see what he could find.

When he recorded the measurements, he smiled and shook his head, almost broke out laughing when he saw how big it was. He wondered what kind of nutcase would take such a big boat into the springs without getting caught by the authorities.

He sat about ten feet in front of the markings and studied its path. Lucky for him, the depression had not been disturbed.

Suddenly, his eyes narrowed as he cocked his head; standing to attention, he tensely walked along the immense outline. There was a slight curve in the formation that could not have been done by a rigid boat. Add to the fact that the indentation was nearly a foot deep, and it would have had to be a good-sized boat weighing nearly five thousand pounds, one that would most likely get stuck in these parts.

He walked to the water's edge and stood where the crystal-clear water lapped at his boots. With a trembling right hand, he lowered his polarized sunglasses from the top of his head to his dumbfounded eyes and gazed into the water.

His uncertainties were confirmed; he saw the telltale signs of the enormous claws that drove the brutal predator out of the water.

"Ohhhh noo, say it ain't so," he mumbled to himself.But before he could take a step back onto dry sand, he caught a glimpse of the large dark shadow that seemed to gently surface out of nowhere. Its big, green eyes barely breached the water but locked on him like a laser beam.

Like a bolt of lightning, the reptile soared forward and attacked. With no time to run, Jack Morgan instinctively threw his arms up to protect himself and fell backward. The colossal reptile sprang from the water faster than what he thought possible and chomped down on his legs with its massive jaws like a giant bear trap.

Staggered by the searing pain, a piercing scream shattered the quiet calm as Jack grabbed onto the massive jaws, fighting a losing battle while the creature slowly dragged him into the water.

A loud pop registered in his internal contrivance as he unexpectedly became free of the jaws. He rolled over and tried to swim back to shore only to realize his legs were gone, bitten off from the hips.

Wide-eyed and in disbelief of his predicament, he cried out for help until his shallow screams became gurgled with blood. With his mind reeling in turmoil, he knew he had to get out of the water before he could assess his injuries. His shaking hands dug through the sandy bottom, sluggishly clawing his way out.

To his incredulity, he watched the creature slowly crawl out of the water beside him and maneuver his arm with its snout, almost playfully, before chomping down and biting it off. Jack's eyes and mouth popped open to their maximum width from the searing agony as he tried to scream, but nothing came out.

He looked over at the menacing eyes as they seemed to stare dominantly into his. His other arm began to quiver and shake as his life receded with the massive blood flow. A look of puzzlement crossed his expression as he couldn't believe the creature was nudging and prodding him back into the water instead of finishing the attack.

Too weak to fight back, Jack lay on his side and closed his eyes as AlliCroc pushed him back into the shallows. Blackness edged the corners of his mind as he prepared to die when he suddenly felt the massive teeth clamp down on his torso. His last thought was how the devil himself couldn't have thought of a more agonizing way to impose death.

There was no doubt in his mind this hellish creature was playing with him and wanted him to feel every inch of the excruciating pain. Jack opened his mouth to take a gasp of air, only to be viciously dragged under the surface and swallowed.

The two fishermen in the small canoe were just around the bend, about seventy yards from the mayhem when they were startled by the ear-piercing scream.

"What in tarnation!?" one asked, "Was that the trapper fella screamin'?".

"Let's get the hell out of here!" his buddy shouted, dropping his rod and reel and grabbing a paddle. He looked back at his partner, who was sitting with his mouth gaping. "Paddle hard! I think it's coming this way!"

True as the words left his lips, a giant wake ignited in the tranquil water as the gargantuan reptile shot forward and swam at full speed in their direction. Only its snout and eyes were above the surface as it rounded the bend in the river.

The overweight fisherman was so frightened his body refused to react. His buddy was slim and muscular and impulsively threw out the paddle and dove overboard, swimming as fast as he could to the embankment ten feet away. His hands and feet found the sandy bottom, and he tore up the embankment like a wild animal.

Only when he thought he was safe did he turn to see his fishing buddy of thirty years half standing in the errant canoe as if he wanted to swim for it, but it was too late.

"Stay in the canoe and brace yourself!"

Too late. The giant reptile's head was completely out of the water with jaws wide open, less than twenty feet and closing fast. In the next instant, a loud crash scared the birds out of the trees as they fled for their lives. The man was thrown into the water on impact when the reptile crumbled the aluminum canoe like an empty beer can and continued swimming, disappearing underwater.

The overweight fisherman poked his head out of the water and coughed a lung full of water. Looking around and surprised to be alive, he gazed up the embankment at his pale-faced friend, "Help me outta here," he struggled to say, his body in a state of shock.

"Don't move! That gator just swam right below you and stopped," his friend tried to whisper, staring into the crystal-clear water from the top of the embankment. "Stay still and try not to panic. We know it just ate that poor trapper, so I don't think it will strike again. I heard alligators don't eat again for a long time!"

"Well, it sure hit the canoe like it's still hungry!"

His friend agreed and didn't reply.

Finally, "It looked more agitated than hungry."

Time seemed to stand still as the two men locked eyes on each other and wondered how they had gotten into such a mess.

The water was so unblemished that the man standing on the embankment could see the reptile clearly sitting at the bottom and couldn't believe what he was looking at. The immense size of the reptile was just unbelievable and the incredible amount of teeth made it look like some kind of prehistoric monster.

His friend in the water noticed the concerned look on his face and looked below the surface to see the reptile's head tilt to the side to get a better view of him.

"Ok...Listen, if that croc was going to eat you, you'd be eaten by now. Keep your eyes on me and very, very slowly float on over toward shore...When your feet touch the bottom, slowly walk out," he whispered, his left leg trembling.

"Croc? Why do you think it's a croc?"

His friend didn't have the heart to tell him that he was staring at teeth the size of his hand sticking out of the sides of its jaws. Even from the eighteen-foot depth, the grotesque teeth looked like a horror film.

The man in the water swallowed hard and tried to muster his strength. Floating with his legs tucked under his fat body made him look like a Buddha statue as he edged closer to the embankment.

Suddenly, the reptile stirred and rose to the surface between its prey and the grassy shoreline. Its snout brushed his chest in a strange jester as if to insult his plans of escape.

"I peed, I pissed my pants," he cried out, cracking under the stress. "That's why it came up...because I pissed my pants," he continued, becoming hysterical.

"Quiet down, I'm going to try and distract that sumbitch," his buddy cried out, his voice trembling. He looked around and found an old tree branch about five feet long with a few dried leaves still attached. Bending over to pick it up, he was surprised at how stiff his body responded. Grunting like an old man, he snatched the branch, wishing it was thicker than the paltry one-inch diameter that it was and threw it in the water to the right side of the reptile, hoping to divert it.

The leaves fell off before the branch hit the water, and it barely registered a splash, "Damn it all to hell. You lousy croc!" he shouted in frustration.

At that moment, the massive reptile turned its giant head and hissed as it stared straight into his eyes. The blood drained out of his face, and his mouth dropped like an anvil at the sight of the deadly creature's eyes. Taking a step back, he tripped and fell down the other side of the mound.

On the brink of passing out and too scared to get up if he could, his ears still functioned enough to hear the agonizing cries and the unmistakable sound of bones snapping like twigs. He tried once more to get up, but the severing screams were too much for his senses, and he lay there curled up, covering his ears.

As if a switch turned off, quiet calm was suddenly restored, and he opened his eyes. He lifted his head and took a quick look around to make sure the hideous reptile wasn't coming for him.

When it looked clear, he slowly stood up and walked back up the small hill. Not wanting to see the grisly remains of his friend in the water, he turned his head and closed one eye before scanning the water. To his amazement, the clear-blue water was returned to normal, not a trace of his friend or the reptile.

Feeling sick, he crouched down and began to cry. Holding his head and shaking it from side to side, he suddenly stopped and looked dead ahead across the water. There it was, the satanic eyes and ferocious head sat just above the water...watching him with what looked like an evil grin, daring him to come closer.

The unmistakable sound of an outboard motor cut through the nightmarish trance he was in, and he looked upriver to see a party boat cruising his way. He turned his head back to the reptile, and it was gone.

"Stop! Turn around! Get outta here!" he shouted to no avail, standing at the top of the embankment and waving his arms.

The party barge looked to be about twenty-five feet long as the captain put the boat in neutral, "What's wrong, pal?" he shouted as a pontoon floated up to the sand.

"There's a giant gator in here! It ate my friend!"

The boat captain looked at his friends and joined them as they searched the pristine water. Giving the man a peculiar look, he grabbed the radio and called for help.

7

More than twelve-hundred miles away, Don Henderson was standing in his barbershop cutting hair in Wichita, Kansas.

The barbershop was in a strip shopping plaza near downtown and had a respectable number of customers. Three barber chairs were set up in front of large mirrors, but Don had only hired one other barber.

He would cut men's regular-style haircuts while the other barber would handle what Don called "Kiddie Cuts." It did not mean that he only cut kids' hair, but he would do what Don called weirdo styles, the styles where they drew designs with razors and whatnot. Don despised these trends but didn't mind taking money from those what he referred to as, special individuals.

The shop had wood panel walls and a hickory smell, making it feel more like a cozy lounge than a barber shop, and if you wanted, you could even have a drink from a little bar table set up in a corner.

He chatted with the regular customer sitting in the chair while a small television hung on the wall. It was tuned in to the local news to add fuel to the mundane conversations.

What caught his ear on the television was completely unexpected. His heart sank to the pit of his stomach, and he could feel its thundering pulse in his neck while his mind raced.

Before they went to a commercial break, the newsman said, "And coming up after this short break, what lurks below in the springs at Clearview State Park in Florida? Eyewitness watches a gigantic creature attack and kill his fisherman friend; a trapper is missing after the fisherman hears loud screaming, and two divers are missing…stay tuned, and we'll be right back."

"Did you hear that?" Don asked, looking like he'd just seen a ghost.

"Yeah, that's Florida for you," the customer smiled. "You would never catch me swimming in Florida. That's right, not even in a swimming pool. They say in Florida that every single place that has water, could have an alligator in it. One time, my little niece and her boyfriend were down there, and you know what? That's right. They were about to jump in the swimming pool at a Holiday Inn when they spotted a gator! Believe That? No sir, you will never catch me in that…."

"Quiet! It's on," Don cut him off when the news returned.

Don stopped cutting the man's hair, rushed over to the television remote, and turned up the volume.

He sat in a chair and watched a newsman interviewing a distraught fisherman inside Clearview State Park.

"I'm standing here on the banks of the Ichetucknee River with a local fisherman who doesn't want to reveal his identity," he said, the camera not showing the man's face. "Sir, what happened here earlier?"

"My friend and I were fishing over there," he pointed, "And were attacked by the biggest monster I've ever seen. It was well over thirty-five feet long."

The newsman gave him a contradicting look, then turned to the camera, "I don't believe alligators get that big, do they?"

"This was no ordinary gator. It looked more like a prehistoric monster. It had twice as many teeth sticking out of its jaws, and I'm not exaggerating about the size."

The cameraman could be heard smirking as the camera shook, and the newsman looked down at his notepad, "Ok, so what did this large reptile do?"

"It attacked our canoe and ate my buddy."

"You also said you believe it killed a trapper around the bend inside Clearview Springs State Park?"

"Yes."

"Ok, thank you, sir," replied the newsman, ending the interview as he watched a police officer and park ranger escort him away to get a statement for their investigation.

"So, there you have it. Is there a giant reptile lurking below? If so, did it attack the fisherman? The trapper? The two divers? We'll let you know when we know. Until then, this is Jim Simpson from WJBC News."

Don turned the sound down and sat motionless in the chair.

"Are you ok, Don? You look pale," the customer asked.

Don Henderson was pale, and for good reason. Years ago, it was he who talked his two bio-chemist acquaintances into splicing the genes and DNA that eventually led to the birth of three, what they called AlliCrocs.

Don was at a loss for words. His first thought was that there was no way in the world he would risk his life and go back down there and try to save his reptile. He assured his old friend Virgil Goodman and his crew, who had hunted the first creature, that this one would never be found. It would live out its life in the wild, far from civilization.

But, if this truly is the other AlliCroc it is the only one left. There's not or ever will be another reptile like it on the entire planet, he thought. I could make millions! All I have to do is trap it and put it in a secure...very secure location and have a one-of-a-kind attraction. People will come from around the world just to see it! He kept thinking.

He quickly finished cutting his customer's hair and sent him on his marry way, practically shoving him out the door.

The first thing he had to do was find out where the hell Clearview Springs was, then go down there and snoop around, find out what the locals are saying and find out who's hunting it.

Hopefully, not Captain Bloodfoot, Randy Taylor or his old friend Virgil Goodman and his crew. After meeting them last time, it was clear they all wanted to kill him.

The sun was slowly receding on the western horizon with flaring luminosity as the Endurance cruised at top speed a mile offshore, heading in a southerly direction after spending the better part of a week salvaging a sunken ship off the coast of Port Charlotte.

Captain Virgil Goodman stood at the helm in good spirits, smoking non-filtered camel cigarettes and sipping a coffee cup filled with apricot brandy. A handsome, rugged man with a well-built, five-foot-ten-inch frame and piercing green eyes, his dark, leathery tan from many hours spent on the water made him look like quite the adventurer, which is precisely what he was.

Born in Wichita, Kansas, the son of loving parents, Virgil and his younger sister had a cheerful childhood. This would soon change when he became a teenager as his father, the most reputable auto mechanic in town and owner of a full-service automobile station, tried to groom his son to work and one day take over the business.

At the age of seventeen, after wracking his knuckles on persnickety nuts and bolts under the hood of countless cars, he decided to change his life and join the army as a paratrooper. When he got out of the armed forces, he and a friend by the name of Don Henderson had saved enough money to buy a shrimp boat down in New Orleans. When that little adventure ran its course, Virgil hitchhiked his way to Miami and got a job as a deckhand on a tugboat in the Port of Miami.

From there, it didn't take long before he received his Captain's license and became Captain of a tugboat in Port Everglades. A quick two years after that, he found the girl of his dreams and married her. They quickly started a family and became proud parents of a daughter and two sons.

After years of dedicated service to the company, Virgil and his crew inadvertently became tangled with capturing and killing a large predator with the help of a world-renowned hunter named Captain Bloodfoot. Not long after the hair-raising experience, a distinctive bond between Bloodfoot and the crew forced them to Socotra Island to help free Bloodfoot from the capture of pirates.

It was after these two life-changing events that Captain Virgil decided to purchase a salvage vessel and offered his crew a spot on the boat to set out for their own adventures. Working with Captain Bloodfoot opened their eyes.

"Aye, Captain, hell of a day, eh?" Ian shouted as he scampered into the wheelhouse with a six-pack of Heineken.

Virgil looked at his new adventure-seeking deckhand out of the corner of his eyes and let out a breath of cigarette smoke before replying, "Can't complain at all. This job was a complete success."

"I hope you had as much fun as I did," he smiled and stood next to the captain. "I'll spot you a few hours so you can get some rest," he continued, squeezing Virgil on the shoulder.

"Just keep her straight between the shore and horizon," Virgil replied, relinquishing the helm, "I want to dock in Port Everglades before tomorrow night."

Virgil watched with amusement at the way Ian took to the helm like a kid to a candy store. While purchasing the salvage tug down in Panama less than a year earlier, he and his two-man crew met Ian while celebrating in a local watering hole called La Rana Dorada.

While sitting at the bar enjoying their well-deserved cocktails, a team of undesirable Panamanians suddenly appeared in pursuit of the men who purchased the sea-going tugboat. Word had it that they were drug runners and wanted the use of the salvage tugboat.

A fight ensued when the Americans told them in so many words to take a hike, and they quickly found out they were outnumbered.

Suddenly, out of nowhere, Ian crashed into the two largest rogues and continued to battle along with the crew until the assailants were either knocked out cold or ran away, licking their wounds.

Virgil and his crew left the bar with their new friend and invited him to the salvage tug, where they thanked him properly with his favorite drink, a bottle of Crown Royal. While talking in the galley, they found out he was also from Fort Lauderdale and, through a series of misadventures, wound up stuck in Panama.

Although he was half the crew's age, his heart and soul were well-suited with theirs, and before the night was over, Virgil and his two-man crew decided to invite Ian aboard as a deckhand, and the rest, as they say, is history.

As the night wore on and the blackness out at sea turned to quiet cool, the salvage tug, aptly Christened Endurance, continued three miles offshore, traveling south at fourteen knots. The hum of the twin EMD 12-645 E2 engines was music to Chuck's ears as he stood at the stern of the one-hundred-and-thirty-five-foot salvage tug, his guard-duty shift about to end.

Two years before, Chuck and his crewmates took on an adventurous, if not irrational, mission in the Gulf of Aden and became aware of the intricacies of pirates. Now, with their life's investment dependent on the Endurance, Captain Virgil insisted that while traveling at sea in the darkness of night, there would be two of the crew on duty while the other two slept.

Chuck McClowski was the engineer and by far the friendliest of the crew, always ready to help a kindred soul in need. Standing five-foot-nine with a medium build, his dark, tanned, leathery features made him look the part of a seafaring adventurer, which he now considered himself to be. Born and raised in South Florida, he married his high school sweetheart at the age of twenty-one.

Virgil rose from his bunk and stretched as he sat up, put his legs over the side of the bed and slipped into his leather clogs. The unmistakable smell of bacon attracted his attention as he gingerly stepped into the galley for a cup of coffee.

"Bacon at this hour," Virgil asked, pouring coffee into his mug and checking his watch.

"Can't satisfy my appetite, Captain. Thought I'd grab a bite before relieving Chuck," said Bill, peering up at the clock on the wall, which read eleven-fifty-five. "Ahh, perfect timing, still have five minutes before I take watch."

Bill Brighton was tough as a steel bricklayer from Pennsylvania before transplanting to South Florida and landing a job as a deckhand in Port Everglades. He stood five-foot-eleven with arms as thick as a regular man's legs and kept his head shaved bald. The crew never missed a beat when he would put on a white T-shirt, and they'd say he was a dead-ringer for Mr. Clean from the television commercial.

His eighteen-year marriage has stood the test of time with the transition from a Port Everglades tugboat deckhand to the new adventures with the crew and their salvage business. The business kept him from home more frequently, but the reunions with his wife and daughter upon return made it all worthwhile.

Virgil smiled to himself as he watched Bill scamper out the door, balancing two BLT sandwiches and a large glass of milk and walked smoothly with his powerful sea legs toward the stern to relieve Chuck.

Ian had just lit his second Cuban Pinar Del Rio cigar when Captain Virgil stepped in the wheelhouse, "How's it going, kid?" he said, reaching for the bottle of brandy on the shelf and pouring a shot into his coffee mug.

"Aye Captain, approaching Cape Sable and its smooth sailing until we cut through the Straights where we'll hit three to five-foot seas on the Atlantic side," Ian replied with vigor.

The fastest route back to Port Everglades would be to go through the mind-numbing Caloosahatchee River, through Lake Okeechobee and out through Stuart, but Virgil and the crew thought it would be more exciting to go through the Florida Straights where anything could happen, and a good salvage tug was desirable.

Virgil suddenly realized that half of his bottle of apricot brandy was missing and shot Ian a resentful look, but all thoughts of a lecture vanished when he slapped him on the back and pointed at the bottle, "Moderation," he merely said.

Having Ian join the crew was the breath of fresh air they needed. Not to demean his late deckhand who was killed while hunting AlliCroc, Ian was twice as good as any deckhand he had while working at Port Everglades and drank twice as much as anybody he'd ever known.

One out of two was good enough; besides, it seemed he loved the Endurance as much as the crew and got along well with everybody. He also knew how to speak Spanish, which could come in handy at times.

Born and raised in Maine, Ian Torren excelled in his favorite sport, 'baseball.' When he was old enough, he was asked to play on a semi-pro team in Puerto Rico. There, he found the lady that would change his life in the local bar. Within the year, they married and moved to Fort Lauderdale, Florida, where he built his own house remodeling business. Soon after, they were blessed with a baby boy they christened Ian Jr.

One day, when work was slowing and Ian was exploring his options, he jumped at the offer to go down to Panama and work for six months. A run-in with local authorities on a raucous bar incident had drained his bank account, which made it impossible to return to the States when, out of nowhere, the Endurance seemingly docked at his footsteps.

Now, after becoming a crewmember, Ian would yarn every now and then that if not offered the job, he would have had no choice but to board the salvage tug as a stowaway.

Captain Virgil took the helm as Ian leisurely stepped back and sat near a window.

"Don't you want to get some sleep?" asked Virgil, giving Ian a staggered look.

"No, sir, Captain. To me, there's nothing better than sailing the ocean on through the night," he replied, taking a swig of Crown Royal from a flask while puffing on his cigar.

Virgil couldn't blame him. There was nothing like being out on the ocean at night. The blackness and cool breeze felt good for the soul and made him feel like he was the only person in the world, with nothing to see but the beautiful stars and nothing to hear but the splashes of the water being cut by the bow of the tug and the twin diesel engines purring in perfect harmony.

Virgil settled in his captain's chair, lit a cigarette, and continued on course. The two of them were lost in their own little worlds until Ian broke the silence and offered Virgil a cigar, "Try one of these, Cap. They're straight from Cuba."

"Oh? When were you in Cuba?"

"I got them in Panama, but they're from Cuba," Ian winced, shaking his head and knowing he'd never get anything past the sharpshooting captain.

"I see," Virgil replied. Tossing his cigarette out the window and biting off the tip of the cigar. Just then, the satellite phone rang. With an annoyed look, Virgil got up and retrieved the phone from the shelf ahead of the massive steering wheel.

101

"VCB Salvage, who's calling at this hour?" Virgil answered, his watch reading twelve-forty-five A.M.

"Ssssup pal? It's your 'ol buddy Randy," replied the intoxicated voice on the other end. "You'll never guess who I'm meeting at the Anchor Bar tomorrow tonight?"

"Get some sleep, you drunk bastard," smiled Virgil. "We'll be back tomorrow. Talk to me when you're sober," Virgil replied, turning the phone off.

"Important call?" Ian snickered, taking another hit from his flask.

Virgil shook his head and replied, "Just an old friend who's had too much to drink."

"I thought I heard him say his name is Randy. Is that the police officer who helped you guys on that Socotra Island caper?"

Virgil gave him a peculiar look before replying, "Taylor, Randy Taylor. That was him on the other end. You sound like you're talking about a Batman episode. Who says caper?"

"I feel another awesome adventure on the rise," Ian smiled, not knowing how right he was.

Before Virgil could reply, the phone rang again. Virgil looked at the phone and then at Ian, who looked anxious as he, too stared at the phone.

"Want me to answer?" Ian asked on the fourth ring.

Virgil gave him the death stare before answering, "Okay, Taylor, who are you meeting with," he replied, watching his new deckhand fidget in his seat.

"Bloodfoot! Captain Bloodfoot is in town!"

"What the hell?" Virgil grinned.

"That's right, he says he has a business proposition for us."

Virgil's grin turned to a frown as he began to pace around the wheelhouse, "Like I said, we'll be back sometime tomorrow. I'll meet you two at the Anchor Bar. It better not be what I think it is either."

"Me neither."

"Did he sail in?"

"I have no idea. I just got off the phone with him. I tried for some information, but he said we'll talk when I'm sober and hung up."

Virgil couldn't hide the look of dread on his face and replied, "Ok, we'll meet at the Anchor Bar, and again, it better not be anything about the AlliCroc that got away."

"I hope not either, but I did get a disturbing call the other day," a solemn-sounding Randy replied, then disconnected.

Ian sat watching as the captain continued pacing the floor, "Did you say Anchor Bar? The place about a mile from the port?"

"You know of it?" replied Virgil, amazed that Ian seemed to know every bar he'd ever been in.

"Hell yeah, I used to practically live there."

"How come I'm not surprised?"

"My old buddy and I coached Little League baseball close by that bar. It was like our coaches' meeting place."

"What the hell didn't you do," Virgil retorted, "Take the wheel. I've got to talk to Chuck and Bill in the galley."

Before he could step foot off the bridge, Ian spoke with an entreating tone, "Wait a second, Captain, I've been a crewmember for a while now, and whatever you guys are going to plan, I want to be in on it."

Virgil stopped at the door and stood for a long minute before facing his deckhand, staring at Ian as if piercing through his eyes to read his mind, then replied, "Careful what you ask for, sunshine. If it's what I think it is, you may not live to regret it."

Ian gave a puzzled look; he couldn't recall anybody ever calling him sunshine. He took a deep breath before replying, "In for a penny, in for a pound, Captain."

He was about to reply but couldn't find the words. Virgil knew deep down that his deckhand had the spirit of the wild and would give his right arm for the chance to participate. He also began to wonder if he'd ever met Captain Bloodfoot.

"Okay, go get Chuck and Bill up here," replied Virgil.

Sergeant Randy Taylor was sitting at the Anchor bar sipping a rum and coke. He checked his watch for the umpteenth time and looked up to see the bartender standing in front of him.

"Carlos, how are you doing this evening."

"I'm good, Sergeant. How are you tonight? I see you keep checking your watch like you've got an important date."

"I guess you can say that. I'm waiting on some friends."

As they talked casually about the latest events in the neighborhood and other mind-numbing chats, they failed to notice the towering, broad-shouldered man walk through the door and head in their direction.

The patrons stopped talking and cleared out of the way as the heels of his black boots sounded like pile drivers on the concrete floor. At a closer look, you could see what appeared to be an arrangement of shark, alligator, human and an assortment of other teeth attached to a buckle at the boot ankle. The only tooth that looked more hideous than the human incisor was the eight-inch, jagged, conical tooth hanging from around his neck.

Attached to a thick leather belt was a hunting knife with a leather handle that looked like it was made by a primeval warrior. Dressed all in black, he wore a tight-fitting, sleeveless shirt that exposed muscled arms that would make the Terminator look thin.

With his six-foot-five-inch frame and blonde shoulder-length dreadlocks, he looked every bit like the rogue pirate that would make Blackbeard shudder in another place and time.

Randy put his face down in his glass to hide the smile as Carlos stood paralyzed at the massive pirate-looking man who suddenly wrapped a massive arm around the Sergeant.

"Randy!" he boomed, his voice drowning out the jukebox.

"Captain Bloodfoot!" Randy replied, squeezing out of the bear hug and turning to see the giant. "Good to see you've still got your head," he smiled and shook hands, which he immediately regretted when the bones in his hand cracked.

He was referring to the incident that took place a few years earlier when Randy, Captain Virgil and his crew had to fly to Socotra Island and save Bloodfoot from Somali pirates who threatened to behead him.

Carlos stood awestruck behind the bar and nearly wet his pants when Bloodfoot turned his head and stared him down with a wicked grin, "Carlos, the bartender with a bat," he remembered, extending his hand so the bartender could shake it. Carlos didn't know if he should run or stick out his hand.

It was a few years earlier when Bloodfoot first entered the Anchor bar, and a raucous fight with the local police ensued. They say not to judge a person by the way he looks, but the local police saw otherwise and tried to arrest him at first sight.

Carlos thought it would be good for the bar if he helped the police, so he jumped from behind the bar with a baseball bat and tried to skulk up on the pirate from behind. Lucky for him, Bloodfoot turned and gave him a look that made him change his mind and run.

"I...I'm...I'm sorry about that, I was just..."

"Save it, kid," Bloodfoot interrupted. "No hard feelings. I'll have a bottle of your Sailor Jerry rum and two glasses."

Randy was about to check his watch again when the door opened and in strolled Captain Virgil and his crew. Virgil smiled and shook his head as Ian seemed to greet everyone in there like old friends.

Carlos looked up and saw them heading over. He looked lost in thought as he realized he was the only male on staff this evening and hoped this motley crew gathering would remain civil.

A quick look at the man bringing up the rear made him smile with relief and ring the tip bell, "Ian! Is that my brother from another mother?"

"Carlos, my man!" Ian greeted. "How's my favorite bar been holding up since I was here last?"

"Great. A lot of patrons have been asking about you."

"Well...the man is back in town!"

Bloodfoot took the rum bottle and another four glasses and headed for an empty table in the back corner, followed by Randy.

Virgil, Chuck and Bill spotted them and headed over, while Ian stepped behind the bar and kissed the barmaid.

"Captain Bloodfoot, how's our favorite pirate," Virgil said, grabbing his shoulder while shaking hands.

"Livin' the dream, Captain," he replied, with a warm reception. "I heard you fellas have got your own dream in fruition," he continued, shaking hands with Chuck and Bill. "Who's the welcome guide?" Bloodfoot smirked as he looked over Bill's shoulder toward Ian, now sitting at the bar surrounded by patrons.

"Our new crewmember," Virgil replied.

"Seems like a chatty fella," Bloodfoot beamed, squinting his eyes as he sized Ian up.

"He's a good man, fits in well," Chuck declared, taking a seat.

They chatted about their exploitations and what they've done since their Socotra Island adventure. Captain Virgil gulped down the gut-wretch liquid in his glass and cut to the chase, "Okay, Bloodfoot, what's the deal. I certainly hope it's not about hunting for that AlliCroc that got away," he said flatly.

Bloodfoot looked them dead in the eye as Ian finally joined them with a new bottle of rum, "Greetings, my friends, my name's Ian," he said, shaking hands with Bloodfoot and Randy.

"Bloodfoot," he boomed in a low but intimidating growl, shaking his hand and taking note of Ian's rough, calloused hand.

"Taylor, Randy Taylor," replied Randy. "I've seen you around here. My nephew also played on your Little League team a few years back."

"Good times, mate, good times," Ian replied with a smile.

"We've got business to discuss, Ian. If Captain Goodman here thinks it's okay for you to be here, you can stay. If not, we'll have a drink when it's over," Bloodfoot said point-blank.

"Ian's part of the crew. He stays," Virgil confirmed.

"Ok, good, let's get down to business," replied Bloodfoot, filling the glasses. "A month ago, people were attacked by what they said was a giant gator. They haven't seen it, but grisly remains are consistent with a large reptile. The attacks continued in different areas before abruptly stopping. The latest attacks happened last week at Clearview State Park. This time, a witness says he saw a reptile over thirty-five feet long."

"I received a call from a Hollywood police officer vacationing in Clearview State Park, who says he's seen the reptile," Randy cut in.

Virgil sat back, absorbing the conversation, when Chuck asked, "What makes you think it's the other AlliCroc?"

Randy took a swig from his glass and replied, "The man said it was about thirty to forty feet long and looked like an armor-covered prehistoric monster."

"The town's sure keeping a pretty good secret about it," Bill chimed in.

"The attacks were reported as a large, unruly gator. The mayor hired a local trapper by the name of Jack Morgan, who went out to set traps one morning and was never heard from since," said Randy. "Then, a day later, a fisherman reported that Jack and his fishing buddy were attacked and eaten by a monstrous gator, or in his words, a prehistoric-looking monster."

"Did you tell the mayor what we went through when we dealt with the one down here? Can you imagine how much bigger and smarter this one must be after all these years?" Virgil finally spoke.

"I did. This time, the mayor took it more seriously and got the National Guard on it. After a few days of splashing around, they gave up when they found no trace of the reptile. Days later, another victim was reported, and the mayor was somehow able to get the guard back for another hunt. After several hours, they again couldn't find the damn thing and discontinued their search. The mayor protested and was told in so many words that the National Guard were soldiers, not hunters. But they did manage to take a photo from the banks of the river," Randy continued, taking a photograph from a file and passing it around the table.

Each crewmember let out a heavy sigh when they saw the three-foot-long footprint of a reptile with dagger-like claws. Virgil tossed the photo to the center of the table and shook his head.

110

"On behalf of the crew and I, there's no way in hell we're going through that mess again."

"If the National Guard can't find that monster, what makes you think we can?" Chuck continued.

"It's what I do," Bloodfoot replied keenly. "This time, we know what we're up against."

"That thing has been loose in the wild for years. Remember how fast they grow? I can only imagine how big this one is," Chuck countered, reaching in his shirt pocket for his pack of cigarettes.

"Eyewitnesses say it's about thirty-five to forty feet…give or take," replied Randy, his hand physically shaking his half-empty glass.

"I really don't know why you think we'd go through this again. That first AlliCroc nearly killed us all," Virgil continued.

"What if I told you there's a million-dollar bounty on its head?" Bloodfoot grinned, draining his glass.

Virgil, Chuck and Bill looked each other in the eye for a long moment. Ian started to speak but Bloodfoot gave him the evil eye, and he reconsidered his place amongst the crew.

"With that kind of money, there'll be every half-baked hunter in the state up there looking for it."

"The offer only extends to me, and I will split it with you because I need your help. We are the only ones that know what that reptile is capable of."

"We got lucky the first time. That damn reptile almost killed all of us, and this one is bigger," Virgil reacted.

"Do it or don't, just let me know. I was hoping we could work as a team. I know we can find and kill that beast. Yes, it's huge, and I can't do it alone," Bloodfoot shot back, excusing himself to go to the restroom.

They watched as the giant ducked his head to go through the restroom door. Lost in thought, they missed the four patrons exit the restroom as if scared for their lives.

A few minutes later, Bloodfoot returned to the table and was happy to see the crew conversing about the hunt. The conversation ended when he sat down.

Another bottle of rum found its way to the table by the ever-pleasing Carlos, who was hot on Bloodfoot's footsteps, "This one's on the house," he said, as he nearly tripped on the man's heels.

"We're going to need some pretty big weapons if we're going to hunt that heinous reptile," said Virgil, digging in his shirt pocket and retrieving a pack of camel non-filtered cigarettes.

"Take a walk with me to the trunk of my car, gentlemen," Randy replied as he stood up and walked toward the back door.

They looked at each other with no surprise as they got up and followed him outside. Ian stayed behind as if guarding the rum bottle until Bill nodded his head for him to follow.

"Should I bring the bottle?" Ian panted.

"Who's going to take a rum bottle from Bloodfoot," Bill snickered as he clutched him on the shoulder and steered him out the door.

Outside, Randy opened the trunk of his police-issued Crown Victoria and opened one of three cases, "Feast your eyes on these monster killers'" he said with a beguiling grin.

Bloodfoot reached for one of the mammoth rifles but was stopped by Randy, "Not here."

"Well, what the hell are they?" Bloodfoot growled, his displeasure not hidden.

Randy closed the trunk and motioned the crew back into the bar. Once seated, the grin left his face, and he was all business. "Sitting in the trunk out, there are three .905-caliber rifles. The rounds fire about twenty-one hundred feet per second, and the recoil will knock you on your ass.

".905-calibur? If what you're saying is true, you're talking about shoulder-mounted cannons. Who makes something like this, and how did you get your hands on them?" Bloodfoot questioned.

For the first time since they met him, the crew saw the staggered look on Bloodfoot's face.

"Remember my old buddy Walter from the Gulf War?"

"I don't think we'd ever forget him. He's the guy who supplied you with the pancor shotgun," replied Bill.

"That's right. Well, he knows a friend who knows a friend that works at the factory in Ohio that made them."

"We can probably use a couple more, don't you think?" asked Bill.

"The three in my trunk are the only ones ever made," Randy replied with an exulting tone.

"Randy, Bloodfoot, excuse us for a few minutes while we step outside," said Virgil, lighting his cigarette and standing.

Chuck and Bill got up from their chairs and followed the captain out the door while Ian sat, staring at Randy.

"Are you not part of the crew?" Bloodfoot asked forebodingly.

Ian took a long stare at the pirate and replied, "I am."

Bloodfoot returned the gaze as he watched the newcomer finish his drink and slowly get up from the table to join the crew outside.

"Nice kid, but there's something unsettling about him that I don't like," Randy muttered.

"He's fine," replied Bloodfoot, "I might just have to tweak him a little if he decides to join us for the hunt."

The crew was huddled by a tree in the far corner of the parking lot, discussing the pros and cons of Bloodfoot's proposal, when they stopped talking and looked over to Ian as he approached.

"I'm in. Let's go get some gator."

"You have no idea what you want to involve yourself in," replied Chuck.

Fifteen minutes later, after agreeing that the arsenal being brought this time would probably turn AlliCroc into sushi and the reward money would pay off the salvage tugboat, they agreed to do it.

Captain Virgil also explained to Ian how distressing the monster is and that nobody would think less of him if he stayed behind. Ian's only reply was, "One for all and all for one." They thought he was drunk and let it slide until morning.

The crew went back into the bar and took their seats at the table.

"OK, count us in. This time, it looks like we can be better prepared. Bloodfoot, what's your plan?" said Virgil.

"Ian, I don't know you, but if you're a crewmember aboard the Endurance, I assume you've got adventure in your veins, and I welcome you to join us," Bloodfoot thundered, holding his glass up for a toast.

They toasted their forthcoming hunt and took turns filling Ian in on the mutant reptile. After a couple of hours, they agreed to meet the next morning on the Endurance to discuss the plan of attack.

8

The sun peaked out from the grey clouds like a spotlight on the cool, clear waters at Rattlesnake Jake's Swamp Adventure but quickly disappeared into darkness as another thunderstorm threatened the small group of thrill-seekers. It was midweek, and the inclement weather added to the eerie adventure.

Jake Brady, his real name Kevin Brady, owned a private stretch of land near the Fort White Wildlife Environmental Area along the Santa Fe River. Family-owned for generations, it was now his turn to continue the family tradition of providing small groups of adventure seekers to walk knee-deep in the mucky swamp along the river and view wildlife like Indians once did.

On this particular morning, Elaine and Marge Newton stepped out of their car and pulled out their hand-carved walking sticks made out of solid oak. The four other adventure seekers were sitting under a tree canopy, watching as the new arrivals sprayed a thick coat of mosquito repellant all over their faces and arms. Marge used vinegar and water, while Elaine took no chances using Off.

Coming straight from vacationing in Mount Dora, the two sisters-in-law decided to check out the wildlife at Rattlesnake Jakes.

With a perpetual smile that she could never hide on these trips, Elaine turned to say hello to an older man as he approached.

"Good morning, sir," she said with a friendly tone.

"Good morning to you too, young lady," he smiled. "You ladies look like you've done this before."

"No, this is our first time," Marge replied.

"Well, you two sure picked a day with inclement weather to start a new adventure. I hope you enjoy it."

"As long as we see squirrels and iguanas, I'll be happy," said Elaine.

"Oh? Those are very common around here. Have you seen them in the wild?"

"I live in Fort Lauderdale. I have a backyard full of them."

"Ok then, I'm sure you'll see those and a whole lot more."

"Hopefully, they come out in this weather," Marge added. "At least if it's only drizzling, it might keep the mosquitos away."

"It looks spooky, did you ever see alligators?" he continued, suddenly not smiling.

"We've seen lots of them. They tend to stay away, but if they get too curious, I will poke them away with my stick," Elaine said valiantly. Marge smiled to herself and gently peeled the price tag off her brand-new shiny walking stick.

The worried look on his face was priceless. Elaine and Marge closed their car doors and headed for the rest of the group.

"Hmmm, my phone hasn't got a signal," Marge said.

"Nobody has a signal out here, especially on rainy days like today," said the man following.

They met with the rest of the group and made small talk until an old, white Dodge pickup with a vanity plate of a Jolly Roger cruised up the rocky drive and stopped.

Kevin exited the truck and tripped over a root as he made his way to his customers, "Greetings, my friends, looks like we might get a little wet today," he crooned, looking up at the sky. "My name is Kevin; I will be leading this swamp walk. Raise your hand when I call your name so I know who you are if you get eaten by something," he smiled. "Elaine...Brian...Marge...Hector...Jake... and Marvin."

"Nice truck," whispered Marvin with a smirk.

Kevin turned his head and smiled as he looked at the pickup. There was a cracked windshield from a stray baseball and a dent on the side, but otherwise, it was Kevin's pride and joy. "Thanks, kid. I call her the White Pearl." *There's always a smartass in every group*, Kevin thought to himself. But at thirty bucks a pop, he was willing to deal with it for a couple of hours. The only problem was that he was also dealing with a slight hangover.

The small group gathered around a picnic table and listened as Kevin gave instructions and handed out fiberglass walking sticks

119

that looked like they had been stored at the bottom of the river. Elaine and Marge declined as they raised their personal sticks.

The smart-ass kid suddenly pointed, "Wow! Check it out. What caused that wake?"

Kevin opted to just roll his eyes and pray the kid wouldn't be too much trouble until he heard the wake crashing into the marsh. He turned and gazed out over the grey, rainy bog and shrugged, "It must have been a manatee or something."

Anticipating their moves and cunningly hiding from the National Guard as they hunted the elusive creature in and around Clearview Springs, the thirty-eight-foot reptile managed to swim undetected out of the Ichetucknee River and into the Santa Fe River.

Driven by endless hunger pangs that furthered its aggressive behavior, AlliCroc couldn't resist a manatee as it swam indifferently in the swampy area on the outskirts of the Fort White Wildlife Environmental Area.

The truculent predator slowly stalked its prey as it fed on the grassy shoreline. At thirty feet away, the manatee detected danger that sent AlliCroc's Integumentary Sense organs tingling. The aggressive reptile became incensed and sprang from the bottom and clamped onto the manatee with its massive jaws, ripping through flesh and bones as it pulled it underwater toward the center of the river before it could reach the marsh.

Hitting its prey with the force of a freight train caused the wake witnessed by the sixteen-year-old named Marvin.

After days of hiding and slipping out of constricted situations without eating, AlliCroc feasted on the manatee like a ravaging monster, careful not to let pieces of the slippery flesh rise to the surface to be detected by the hunters if they were near at all in this isolated area.

When finished with the fatty feast, the hideous reptile detected a pressure drop near the marshy bog near the shore. AlliCroc sat still and took note of not one but many potential quarries entering the water.

With the abundant leaf droppings from nearby cypress trees like the Bald Cypress, the water of the slow-moving river was dark-brown and impossible for the gargantuan reptile to be detected underwater.

It suddenly perceived that there were seven individual entities moving sluggishly between Cypress trees and thickets along the shore. AlliCroc slowly rose to the surface, careful not to cause a ripple in the water. The hideous snout and malicious-looking eyes gradually breached the surface.

Hunger spasms swiftly resumed and nearly drove the reptile into a rage as it slipped below the surface and sank to the bottom, crawling along in an ever-closing attack.

Its first instinct was to rush in and devour the prey, but AlliCroc was aware of the loud, high-pitched screams the quarry could make, which could bring the hunters back.

Certain that it could wipe out the entire group in one menacing sweep, the well-developed thought pattern the reptile was experiencing made it aware that if one of the prey was able to escape, its whereabouts would be known, and the hunters would come searching. The reptile thought it would be better to follow along and wait for one unsuspecting prey to separate from the group, where it could be quickly eaten before the others knew what happened.

"Damnit! These mosquitos are killing me," Squealed Marvin.

Elaine turned to see the irritant young man slapping the back of his neck and arms. She gave a slight smirk as she pondered how the obnoxious kid could possibly go wading through the swamp without putting on mosquito repellant.

"Marvin, I have a can of OFF if you want to use it," she said.

"Sure, I'll try some of that and die of skin poisoning instead of malaria," he replied spitefully.

"Forget it. Get malaria," Elaine replied, returning his arrogance.

Kevin was not as patient as his adventurous clients and fell back to where he could talk to Marvin. "Look, kid, most of these people really look forward to doing this sort of thing. The last thing they want is to have you ruining their venture because you are complaining about being eaten by mosquitos."

"What a mistake I made coming out here, splashing in this filthy swamp," he replied, smacking the surface of the water with his stick.

Before Kevin could refute the spoiled tempest, Elaine spotted an alligator heading over, "Hey Kevin, you might want to stop smacking the water with your stick," she called out, pointing at the gator.

"Why don't you just mind your own damn business?!"

"Sure thing, kid," she grinned. "Just watch out for that little gator swimming your way. It probably thinks you have some food."

Marvin froze and turned to see the three-to-four-foot alligator swimming over. As he panicked and tried to hide behind the tour guide, Elaine walked over and nudged it away with her stick when it was close enough.

"Careful, girl, that's not one of your iguana friends," Marge whispered.

"Good job, Elaine," smiled Kevin. "See, Marvin, that's one of the reasons we have these sticks. Now join us or waddle your way back to the camp. It's your choice," he continued, making his way up to the front again.

Marvin stood with an intense look, waste-deep in dirty brown water and mosquitos eating him alive. His reply came quickly, "Sorry everybody, this is not what I thought it would be like. I'm going back to the camp and wait for you guys," he said, his shoulders hunched forward.

"Ah, c'mon Kevin, you can walk with me…It'll be fun," offered Marge.

He turned and looked at the encouraging woman and thought for a moment before replying, "Thanks, but no thanks," and turned and walked away.

Hector and Kevin looked at each other before looking over to Marvin's father, "You might want to try to stop him," Kevin informed. It's not such a good idea to walk around by yourself out here."

"No, not this time, let the kid go back and wait for me at the car. He's not going to ruin another trip of mine," said Brian, spearing the swampy bottom with his walking stick in frustration.

"There's snacks in the back of my pickup when you get back, just don't touch the red cooler," Kevin shouted, turning to the others with a slight grin, "The red cooler is for the grownups."

They watched Kevin's wake when he disappeared around a bend before turning to continue their exploration. Not a word was said about the young man who dared to brave the mosquitos by himself.

Suddenly, Hector swallowed hard and pointed, "Kevin! There's another gator coming in at us to your left!" he gasped.

Elaine smiled and walked next to the leader, "I've got this," she said, poking the average-sized alligator on the side of its head with her walking stick, causing it to change course and swim away.

"Whew! That was close!" said Marge, maneuvering herself between the others.

"You're next to try out your new stick, Marge. That won't be the last one we're going to see out here," replied Elaine, smiling and giving the guide a wink.

"She's right. We see 'em out here all the time. No need to panic; just push 'em out of the way like she did," Kevin added.

"Well...uh...maybe we should go back and warn Marvin," said the concerned father.

"He's probably halfway back to camp by now," Jake grumbled.

"If ya'all wanna go back, we will. If not, we've got another hour or so on this trail," Kevin suggested, not caring either way.

"My boy will be fine. Carry on."

Nearly a half-hour later, the group had forgotten their concerns about Marvin as they walked single-file through the knee-deep water, encountering more than a dozen alligators that

125

seemed to swim close enough to satisfy their curiosity before being poked and moving on.

At one point, Marge screamed, "God help me!" in a quaking tone only to find a manatee swim to the surface next to her for a breath of air. The rest of the group held their breath in stun silence, all scared but not willing to admit it.

Kevin did a good job pointing out a Bald Eagle flying at the tops of the canopy of trees and a Black Bear taking a bath up ahead. He put a finger to his lips as he turned and whispered for the group to freeze and stay quiet. Five minutes later, they watched the bear get out of the water and stare straight in their direction before moving on.

"Wow! If that damn bear attacked, we'd have been in some kind of trouble," Jake said.

"Oh, I don't know," Kevin looked at him with a sly smirk, putting his trusty forty-five magnum back in its shoulder holster.

"What the hell? I didn't know you brought a gun out here," Hector cried out.

"You don't think I put on this long-sleeved jacket for nothing, do you? Man's got to keep his customers safe, doesn't he?"

"Well, I'm glad you didn't have to use it."

"Me too."

Marvin was already dreading walking back by himself. He thought for sure that one or two of the others would follow. Minutes after trekking off, he rounded a bend and saw an alligator slowly swim by within ten yards away. His first reaction was to call for help, but instead, he climbed a skinny tree branch that felt like it was going to snap from his weight.

He waited silently until the reptile was out of sight before climbing down and continuing. His nerves were shot when an iguana darted from a hole in the bank and ran for safety. After realizing it was a harmless reptile, he gathered his wits and determined that they had these tours all the time, and nobody had ever been injured or killed by the wildlife.

Looking around, he figured the campsite was close, just around the next bend. He took a few deep breaths, stuck his stick in the muck and carried on with a brave face.

AlliCroc swam poised in the deeper water at the center of the river, careful not to make a ripple in the water while following the group. Its keen senses are on high alert. The constant battle between the reptile's ferocious appetite and its ability to sneak up on its prey agitated it ferociously, but in order to remain elusive, it had to fight the constant battle to stay in control.

Finally, the moment it was waiting for. AlliCroc sensed one of the people leaving the pack. It slowly rose to the surface until its eyes and repugnant snout once again breached the surface undetected. It watched as Marvin separated from the rest of the group and headed in the opposite direction.

The mutant reptile unhurriedly sank below the surface and began swimming toward the lone quarry, the enormous tail swaying side to side in a smooth manner, propelling the beast toward its prey. It slowed considerably as the brown water got shallower, careful not to stir the surface.

Suddenly, the prey vanished. The agitated creature stopped and waited for the vibration that would trigger its senses. It slowly raised its head and breached the surface with menacing eyes only.

Reassured to see its next meal climbing out of a small group of tree branches and back into the water, it only took seconds before the raging battle between stealth and attack mode drove the creature into a frenzy.

Marvin sloshed forward through the muck and finally spotted the camp up ahead. He was about to take another step but stopped dead in his tracks; something wasn't right. A sudden wave of fear numbed his entire body as he looked down and felt the incredible surge of water flow past his legs. Something big, like a boat, was pushing water in his direction, heading straight for him.

He quickly turned and gasped at the carnivorous jaws gaped wide open and ready to strike. He let out a high-pitched scream at the same time he tripped while scurrying backward.

The monstrous reptile careened over Marvin as he fell over backward, the enormous jaws snapping shut and missing him by inches, but the knee-deep shallow water made escape impossible as the weight of the reptile was crushing.

Marvin lay in the muck with his eyes wide open and couldn't believe what was happening as he watched the monster's hide pass over, its tough belly rubbing over his skin, slashing and cutting as if it contained what felt like knife blades.

AlliCroc stopped abruptly and became incensed for missing its prey. Feeling the quarry under its body, it compressed its massive legs while backing up, crushing Marvin and sinking him deeper in the sediment.

Marvin's life flashed before his eyes. He thought it strange that here he was in the middle of a swamp with a gigantic reptile on top of him, crushing his life out and backing him so that it could tear him to pieces with its jaws, and the one thing on his mind was how he wished he was back home watching cartoons, his mom and dad sitting at the kitchen table laughing and carrying on like every Saturday morning. He wished his dad never wanted to explore the swamp.

As his brain screamed for air, he thought how unfair it was to not even be able to say goodbye to his family.

Suddenly, an incredible blow to the head jerked his head forward. The pain increased as his chin dug deep into his upper chest, and the back of his neck felt like it was ready to snap. The creature was backing up, and Marvin's head was caught on a large bony section of the reptile's lower jaw.

Almost completely buried in the muck with his lungs screaming for air, Marvin knew he had to somehow get out from under the pulverizing monster before his neck snapped or he ran out of air, whichever came first. He tried to move his arms to no avail; they were buried in the sludge. A shroud of darkness engulfed him as he abruptly screamed out and tried to get himself out from under the reptile with all his strength.

Trapped and awaiting the inevitable, his mind's reflex told him to go ahead and gulp the brackish water. Suddenly, all the weight was off him, and the upper portion of his body floated off the muddy bottom. This could only mean one thing, he thought. The reptile was off him and ready to snap its monstrous jaws to finish him off.

He poked his head through the surface and sucked in a breath of air when his heart nearly gave out. There he was, staring eye-to-eye with death. AlliCroc was so close Mathew could smell the vile breath as it exhaled.

Conquered by terror, all he could do was sit and stare at the noxious monster. After a full minute had passed, he wondered why the reptile didn't finish the job and continued the assault. He looked deep into its big green eyes and suddenly felt that it was toying with him. It seemed to enjoy the fear exalting from its prey.

He quickly gathered what was left of his wits and tried to shake out of the sediment. His legs felt like they were held by suction as he pulled free and tried to back up towards the shore. His eyes never left the evil predator as it seemed to sit and watch what he would do next.

He turned his head to see how close he was to the embankment when the reptile hissed loudly and crawled closer. To his amazement, he turned his attention back toward the reptile and confirmed what looked like the evil monster was euphoric while terrifying its prey.

Another quick glance toward dry land and the reptile while gathering his nerves proved unbearable, but it was now or never.

He took a deep, unsteady breath and suddenly bolted out of the muck, screaming at the top of his lungs. He didn't look back to see, but he could feel the reptile give chase. Scrambling out of the water, he tripped and fell on a tree root and rolled over on his back to see the reptile crawl out of the water. The white pickup truck called the *White Pearl* was just about twenty feet away, and he got up and ran straight to it. The doors were locked so he quickly ran for cover on the other side, still locked.

AlliCroc was out of the water and slowly crawled toward him, hissing and growling the closer it got. It was astounding to see the sheer size of the monster when it was completely out of the water.

Marvin was overwhelmed and managed to scream out at the top of his lungs for help. And tried to run, but his legs felt like rubber. As a last-ditch effort, he jumped in the bed of the truck and held his breath.

AlliCroc reached the truck and thumped it hard with its enormous snout. Marvin did everything he could not to scream in panic. His breathing labored, and feeling his heartbeat in his neck, he waited a few minutes, not moving a muscle, and finally worked up the nerve to sneak a peek over the truck bed.

Slowly raising his head until his eyes peered out of the side, he reacted with a gut-wrenching scream when he found he was staring eyeball to eyeball at the most vicious reptile in existence. He instinctively jerked backward, slamming his head against the side panel as AlliCroc continued raising its massive head up and over the side.

The garish hiss expelled from its quivering jaws was insufferably loud as salivate flowed from between its vast conical teeth. Marvin watched in horror as the devilish eyes kept their gaze on him while an enormous claw appeared over the side panel. The sheer weight of the reptile caused the truck to dip heavily on its side as the creature slowly stirred closer, causing Marvin to scream louder.

AlliCroc could smell the fear exuding from its prey and was eager to make its final assault when loud shouting erupted from behind. AlliCroc's sense organs detected the wild splashing and shouts from the people stomping through the water.

The reptile quickly became Agitated by this new threat and turned violently aggressive from the constant battle between hunger pangs and its ever-growing sense to remain undetected. Its cover was blown, so it attacked, crushing through the side of the truck bed. It leaped at Marvin. The ferocious jaws clamped down on its prey and viciously shook its head from side to side, effectively making Marvin look like a rag doll in a shredding machine.

Brian screamed with rage as he and the others watched in horror as his son was torn to shreds. The others stood in disbelief at what they were witnessing and tried to help but had no way of doing it.

AlliCroc backed away from the truck and turned toward them with the remains of Marvin dangling in its mouth.

Kevin wasted no time pulling his gun from its holster firing off several shots at the reptile. The bullets seemed to bounce off the thick hide as AlliCroc dashed into the river and disappeared below the surface.

The swamp tourists stood in shock as the entire scene was over in seconds. They thrashed to get out of the water and feverishly ran up the waterfront to find cover while Brian stood sobbing in the knee-deep water.

9

Virgil left the Anchor Bar and checked his watch as he entered the front door of his house and winced when it read twelve-thirty. His beautiful wife Jeanne was relaxing on the sofa watching a movie and clicked it off when he walked through the door with a dozen roses.

"So...where are you boys off to tomorrow?" she asked cynically.

"Hello, sweetheart, great to see you," he replied, handing her the flowers as she stood and greeted him with a big hug and kiss.

"You bring flowers when you feel guilty, so...what's up?"

"You're forgetting about Valentine's Day, birthdays, anniversaries and..."

"Let's have it," she cut in, pushing him away playfully.

Virgil scratched his head and let out a sigh, "We're going out on the *Endurance* tomorrow. We'll be gone at least a week."

"Wow, another salvage so soon?" she smiled half-heartedly, wishing he could at least be home for a couple of days.

"Not exactly. In fact, it's nothing like that at all," replied Virgil, taking her hand and leading her to the dining room table.

"Captain Bloodfoot is in town and made us an offer we couldn't refuse."

The night went downhill from there. Virgil told her the whole story and what they were planning to do. She protested and carried on like it was the end of the world, then took a deep breath and gave Virgil a hug.

"Are you trying to squeeze the breath out of me?" he tried to joke.

"No, honey, I'm just worried. I remember the last time when you came home, you were so shook up you wouldn't take a bath until you were sure that reptile wasn't in there."

"I don't take baths. I take showers."

"You know what I mean. Even when you went back to work on the tug, you and the rest of the crew wouldn't go near the sides of the damn tugboat for months. That's right, us wives know about that. We constantly received phone calls from the guys on the other tugboats, asking if you guys were ok."

"I know, you're right. But like I said, this monster is out there, and Bloodfoot is the only person that can find it."

"So let him. Why does he need you?"

Virgil broke out of the tight hug, walked to the refrigerator, and retrieved a beer, "He needs our help. Randy Taylor got hold of these special rifles that should make the kill much easier this time."

Jeanne knew she couldn't talk him out of it. She shook her head, put her hands on her waist and replied, "Good luck. I want to see you back home in one piece."

The *Endurance* sat tied to the dock in Port Everglades in the same area as the Port tugboats where they used to work. Virgil sat in the wheelhouse looking at his old tug, *Horizon*.

Feeling sentimental while sipping a cup of coffee with a shot of apricot brandy, he watched the new crew of the *Horizon* as they showed up for work. He spotted one of the deckhands he knew when the man subbed for one of his crew, and he gave Virgil a shout and a wave of the hand as he boarded the *Horizon*.

Virgil was happy to see the man was now a full-time deckhand and leisurely took a gaze inside the wheelhouse with a pair of binoculars. He almost choked on his coffee when he noticed the captain staring back at him with a grin, waving.

It was none other than his old relief, Captain Anton, the snitch who reported him and his crew years back for throwing empty booze bottles under the tug.

Virgil reacted to his wave by flicking his cigarette butt in his direction and walking away from the window.

"Good morning, Captain," Chuck said as he knocked once on the door and entered.

"I guess all that ass-kissing worked out well for Anton. He's now the full-time captain of the *Horizon*.

"Figures. I'm glad we got the hell out of there," replied Chuck.

"You're lookin' a little peaked," Virgil grinned, turning toward the engineer.

"Remind me not to try and keep up with Bloodfoot anymore. That freakin' pirate can drink a case of that gut-rot rum and not blink an eye."

"Ian kept up pretty good," Virgil ribbed.

"Yeah, well, he's ten years younger than me," complained Chuck.

"Where's he at? He's probably hugging the porcelain god."

Chuck shook his head and pointed toward the galley, "He's makin' bacon. Holding the skillet with one hand and covering his eye with the other."

Chuck held his coffee cup as Captain Virgil poured a shot of brandy into it when an uber driver pulled up to the dock. Virgil and Chuck watched as Bloodfoot poured out of the backseat and paid the terrified-looking driver.

"That son-of-a-bitch has quite the presence, eh?" Chuck smirked.

"Absolutely," replied Virgil, watching the uber driver accept the money with a shaky hand and peel off out of the entrance gate as if thankful to be alive.

It was low tide, and the tug was five-foot below the dock as Bloodfoot jumped to the gunwale without missing a beat.

"Permission to come aboard," he said halfheartedly, waving to the two men in the wheelhouse as he slipped into the galley.

"Granted, you pirate bastard!" Virgil shouted with a spirited tone.

"How did Jeanne take the news last night?" Chuck shouted, following Virgil as he headed to the galley.

"I'm supposing pretty much the same as your wife did," Virgil replied.

"Where's Bill?" asked Chuck, stepping into the galley.

"He's in the bathroom," said Ian, sliding bacon from the pan to a plate.

"Head. It's called a head on a boat," laughed Bloodfoot.

They sat around the table chitchatting about the bar they were in the previous night when Bill arrived, nearly tripping into the galley as he raised his leg to get in the hatch.

Ian finished making breakfast, passed the eggs and bacon to the table and sat next to Bill, clearly disappointed his crewmate couldn't keep up the following night. They ate cheerfully and cleared the table when Virgil retrieved the brandy and filled his coffee cup a quarter full.

"Ok, Bloodfoot, what's the game plan," he said bluntly.

Before he spoke, the celebrated hunter sat and looked each crewmember in the eye, "What we are hunting is the same type of creature that we hunted a few years back, only bigger, stronger and smarter. I don't know if you filled Ian in on the reptiles' abilities, so I'd like to review them."

"If you don't mind, I'd like to tell you what I know," Ian spoke.

Bloodfoot raised an eyebrow, "You've been versed on the reptile and still want to join this hunt, so go ahead. You've got the floor."

"I've been told that the reptile known as AlliCroc is one of three that escaped captivity in the Everglades a few years back. The first one was quickly killed by hunters, and the second one met its fate in a bloodbath with you guys. The third one got away and was said to be headed north, which we now know it has, and this is the one we're hunting."

Ian paused to put a wad of Copenhagen dip in his mouth and continued the tale. "The reptiles were genetically altered by two scientists that Captain Virgil's friend, Don...uh.."

"Henderson," Virgil answered, making a face like he just bit into a lemon."

"Yes, Don Henderson somehow got them to make a genetically altered reptile. He thought if he could have a superior reptile, he'd make millions showing it as an attraction, like King Kong or something."

"I'll take it from there," Bloodfoot cut in. "The scientists were making transgenic catfish. They spliced genes of other species into the eggs, causing them to grow larger and faster at an alarming rate."

"It seemed like a good idea to stay on top of the catfish industry," Bill murmured, holding his head.

"Sure was. They grew about ten times larger and, unfortunately, extremely aggressive. They ended up shutting down the operation for fear of them escaping and wreaking havoc on the entire eco system. Don suddenly enters the picture and has them splice genes from a twenty-two-foot saltwater crocodile with the eggs of a large alligator and hatched the deadliest reptile since the Tyrannosaurus Rex," Virgil added.

"Probably more deadly, those mad scientists also gave it something so they could think like a human...A smart human," said Bloodfoot.

Nobody spoke for a moment, which seemed like an eternity, while each man soaked in and reflected on the nightmare they went through the last time.

Virgil finally broke the silence, coolly lit a cigarette and added, "What we're dealing with is an extremely large mutant reptile with razor-sharp teeth protruding from its jaws. It's extremely aggressive and has a non-stop appetite. Don said the AlliCroc can sense a pressure drop in the water from over a mile away."

"Ok, Ian, so there you have it. Do you still want to join us for this hunt?"Bloodfoot, asked.

Ian spit into a paper cup and answered, "I wouldn't miss it for the world."

"Alright, I think you'll do fine," Bloodfoot replied. "Now, let's talk about the game plan. I think it would be best if we hunted on foot, along the waters' edge. We have those three rifles, or should I say cannons, that Randy supplied us with, and I have some shotguns for extra support."

"Since the National Guard was hunting that thing for days without a glimpse, what makes you think we'll find it?" asked Chuck.

Bloodfoot gave him a foul look and replied, "Like I said last night, they didn't know what to look for."

A shout from the dock interrupted their conversation, "Permission to board, Captain!"

"Denied!" Virgil shouted back, hearing the unmistakable sound of Anton, the snitch.

The *Endurance* was making good time as it chugged up the west coast. The calm, warm water of the Gulf of Mexico and a slight breeze were all it took for Chuck, Bill and Ian to troll fishing lines off the stern.

Bloodfoot was in the wheelhouse steering the tugboat while Captain Virgil poured a couple of apricot brandy and lit another camel non-filtered cigarette.

It was decided that they would take the tugboat and use it for home base in case the elusive reptile swam into the Gulf.

"Slow the tug, Virge! Ian just hooked a porpoise!" Bill shouted, running up the port side and sticking his head in the window.

Bloodfoot nearly coughed up his brandy as he turned and glared at the deckhand, "You mean dolphin," he gruffed.

"No, it's an actual porpoise like Flipper," he busted out laughing.

"I thought those mammals were smarter than that," Bloodfoot frowned.

Virgil put the tug in neutral, and the three of them headed toward the stern where Ian was fighting the mammal like a madman. Bloodfoot instinctively drew his hunting knife from its scabbard and cut the line.

Ian turned and gave him a dirty look, "What the hell! I was going to get him in closer and get the goddamn hook out of its mouth!"

"It would have bit your bloody hand off," replied Bloodfoot in a calm, commanding tone.

Ian watched as Bloodfoot walked away and stepped into the galley. Sizing him up and feeling a bit buzzed from a case of Heineken, he set off to have a talk to the burly pirate and maybe teach him some manners.

He entered the galley and found Bloodfoot sitting at the table eating a baloney sandwich.

"Next time you cut my line when I hook a fish, I'm gonna pop your jaw," he threatened with an unyielding grin.

Bloodfoot was amused and just rolled his eyes between bites, provoking Ian. The new deckhand lunged at him, and before he knew it, he was lying flat out on the table with Bloodfoot's hand placed inflexibly around his throat, "I like you, kid. You've got gumption," he smirked, removing his hand and lightly patting his cheek.

Ian knew better than to move a muscle and acknowledged his defeat. The burly pirate stood motionless and looked him dead in the eye before he offered his hand and helped Ian off the table.

"We're on the same team, kid. I expect this was simply a learning curve," Bloodfoot sneered, stepping out of the galley and heading back up to the bridge.

Ian was pacing the galley when Bill stepped in, "You're still standing? I guess he likes you," Bill smirked, patting Ian on the back.

"That son-of-a-bitch doesn't know how lucky he was."

Bill peered at him to make sure he wasn't joking before he could say a word, Ian shook his shoulder hard and added, "That's one scary bastard. I'd hate to get on his bad side," he said with genuine humility, giving Bill a wink as he scooped a pinch of tobacco from his Copenhagen can.

When Bloodfoot reached the bridge, Captain Virgil was already back at the wheel and had the tug plowing northerly again, "Did you slit his throat or just punch a hole through his head?" Virgil asked, lighting a cigarette and casually looking out the windows.

"Nothing of the sort. I just had to burst his bubble and let the porpoise go. I've never in my life seen one of them get hooked."

"I thought they'd be too smart to take the bait," Virgil replied.

"Just goes to show you. No matter who or what you are, there's always some dip shit in the crowd," Bloodfoot replied, lighting a big fat cigar.

AlliCroc took what was left of Marvin and swam undetected down river. Aggravated and intensely disturbed at the thought of retreating when there were seven more potential prey, the ability to think clearly was one of its better ways of survival.

Although it was a constant battle, the predator had to learn to adjust its veracious appetite with the awareness to know when to retreat. The large wake could be seen by the other prey, but AlliCroc knew there was nothing they could do but watch. Satisfied with its humanly meal and not wanting to stick around and risk exposure to any others in the area, the demonic reptile slowly sank underwater and disappeared.

Manatees in the monster's path nearly beached themselves as the long tail thrust from side to side as the indomitable predator swam to deeper water. It began to dive deeper until its giant claws touched the bottom, where it would rest…and wait for another chance to strike at the remaining group.

The dazed swamp explorers watched in horror as the ungainly sight of the wake faded to smooth calm. It was gone, or so it seemed.

Elaine and Marge were numb. Their legs felt like they were attached to cinder blocks as they slowly walked toward the water and tried to talk Brian out of the river. Heart-broken and in despair, they finally coaxed him out of the water, where he nearly collapsed in Marge's arms. Jake came to the rescue and helped guide them to the parked cars.

"Ok, I've got him leaning on the car. Maybe you can sit with him for a few minutes while we figure out what the hell just happened," said Jake.

Leaning against the car with his head buried in his knees, Marge wrapped an arm around Brian but couldn't find the words to say to the grieving father.

When it looked like the reptile wasn't going to return, Kevin headed straight for the truck and tried to pry the door open. The door was jammed, so he broke through the passenger side window and scrabbled for the radio.

"Call for help," Hector demanded, approaching from the passenger side.

"What the hell do you think I'm doing!" he replied, fumbling with the radio receiver, his hands shaking.

Jake was sitting on a tree stump, vomiting at the water's edge, when Elaine saw what looked like a submarine speeding through the water. Her eyes grew large when she realized the demonic reptile was coming back...and headed for Jake.

"Ja...Jake!" she screamed as she stood and pointed at the water.

It looked like a slow-motion horror movie as the malevolent eyes breached the surface and locked on target.

Jake instinctively ducked his head and looked over toward the group to see who was shouting when it suddenly dawned on him that he was in grave danger.

It took a split second to find out the monstrous reptile was closing behind him as the clamor of the wake on the shoreline sounded like a speed boat was making it.

He sprang from the tree stump and began to run toward the parked cars, but it wasn't fast enough to elude the creature. The others watched in dismay as the reptile darted out of the water at the same instant as Jake and swiftly caught him, clamping down on his midsection and savagely shaking its head from side to side.

Jake didn't have enough time to let out a scream before he lay lifeless in the horrendous jaws, but the shocked look on his face and the expression in his eyes as he kept his gaze on his friends, was enough to make the others cry out in horror.

While they were scrambling for cover and trying to get inside their cars, AlliCroc leisurely crept closer to the four remaining vehicles with Jake hanging from its jaws like a dog carrying a prized trophy. The feeling of pure evil overcame them as they watched the reptile take note of each person.

It hesitated when Marge started her car and tried to back away, but before she could get anywhere, the reptile charged and rammed the car head-on, crushing the front end and engine, rendering it useless.

It became disturbingly clear to Kevin that this reptile was not just a cold-blooded killer like any other reptile he had seen on many of these excursions, but it was malicious and manipulative, almost as if it was capable of thinking and plotting out the attacks.

His thoughts were broken as he heard a shrill cry for help from Marge and Elaine. The tortured look on their faces was something he would never forget as they stared at him through the cracked windshield and questioned what to do next.

For one fleeting moment, Kevin thought the loud noise from the other three car horns might cause the reptile to retreat.

"Everybody lay on your horns! It might scare it away!" he shouted.

As the horns began blazing, the reptile backed away from Marge's car and once again shook its head with brutal force, shredding limbs from Jake's tortured torso.

They screamed in horror as they watched the creature flip Jake in the air and swallow his remains in one gulp.

All eyes were on the killer reptile as it slowly walked backward into the water; its evil eyes and vicious-looking grin locked on them as it sank into the river.

All was quiet. Nobody moved a muscle inside their vehicles until they were sure it was gone. Finally, Hector cranked his engine and motioned for the others to climb into his car, but before they could move a muscle, the river burst with spray, and the menacing reptile charged out and rammed the remaining cars, completely destroying them as if hit by a freight train.

Strange as it seemed, the reptile made no attempt to attack the people inside the vehicles. It was almost like it knew the cars were smashed, and it was in no hurry to attack because its prey couldn't escape.

AlliCroc sat watching the people inside their smashed vehicles for nearly an hour before it turned and headed back into the river.

Elaine and Marge quietly got out of their smashed car and walked over to Kevin, their eyes focused on the river, expecting the reptile to return.

"Kevin…were you able to reach anybody on your radio?" asked Elaine, slowly turning to face him, her eyes red with tears.

He looked at her with defeat, "Radio's dead. That damn reptile snapped the antenna."

"Sit tight, I'll go get help," Hector offered, springing from his car.

"Not a good idea," replied Marge, wiping her hair out of her face and looking towards the river.

"And why is that not a good idea?" Hector snipped.

"Because that monster is out there, probably waiting for another chance to single us out. Take a closer look at the water…See those two bumps barely poking through the water over there?" she continued, pointing. Those are eyes. That damn thing is watching us, waiting to see what we're going to do."

Hector squinted his eyes and took a closer look, "I don't see anything. You people can sit tight if that's what you want to do, but I'm going for help."

"Stay here, Hector! I'm telling you to sit tight!" Kevin cut in with a commanding tone. "Marge's right. If you stare long enough, you'll see it. I can see the complete silhouette of its head just below the surface. It's watching us."

Hector wiped the sweat away from his eyes and refocused on the brown water. After a long minute, he said, "Ok, I think I see what you guys are talking about. The only problem is that the space between the two so-called eyes is a good three feet, and that would mean that its head is at least six-feet wide."

"Yes, we know. We saw it eat Jake," Elaine shot back, her eyes blazing.

Hector felt like a trapped rat in a cage. The sweat dripped from his forehead as he nervously paced back and forth, "I missed it. When that monster grabbed Jake, I turned my head and closed my eyes."

"You closed your eyes?" Elaine asked incredulously.

"I couldn't handle it and closed my eyes. I didn't see how big it was when it crawled out of the water," he sniffled.

"Leave him be," Kevin said. "We all face tragedy differently."

Elaine raised her eyebrows and looked at Marge, who gave her a reassuring wink.

"I know this is probably not the best thing to do, but I don't see any alternative," Hector blurted. "I'm going to run for help, anybody want to come with me?"

Brian was mourning the death of his son and stood silent near the rear of the truck, staring at the repulsive reptile as it returned the glare. The menace in its eyes was nauseating, but he kept his gaze before surprising himself and the others with a quick reply, "I will go with you," he said, in a trans-like state.

"Not a good idea," Kevin said again.

Hector frowned as the words left his lips, "Do you really think it's going to chase us through the damn woods?"

"I have no idea, but I wouldn't want to change it. I think we should stay here and try to get this damn radio working so we can call for help."

"Call the cavalry, eh?" Hector scolded.

"I was thinking more like the National Guard," Kevin replied seriously.

"What the hell are you talking about?" Hector blew-up. "Aren't you used to seeing these kinds of gators? All we need is a couple of your redneck backwoods boys to show up and shoot that damn thing with a shotgun."

151

Kevin stood up and took a long look at the delusional man, then replied, "Look, mister, I've been out here many, many times and never once had I laid eyes on such a hideous reptile like this. I would never think it possible for such a reptile to have a look in its eyes like a menacing, cold and calculated evil killer.

"What the hell are you talking about?" Hector repeated, standing up and scratching his head. What makes you think the National Guard would come out here?"

All eyes were now on Kevin. He took a deep breath and swallowed hard before continuing, "Ok, this is what I think. I sure hope it ain't so, but this is exactly what I think. A few years back, I followed a story in the news about a huge alligator attacking people in and around Port Everglades. Nothing about the story made sense on the local news stations; it was as if the media was downplaying the attacks. They pretty much tried to keep it quiet until one day on live television, there was a thirty-five-foot creature standing on the jetties at the Port Everglades inlet."

"Creature?" asked Hector with a curious look.

"They said it was some kind of anomaly croc or something, which didn't make sense. I'm a nature lover and think I know a thing or two about alligators and crocodiles, but this thing looked like a cross between both… on steroids."

"I remember reading about it," Marge said, "But didn't they kill it?"

Elaine stared at Marge for a long moment before grabbing her wrist and shaking it, "Does that thing in the water look like a regular gator to you? That thing is over thirty-five feet long, and the teeth…Did you see the teeth?"

"This thing looks exactly like the one on the jetties! I can't believe I didn't think of it. We must keep cool heads because we are in deep you-know-what," Kevin added anxiously.

"And you know what's even scarier?" asked Marge.

Kevin just looked at her.

"What's scarier is the fact that it seems to get excited when it detects fear…like it can taste it!"

Kevin walked up the dirt road with the others trailing behind and unlocked the door to the small wooden shack used as the welcoming center, where tourists could buy souvenirs and snacks.

The ten-by-ten wood room stood on cinder blocks a foot off the ground and was Framed out two by fours, with T1-11 wood panels as walls.

"I really don't think this is such a good place to hide out in," said Elaine. "If that reptile launches another attack, it will plow through this shed like matchsticks."

"I know. Back up everybody, we're not hiding out in here. I'm going inside to retrieve my shotgun from behind the counter," replied Kevin.

The calming moment was quickly shattered when Marge suddenly stood erect and shouted, "Hector, get back here! That monster will catch you in seconds!"

Everybody tensed and looked over to see Hector sprinting up the gravel trail and then to where the reptile had been lurking. Their hearts sank when they witnessed the colossal head rise out of the water and turn towards the fleeing prey.

"No, no, no! This can't be happening!" Kevin screamed out.

They watched in awe as they scrambled inside the shack. The water swirled at least thirty feet behind the reptile's head, and the gigantic tail splashed the surface and propelled the prehistoric-looking beast toward the embankment. Its sheer strength and enormous girth were overwhelming.

"Hector!" Elaine shouted out, busting out in tears. "Run for your life!"

AlliCroc swam like a raging torpedo and used its massive claws to plow through the muddy embankment and onto the rocky path, hissing and growling as it turned to look at the people hiding in the shack before continuing its course toward Hector. The ferocious power it possessed was inconceivable as they watched it run. The speed of such a gigantic reptile was frightening.

Hector's legs felt like lead weights when he slowed to a steady jog, believing he was clear of danger. He stopped to catch his breath when he heard Elaine scream out his name. Thinking that his friends were under attack, he turned to head back when he heard branches snapping like twigs and felt the thunderous pounding of the ground he was standing on.

He thought his eyes were playing tricks on him when he saw the horrifying site of the reptile speeding up the path like a city bus. Its girth was so massive that branches and flora on the sides of the path snapped and fell behind.

Stunned by the dreadful spectacle, Hector's legs simply gave out. Fighting to stop from just curling up in a ball and crying, he swiftly gathered his strength, picked himself up off his knees and ran.

Thoughts went through his mind as he couldn't believe such a massive alligator would be chasing him for such a long distance. He always thought they were lazy, at least the regular-size ones. He remembered reading that they were fast reptiles and would give chase for a short distance, but this damn thing seemed to pick up speed the further it ran.

Then he remembered reading somewhere that if you were ever chased by an alligator, to run in a zig-zag direction because the reptile was not as agile, but that would do him no good because the thing chasing him took up the entire path, and there was nothing on either side except swamp.

His train of thought broke when he faltered on his own two feet and face-planted into the gravel. Bleeding from scrapes on his nose and forehead, he again fought the urge to give up, picked himself off the ground and continued running.

The main roadway was only thirty yards away when Hector collapsed after a loud pop from his knee. The horror in his mind was unbearable when he realized he couldn't get up. Wheezing and out of breath, he turned in time to see the colossal jaws open and hit him with such force that it knocked out what little wind he had left. It took him a couple of seconds to comprehend the fact that he was in the jaws of the hideous beast until they abruptly compressed and drove the six-inch conical teeth through his body.

A blood-garbled scream was heard as blood sprang from his body like a fountain. He screamed out one last blood-soaked time before he felt the smooth, warm sides of the monster's throat as he was being swallowed.

AlliCroc lifted its head skyward and closed its eyes, relishing the pungent taste, opening and closing its massive jaws and finally swallowing what once was Hector.

10

Minutes went by, although it seemed a lifetime, as the wildlife explorers hunched behind the battered truck. If not under the circumstances, it would be laughable to see how they piled into the shack to seek safety after talking about it being a bad idea.

Elaine swallowed hard and leaned over toward Kevin, who continued working feverishly on the radio, "It's been a while since we've heard from Hector. Do you think he made it?"

Noticeably shaken and infuriated about the broken radio, Kevin fought the urge to scream and jump down her throat. He simply crawled out of the cab and wiped the sweat off his forehead before eyeing her and then looking down the rocky path.

"Well…let's see, we have two choices," he replied derisively. "We could walk up the path to see if he made it or stay here and pray like hell that somebody comes along and saves us."

"Well, what the hell kind of swamp guide are you!" Marge asked, standing with her hands on her hips.

"Look, ladies! I've been doing these tours for years! Never! And I mean NEVER! Have I seen a monster like this," Kevin retorted, crawling back into the truck and stretching his back.

"I'll bet you don't even have a…"

"Okay, stop!" Marge mediated, "We've got to stay calm and think about our options. Sorry, Kevin, we're all understandably aggravated. We've got to work together if we're going to make it out of here."

She was right, and they knew it. Kevin took a deep breath and let out a heavy sigh, "All right, you're right. If we are going to make it out of here, we've got to try and stay calm. If Hector made it out to the main road, he would have to keep running for about four miles before he reached an old gas station."

"And if he didn't make it?" Marge added.

Kevin was on his last nerve and gave her a look before replying, "I guess we'll have to grow wings and fly."

The two of them stood with hands on their hips and raised eyebrows until Kevin shrugged his shoulders and continued with the decrepit radio. A minute later, he smacked the radio and crawled out of the cab, "Damnit! Hector had to have made it. This kind of nightmare only happens in horror movies! I can't believe how fast that...that monster swam out of the river and chased him!"

"Hector was running pretty fast...I'm sure he made it to safety," Elaine cut in, trying to stay positive and believe what she said.

As the morning wore on, all eyes continued to focus up the path, waiting for a sign of Hector. Marge checked her watch for the umpteenth time and seemed to find comfort by telling the others they had now been waiting over two hours and that help should arrive shortly.

Elaine and Marge stood guard while Kevin tried in vain to get the radio working. Brian, who had been unresponsive since watching his son get killed, suddenly stood and wiped his eyes.

Marge's supportive smile faded as he looked at them through red, glassy eyes, then turned to look up the rocky path.

"Brian? Brian, please come over here," said Marge.

In a trans-like manner, he scuffed his feet and started to slowly walk in the direction that the devilish reptile took. Ignoring the calls from his friends, he began to pick up his pace.

"Brian! Where the hell are you going? Get back over here until help arrives. I have no idea where that gator is!" Kevin demanded.

He stopped walking and slowly turned to face the others. His face was cherry-red, and tears streamed down. "Gator...It's no gator. That beast is from the bowels of hell, killed my boy, and I'm going to kill it."

"How do you intend to kill that thing," Kevin continued, motioning with his hand for the others to stay back while he walked toward the confused father.

"Do you really think I'm going to just sit here and wait? It killed my boy."

159

"Look Brian…I know how you must feel, but you're right. That thing is no ordinary gator. I've been out here all my life and never seen anything like it."

"I can't just let it go."

"Of course not, but let's get the hell off this path and take shelter behind my truck. When we get back, we can plan to come back with more people and hunt the thing."

"You take shelter. I'm going to kill that hellish reptile."

"Now look, Bri…" Kevin stopped talking and froze in terror. He turned his head slightly to confirm what he saw from the corner of his eye. Not ten feet off the side of the rocky path, the large head surfaced from under the water. The green eyes stared with deadly desire as they seemed to glare at him.

Brian had no idea why the guide stopped in mid-sentence and obviously care less as he turned and walked away.

"Don't move!" Kevin whispered tensely.

AlliCroc slowly turned its massive head and locked eyes on Kevin. This one, it sensed, was more afraid than the other and easily within reach.

Kevin was awestruck as he sensed the wild reptile looked like it was making a decisive decision on who to attack.

His heart skipped a beat as he felt every muscle in his legs tense and wondered if he'd be able to outrun the menace. Before he could make up his mind, the enormous reptile opened its massive jaws, hissed a heart-wrenching, guttural sound and leaped forward at a startling speed.

"RUN!" Kevin screamed out as he turned and bolted back toward the wrecked pickup truck.

Elaine and Marge were already inside the smashed cab of the truck when they witnessed the reptile launch itself out of the water and chase Kevin.

With seconds to spare, Elaine opened the door and waved Kevin in. A quick glance behind him was all the dumbfounded guide needed to sprint faster and dive through the open door, slamming it shut at the same instant the massive head plowed into it.

The truck was hit so hard that it upended and landed near the muddy bank of the river. The three occupants tried to remain calm as they assessed the situation. Elaine and Marge were preparing to escape the truck, but the monster was too close. Kevin assured them they would not make it to safety and was able to change their mind and remain in the dilapidated vehicle.

They watched as the reptile continued to take great pleasure in seeing its petrified prey. Its nostrils flared with the delightful smell of fear as it meticulously tried to chew through the door. When it looked as if the thin metal doors were about to surrender and fall off, the reptile stopped its attack and peered inside.

Again, all suspicions were dreadfully confirmed that the evil reptile could think and calculate a plan to get its prey when they witnessed the hideous eyes look at each one of them as if to see which one it would eat first.

The back of Elaine's head was under the dashboard as she continued to maneuver deeper when her hair became snarled on a wire. She frantically yanked it out and stared for several seconds before calling out to Kevin, "Hey! Does this wire connect to the radio?"

Kevin quickly looked down to see what she was holding in her hand, "Damnit! It's the missing antenna cable to the damned radio!"

"Where does it go?"

"Get up and switch spots with me. You'll never get it!" Kevin shouted as he literally picked her up and threw her to the side.

The reptile began a new tactic as its massive head slammed into the side of the truck and pushed it closer to the water.

"Hurry up! It's pushing us into the water!" Marge screamed out.

The two women watched in horror as the truck slid into the murky water. Marge screamed for the malevolent reptile to stop and, at one point, kicked its snout as it continued its assault.

"Ok, I got it!" Kevin shouted as the first sign of water began to flood the floorboards. He grabbed the mic and switched the dial, "Come in, anybody! This is Rattlesnake Jake's Swamp Safari! I have a deadly emergency at my camp!"

Static was the only reply as he repeated the emergency several more times. Finally, "This is the *Water Rat*. I hear you loud and clear. I'm headin' yer way 'bout a mile out. Come back."

"Stay clear, *Water Rat*, we have a deadly situation with an enormous reptile…I repeat, stay clear. Call the Sheriff and tell him to bring his deputies and heavy artillery!"

There was a pause on the other end before the reply, "Uh…is this a prank?"

"It's the same monster that was in South Florida a few years ago! Call for h…," the radio went dead. The water flooded in under the dashboard and shorted out the radio. Kevin slammed the mic down and hoped his message had been taken seriously, and that help was on its way.

"Why didn't you want him to come help?" Marge said hysterically.

"He's a drunken sod that would have just gotten himself killed," Kevin replied, looking out the window and watching the devastating creature nudge the side panel.

"What's the plan?" Elaine asked, trying to keep a cool head.

"We've got to get out of here," replied Kevin, breaking the driver's door window with his elbow. With all the melee, Marge couldn't help but wonder how he broke the window with his elbow. She had always heard you needed a sparkplug or some other pointed device. Kevin must have had the help from brute force and adrenalin…or a pointy elbow.

Her thoughts were broken when AlliCroc let out a hair-raising growl that made them all shudder. Kevin and Marge locked eyes for a split second after they saw the reptile stop and gaze inside the vehicle when the window broke.

It was now a fact; the creature was relishing the idea of taunting its prey. Elaine screamed at the sight of the big green eye staring at her with none other than pure evil.

"What's it doing!?" screamed Marge. "That freakin' thing looks like it's having fun watching us panic. Why doesn't it just try to eat us!"

"Let's go. I think it locked the jaws on the wheel well. It looks stuck. Let's get out of here," said Kevin.

"Come on, Marge, follow Kevin. This might be our only chance to escape!" Elaine shouted, grabbing her elbow and forcing her behind Kevin, who was already halfway through the window.

The cab was now flooded, and only a foot near the roof was still dry. Kevin's legs disappeared as he swam out and Marge wasted no time following. When it was Elaine's turn, she took one last look at the menacing reptile and was happy to see that its jaws appeared to be stuck on the door and wheel well. She was halfway out and sitting on the armrest when AlliCroc stopped pushing the truck. Her head barely breached the surface of the water when she felt the hot stench of the reptile's breath down her neck.

Instant goosebumps sprouted from her body as she quickly turned and stared eye to eye with the creature, only inches away.

164

Her limbs went numb as she tried to move away, so she just sat as if hypnotized, watching her reflection in the devilish eyes. The sound of her two friends swimming for safety left an empty pit in her stomach as she waited for the inevitable.

Suddenly she heard shouting behind the reptile, and out of nowhere, Brian leaped on the predator's back, poking at its eyes with a skinny tree branch.

She watched helplessly as the horrific eyes retracted and what looked like metal-plated eyelids closed tight. Brian's branch broke and he quickly retrieved a coral rock the size of a soccer ball and began bashing the reptile's head to no effect.

AlliCroc slowly rolled into what is called a death roll, taking Brian down into the water and tearing him to shreds with the armor-plated scutes covering its body.

In shock and still unable to move away, Elaine watched helplessly as the reptile methodically tore its prey to shreds. She suddenly felt an arm wrap around her waist and whisk her out of the truck toward the safety of trees near the water's edge.

"Elaine! Snap out of it! Brian's gone, and we need to get the hell out of here!" Kevin tried to whisper.

Kevin swam with her downriver about twenty yards until Marge's arm plucked her out of the water.

"What about Brian?" Marge whispered as they hid behind a tree and watched the carnage.

They watched with a disheveled look as the reptile let Brian crawl out of the water before it placed a giant claw on his back to stop him. They weren't prepared to watch what happened next as it bit his limbs off one at a time. The screams were piercing and guaranteed to haunt them for the rest of their lives.

"He's gone," replied Kevin, the bile rising through his throat.

"We've got to get out of here," Marge tearfully announced.

They took one last look at the monster before exiting the river and ran through the marshy thicket. They kept their pace through the winding trail, fighting spasms and fatigue as they wallowed along, and twenty-minutes later, they reached the roadway and slowed to a walk.

Beaten, bruised and unable to comprehend the surreal nightmare they had just come from, Kevin cleared his throat and spoke, "There's a gas station just up the road a little further. We'll call for help and wait..." he stopped, cleared his throat again, "We'll wait for help to arrive."

Elaine and Marge were unable to speak. They just stared down at the road and nodded their heads.

11

The orange and red color of the sunset looked like a fireball as it wafted below the horizon while the *Endurance* broke away from a weed line it was trolling on and headed for the Suwannee National Wildlife Refuge less than a mile away.

Bill and Ian were busy reeling in their fishing lines when the captain blew the whistle for Bill to ready the anchor. When the salvage tug was near the mouth of the Suwannee River, Captain Virgil slowed to a stop and poked his head through the wheelhouse window, shouting for Bill to drop anchor. A minute later, Chuck was given the green light to shut down the engine.

While descending the stairs, Virgil shook his head while glancing at the pirate-looking hulk standing motionless on the bow. Making his way down the portside of the tug, he met Chuck as he climbed out of the engine room hatch.

"Bloodfoot still looking like an ornament?" he snorted.

"He is," replied Virgil. "But don't knock him. He's been doing it for a long time and always seems to find his target."

For the next two hours, the tugboat crew watched with fascination at the way the hulking hunter stood on the bow and searched the water, shoreline and everything in-between for the elusive AlliCroc. At one point, Ian thought it would be a good idea to sneak up behind him and slap him on the head with leftover squid chunks and ballyhoo that they were using for bait. Virgil egged him on, knowing that the wily pirate would probably turn around and knock him out cold with one punch to the head before Ian could convey his assault. Luckily, he seized the advice from Bill to stay clear.

Bill and Ian reeled in the last two fishing lines without a trace of a bite as Virgil and Chuck walked to the stern, "Looks like we're eating peanut butter and jelly sandwiches tonight," Chuck scoffed.

"Not to worry, we still have tuna steaks in the fridge from yesterday's catch," Bill announced, scratching his baldhead, wishing he had caught something appetizing lurking below the weed line.

After converging with Bloodfoot, Virgil walked back toward the stern. Checking his watch, he announced, "Okay, while Ian's cooking up some tuna steaks, we'll prep the skiff for a little night cruise up the Suwannee and see if we can't find AlliCroc."

"How are we going to find it at night?" asked Ian.

"If it's near, it will probably find us," Chuck added awkwardly.

"Just look for the giant glowing eyes when the spotlight hits them," said Bill, gathering the fishing poles.

"No spotlights tonight, fellas," a booming voice echoed from behind. Captain Bloodfoot made his way to the stern and sat on the gunwale, "AlliCroc has remained elusive all these years because it can think like us. We will cruise quietly upriver for a few miles at slow speed. The Yamaha should keep a low hum, enough for AlliCroc to know we're there and for us to hear it coming to attack."

Bloodfoot noticed the peculiar look Ian gave and added, "Remember, this reptile is a hybrid. And the psychotic people who made it gave the damn thing the intelligence to think and plan its attacks accordingly," he grunted.

The goose bumps were visible on Ian's arms, "Bastards."

After a quick tuna-steak dinner and a couple shots of rum and apricot brandy for good measure, the crew threw some amazingly large arsenal into the eighteen-foot launch and were ready to go. Ian nervously lit a cigar and prepared to step into the zodiac when Virgil announced, "Sorry, Ian, you stay behind and keep the *Endurance* secure."

Ian took a confused step back and protested, "What the hell does that mean?"

"Means you're staying on the tug," replied Virgil with a cunning glare.

Ian knew better than to challenge the captain and stepped back as Virgil jumped into the inflatable.

"We need somebody to stand by on the tug. You wouldn't want to come across that reptile tonight," Bloodfoot added, taking a good look at the water before stepping into the small vessel.

Ian didn't try to hide his disappointment, and it showed as he cast the lines and stepped back. Virgil cranked the outboard to life, looked up at him, and said, "Put the night vision goggles on and continue searching around the mouth of the inlet. Raise us on the VHF if you spot it. Stay in the wheelhouse, and don't go near the water. This damn reptile is devious."

"Good luck and I will be standing by in case you run into trouble."

The last remark made everybody in the zodiac turn to Ian with curiosity, "Don't even try to take this tug up the river," Virgil frowned, putting the motor in gear.

They rode in silence through the mouth of the Suwannee River and disappeared in the darkness while rounding a bend.

Ian stood on the bridge watching through the night vision goggles and snickered at the only thing he could see: a small light at the bow of the zodiac from the large cigar Bloodfoot held between his teeth.

"Why the sudden change of leaving Ian behind?" Bloodfoot casually asked.

"The kid was shaking like a leaf. It wouldn't be good for him or any of us if we were attacked and he saw that thing for the first time in the dark. I'm thinking that if we survive this little boat ride tonight, and we don't kill AlliCroc, Ian will have plenty of time to see that thing in the daylight," replied Virgil, flicking a cigarette butt into the water.

Bloodfoot sat back with a slight grin. He felt honored to have the captain along for the hunt. Not many men would take the time to notice the minute details about his crew like Virgil.

An hour later, they were nearly two miles upriver. The quiet hum of the outboard nearly put Chuck to sleep before Bloodfoot's booming voice reverberated, "I think now is a good time for you two to turn on those spotlights."

"I thought we weren't using them tonight; do you think it's close?" asked Chuck.

"Hard to tell. But we haven't had much luck without the spotlights. If it is close, hopefully, we can spot it with the light and prevent a sneak attack."

Chuck and Bill were more than happy to turn on the hand-held spotlights. Chuck scanned the shoreline while Bill searched the water. Virgil sat behind the wheel and lit a cigarette, watching the burly pirate standing on the bow like a statue.

When they traveled as far as they thought they should go, Virgil cut the motor and let the Zodiac quietly drift back downriver. The ebb tide was at its peak and enabled them to quietly continue their search. If the creature was out there somewhere, they hoped to catch it off guard.

All at once, Bill shuffled and flinched as the light from his spotlight landed on two big and bright eyeballs staring back at him, "Uh…Guys, look at those eyes. I hope that's not our reptile."

"It's not," Bloodfoot replied, without batting an eye, "Pretty big son-of-a-bitch though, but not ours."

Virgil and Chuck made eye contact and smiled when Bloodfoot replied with a country twang in his voice but fought the urge to needle him as he told them once before that wherever he goes, he blends in with the environment. That being known, they figured the Suwannee River was a perfectly reasonable area to have a country twang.

"Sure as hell, a big one," replied Bill, shaking the light in its eyes and trying to get it to move.

Bloodfoot finally moved his head to look at Bill, "It's big, but not big enough," he grumbled, irritation creeping into the sound of his voice.

At this point, Virgil laughed, "C'mon, Bill, did you have your eyes closed when we hunted the last AlliCroc?"

"Just want to know how he's so damn sure that thing isn't thirty-something feet long, that's all," Bill protested, not wanting to be the butt of jokes for the rest of the evening.

Bloodfoot took it in stride and turned to Bill, "Measure the distance from the snout to the eye ridge and convert the inches to feet."

Bill was floored. He didn't know if the pirate was going to turn and attack him for questioning him or what, so he balled his fists and prepared for the worst. Relieved that it was just a small lecture, he relaxed and wiped his brow while Bloodfoot returned his attention to the bow and lit another fat cigar.

Chuck checked his watch and reported that it was getting late and suggested it would be a good idea to head back to the *Endurance*. All agreed, and Virgil cranked the motor and steered toward shore before making a wide turn.

"Keep those spotlights shining, fellas. If that monster's out here, I don't want it to take us by surprise," said Virgil, flicking his cigarette butt into the water. No sooner did the butt hit the water when a large splash seemed to come out of nowhere.

"Kill the engine!" Bloodfoot roared, twisting off the bow and landing on all fours with his trusted hunting knife firmly gripped in his hand.

Virgil killed the engine and reached for one of the .905 caliber rifles while the Zodiac slowly drifted downriver. Chuck and Bill were lying on either side with their giant rifles pointed over the gunnels and ready for action.

"What do you think, Bloodfoot?" Chuck whispered, seeing that the burly hunter was sitting on his knees with both hands in the water.

173

"It's not AlliCroc," he replied, slowly flexing the hand gripping the knife. "There's a hungry reptile approaching, but it's not the one we're looking for."

Before anybody could advise that it wasn't such a good idea to stick your hands in the water where something huge just splashed in total darkness, a large alligator head breached the surface and snapped at his quick-moving hand.

With lightning speed, Bloodfoot grabbed the twelve-footer and stabbed it dead-center between the eyes. The gator hissed and tried to roll, but Bloodfoot kept his grip and stabbed it three more times.

Drifting lifeless in the bloodied water, Bloodfoot calmly grabbed the tail and proceeded to cut it off.

"What the hell are you doing?" asked Virgil, watching the lifeless alligator drift away and sink.

Bloodfoot finished washing his hands in the river and stood facing Virgil with a trivial grin, "Well, since Bill and Ian can't catch a damn fish, I thought we might try some gator tail for a change."

Virgil shook his head and lit another Camel cigarette, "Very thoughtful, next time let us know your plan." He took his seat, cranked the motor and pressed the throttle to its limit, "We're done here, let's get back to the tug."

On the ride back, Bloodfoot puffed on a cigar and watched Bill and Chuck chatting. He raised his eyebrows when they looked

174

over at him and asked, "Don't you need a license to hunt alligators?"

Bloodfoot smiled and replied, "Yes."

It was after midnight; Ian had chunks of alligator tail cut up like steaks while Bill wrapped them in foil and stored them in the freezer. Virgil and Bloodfoot sipped apricot brandy at the table and leisurely talked about the Suwannee River. The solid oak table and the wood décor on the walls made the galley look warm and comfortable, and Bloodfoot showed his gratitude for the decision to take the *Endurance* by bringing a case of his favorite rum and apricot brandy.

Chuck leaped through the galley hatch in a fresh pair of khaki shorts and a denim shirt with a towel wrapped around his neck, "Looks like we have enough gator tail to feed a small village," he said, pouring himself a cup of coffee.

"Gator tail with some old bay," Ian replied, whipping up a bowl of coleslaw. "We'll eat like Kings."

"You'd make a fine woman proud," Chuck joked, patting him on the back.

"Yup, a fine woman who doesn't cook," Bloodfoot grunted, draining his glass with one gulp and lighting a stogy.

"Listen, pirate boy, you don't have to eat it," Ian retorted, turning toward the table and shaking the spatula at him.

"Whoa, looks like I hit a chord," he grinned and blew smoke at the utensil.

"Easy Ian, he's only playin' you," Bill cut in before Ian had the bad idea of dueling it out with Bloodfoot.

"You do the cooking, and I'll do the hunting," Bloodfoot added for good measure.

After they settled down and relaxed, making sure the two weren't going to battle it out, they talked about their previous adventure at Socotra Island, then reminisced about the time they hunted the first AlliCroc.

"What's the game plan for tomorrow," asked Virgil, reaching in his shirt pocket for another camel non-filtered cigarette.

"Tomorrow, we should go into town and introduce ourselves to the mayor. From there, I want to talk to the park rangers at Ichetucknee State Park," Bloodfoot replied, refreshing his glass of apricot brandy and relighting his cigar.

"A necessary evil, I suppose," grunted Virgil.

"I will call around for a rental car," Ian added, reaching in his mini humidor and retrieving a larger cigar than Bloodfoot's stogy and giving him a pleasant look.

"No need, Ian. Randy Taylor is picking us up in a chopper," Virgil replied.

A surprised Chuck straightened up, "When the hell did you find that out?"

"He radioed just before we dropped anchor. He asked to keep it quiet until he arrived so he could surprise you guys."

"If he wants to surprise me, he will stay and join us for the hunt."

"I believe that is his game plan."

"Works for me," shrugged Bill.

"I don't mind him coming along for the ride, but I don't want too many captains on this outing getting in my way," Bloodfoot professed, staring unblinkingly at Virgil, testing his reply.

Without a scowl, Virgil emptied his glass and inhaled his cigarette, "There will be no problem there. You are the hunter; you make plans to catch and kill AlliCroc. I'm the captain aboard this vessel. What I say goes. Sergeant Taylor wants to come along to help. Since he's proven himself to be an asset from the last time, I think it's a great idea that he feels the need to risk his life with us again."

The concerned crew watched and waited in anticipation for Bloodfoot's reply, hoping the two strong-minded captains wouldn't start quarreling.

Bloodfoot cleared his throat, looked around at the crew and replied, "I wouldn't be here if it were any other way."

177

"Good, now let's get some sleep. I don't want a lethargic crewmember getting eaten while trying to stay awake tomorrow," Virgil replied, heading to his cabin.

Bloodfoot shook his head. Still grinning, he held a hand up, stepped out of the galley and headed for the extra bunk in Ian's quarters. Chuck and Bill sat with a look of relief while Ian looked puzzled, "What the hell was that all about?"

Bill smiled while Chuck explained, "We've got two strong-minded captains on this boat. Captain Virgil is a real captain with commendable leadership skills and Captain Bloodfoot commands a pirate ship that looks to be transplanted from another place and time. He calls himself captain, and that's all we know, but who's going to doubt him?"

"Looks like Virgil does," Ian quipped.

"Those two go at it every time they see each other. It used to be scarier, but now I think they do it just to keep us on edge," replied Bill.

"Thanks for the notice. See you guys in the morning," Ian said, leaping out of the hatch and heading to his quarters.

When Ian entered his room, he caught Bloodfoot checking out his cigar collection like a kid in a candy store. After a quick scan to make sure none were missing, he said, "Which one would you like, matey?"

"You have quite the collection, Ian. My stock in you has just gone up a notch," Bloodfoot smiled, picking up a big, spicy-looking one.

"What you are holding is a Don Collins cigar. I picked up fifty of them straight from the factory in Puerto Rico," Ian proudly said.

"Factory?"

"From the oldest cigar factory in the entire Caribbean," Ian continued, boasting.

"Yes, I think I know the one. It was built on the site of the old Taino festival in 1506," Bloodfoot said, staring at him with a devil-may-care grin.

Ian's smile faded as he returned the glare, "You've been there?"

"Yes."

"Ok, so there you have it. These are my Cubans, and these are my Dominicans," Ian continued, pointing at two other humidors.

"Which of the two do you like better?"

"If push came to shove, I'd have to settle for the Cubans," Ian replied thoughtfully.

"I prefer the Dominicans myself. The Cubans tasted better before the island became communist. Now, the cigar makers don't get paid enough, and it reflects in the product," said Bloodfoot.

Ian showed Bloodfoot more of his collection while they puffed their stogies.

Bloodfoot reached into his bag, produced a bottle of Sailor Jerry and said, "We can't sit around smoking the sacred herb without a shot or two of this."

Ian laughed, "Sacred herb?"

"That's what they called these cigars. Sacred herb or Queens herb, if you will," Bloodfoot added.

Before long, as they were talking it up and playing liars poker with five-dollar bills, a loud pounding was heard from the other side of the door before it sprang open.

"What have we here? Is this a party? Virgil asked, walking in the smoke-filled room with a bottle of apricot brandy.

It was early morning; the sun had just risen above the horizon as the small Cessna 402 private plane landed at a secluded landing strip near Fort White.

As the door opened, Don Henderson ducked his head out and looked around before stepping down the small flight of stairs, stretching his back as if he had just been released from a can of sardines.

He arrived earlier in the night on a conventional flight at Gainesville Regional Airport on a straight flight from Wichita, Kansas, then hopped on the Cessna to take him covertly to the isolated landing strip so that he couldn't be easily traced if things got out of hand.

As planned, an old associate of his met him in a dark green minivan and they loaded Don's suitcase and disappeared to the nearest diner for breakfast.

"Jeez, it's hotter than a stripper's ass," Don said as he climbed into a booth.

"So why are you here? And why the hell are you trying to get me involved?" his associate, Johnny Lee, replied.

Johnny Lee was one of the two biochemists who created the AlliCrocs. The last time Don spoke to him was when he took the three hatchlings to the Everglades Sanctuary before a remorseful Johnny and his cohort could destroy them.

"You know damn well why I'm here. I also know that you are interested in AlliCroc just as much as I am, or you wouldn't have answered my call and picked me up."

"I watched the news. What makes you think it's AlliCroc?"

They stopped talking when the waitress came and took their orders. Don ordered four pancakes, a western omelet, French toast and bacon, while Johnny ordered a bagel.

"You fat bastard. You eat as much as the alligator."

"And you eat like whining butterfly, you skinny Korean weed."

They broke out laughing and kept the façade until the waitress was out of earshot.

"There's a witness that swears the reptile is over thirty feet long."

"Well, it should be. The other one was thirty-five feet long," Don bellowed.

Johnny took a sip of tea and reasoned, "Ok, maybe it is AlliCroc. But what are we going to do? Try to catch it?"

"Say we do? Do you know what kind of an attraction that thing would be? People will come from all over the world to see it. You and I will be millionaires," Don boasted, his voice getting louder and louder as he talked.

"Shhh, quiet down. I thought you wanted to do this quietly," Johnny retorted.

Don looked around the diner and was glad nobody was looking. He wiped his mouth with the napkin and leaned in, "You're right. I'm sorry. I tend to get out of hand when I think of the potential in all this."

"Look, I don't think I want to go through with this. How are you planning on catching that reptile?"

Don bit into a piece of bacon and stared at Johnny. A full minute went by as the biochemist watched Don finish off the plate of bacon, staring at him.

Finally, Don leaned forward and replied, "I'm going to borrow your minivan and snoop around at the ranger station at Clearview Springs Park. I'll ask around and see if I can find out who's hunting AlliCroc. When I find out who's hunting it, I will persuade them not to kill it."

"You must be mad," Johnny replied, shaking his head.

"No. I'm quite happy, actually. In my bag, I happened to get hold of a drug called carfentanil. All I have to do is get the hunters to agree to shoot it with the drug, and it should render AlliCroc unconscious until we can haul it to a safe place."

"And where might that be?"

"I'm going to contact Chief Bhim with an offer he can't refuse. He will restore the tank at the Everglades Sanctuary where we raised the three AlliCrocs."

Johnny gave him a distasteful scowl and replied, "Didn't Chief Bhim lose a son to the AlliCroc?"

Don glared back, "Let bygones be bygones, eh? This is the last AlliCroc. There will be no more like it. Once he gets a taste of all the money and fame he's going to get, he'll gladly give up his mother," he chuckled.

"You are a sick man."

183

"If so, then so are you. I don't see you walking away. I'm sure you wouldn't mind being a millionaire. What are you doing these days? Still working for peanuts?"

"I'm waiting for a reply on a grant to…"

"Peanuts! A smart guy like you should be making good money, not begging for grants," Don shot back, his voice overbearing.

"Quiet down."

"Again, I apologize. This talk just gets me so worked up. You know what I'm doing? I'm cutting hair in a barber shop. Can you believe it?"

The waitress returned with a concerned look, "Is everything ok? Can I get you some more coffee and tea?"

"We're fine. Just give me the check," Don grumbled.

The waitress gave him the bill and walked off when Don continued, "Look, I need to know right now, are you in this with me or out?"

Johnny took some time to think before replying, "I'm in. You heard of Barnum and Bailey? Well let's catch our attraction so the world can come see the amazing beast from Henderson and Lee."

"Great answer. Now let's go talk to some park rangers," Don replied, climbing out of the booth without leaving a tip.

The dark night gave way to the dull, yellow-inspiring morning sunlight. Captain Virgil and Chuck were drinking coffee in the galley while Bill, looking annoyed, was trying to cast a fishing line at the stern of the *Endurance*.

Hearing the few choice words the deckhand was spewing, they decided to walk out and see what was going on.

"What's the problem, Bill?" asked Virgil, reaching in his breast pocket for a pack of cigarettes.

"Wait for it… Wait for it…."

Virgil looked over to Chuck, who just shrugged his shoulders. Without warning, the fishing line went rigid, and the pole bent downward like it was about to snap.

"Damn it!" Bill roared.

"Reel it in! Reel it in!" Chuck gasped.

"I'd like to reel it in with a hook through its head," Bill retorted.

Just then, Bloodfoot's head broke the surface with a gleaming grin, "Reel it in, fisherman. I've got breakfast!"

Virgil and Chuck leaned over the gunwale and noticed blood in the water, "Did you get eaten by a shark, or did you spear something?" Virgil asked.

Bloodfoot swam with one arm to the ladder on the starboard side of the salvage tug and with the other hand, he pulled up a nice size almaco.

"Junk fish, throw that amberjack out. They're full of worms," Bill chided.

"This here is an almaco. Don't you know the difference? Kind of rare for these parts, but here it is," Bloodfoot retorted as he heaved it over the gunwale. "Breakfast tacos and scrambled eggs on me this morning," he continued, climbing up the ladder.

Bill swallowed his pride and gave Bloodfoot a hand on deck, "Where the hell's Ian," he grumbled all the way to the galley.

Virgil checked his watch, confirming it was seven-twenty and replied, "Sleeping, the kid had a rough night last night."

"He's going to wake up and gag when he smells what Bloodfoot caught," Bill griped.

Bloodfoot was showered and standing at the stove in the galley cooking his catch when Ian finally poked his head in, "Aye, Captain, what smells good?"

Virgil and Chuck sat at the table, watching the expression on Bill's face and waited for the response, "Bloodfoot scrambled fish worms," replied Bill.

Bloodfoot ignored the jab and turned off the stove. He brought the fish tacos and scrambled eggs to the table and sat down, "This will put some hair on your chest, big fella...now let's eat."

Everybody dug in and was surprised at how good it tasted. Even Bill had a look on his face like it was the best thing he tasted in days, "Well, I stand corrected. Amberjack does taste good when freshly caught."

"You really don't know the difference between amberjack and almaco, do you?" Bloodfoot grinned. "Okay, let me tell you. The most notable difference between the amber and the almaco is the second dorsal fin. The almaco fin is more than twice as high as the spines in the first dorsal fin."

"And that makes it tastier than amberjack?" Bill cracked.

"Hell no. Almaco just sounds better than amberjack," Bloodfoot smirked. 'Not to mention that the meat is firm and white, and a lot of people I know prefer it better than snapper."

Minutes later, the sound of helicopter blades was heard twirling overhead and they scrambled out of the galley to see the commotion. A green Astar 350 B2 helicopter with floaters hovered over the *Endurance* before edging twenty yards off the port stern and descending to the calm blue water.

They watched as the engine shut down, and none other than Randy Taylor and Christi, a member of Captain Bloodfoot's crew, opened the door and gave them a wave.

"Hello, Captain, permission to come aboard?" he shouted.

"Granted!" replied Virgil, lighting a cigarette.

"Who's the lady?" asked Ian.

"She's one of Bloodfoot's crew. We met her on Socotra Island," replied Bill.

Randy and the helicopter pilot carefully unloaded a box-shaped item into the water and it exploded with air, minutes later revealing a small inflatable Zodiac with a wood sectional bottom that they had to put in place. When completed, he jumped in and was carefully handed a twenty-five horsepower Yamaha outboard from the pilot.

"Easy, does it? You look like you're going to break your back," Bill shouted with concern.

"No problem," Randy winced. "These newer outboards only weigh one-hundred and twenty-six pounds."

"No problem on dry land, but handed over from a helicopter to a portable floater…not so much," Chuck added.

"I'll manage."

In less than ten minutes, Randy attached the outboard to the zodiac, connected the gas tank and cranked the motor. The helicopter pilot could have just shoved the boat with his foot, and the momentum would have let it drift over to the tug, but the crew just watched and smiled, as they knew it was probably a new toy for Randy to show off.

As the zodiac idled over, Ian grabbed the line that was thrown to him, and Randy gave Christi a hand over the gunwale after he cut the motor.

"Greetings from hell, my friends," Taylor said, throwing his leg over the gunwale. "We ready to do this again?"

"No, but nobody else wants to do this," Chuck replied.

"Always ready for a challenge," Bloodfoot countered.

"I thought you said you wouldn't be joining us," Virgil stated flatly.

"After we left the Anchor Bar, I was driving home when all of a sudden it hit me…Why the hell would I miss out on this hunt? So, I changed my mind," Taylor replied haphazardly.

Ian tied off the zodiac and followed the men into the galley where they briefly talked about their adventures and the latest hunt they were now facing. They greeted Christi when she boarded but never asked why she came along. Bloodfoot took notice and finally told them.

"Since nobody asked why Christi is here, I might as well tell you. Christi is my eyes and ears when I hunt. I'm usually too focused on what I'm hunting to see what else is going on around me. Sometimes, if I'm headed deep down a dark path, she points me back in the right direction, so to speak."

"Say no more. She'll fit right in," said Virgil.

"Fine by me," replied Chuck.

"I'm sure," Ian stood up and winked at Bloodfoot while Bill just nodded his approval.

An hour later, they bid farewell to Christi and Ian and made their way to the helicopter. Chuck was a little surprised that Captain Virgil had no reservations about leaving her aboard with Ian to watch the salvage tug and monitor the radio.

The plan was to keep her aboard the *Endurance* for the duration of the hunt. They would keep radio contact for updates and a satellite phone call every two hours if there was no radio contact. Failure to make the phone call would be considered that the team was in grave danger and Christi would notify the authorities in the area.

Ian was chosen to stay behind only because there was not enough room on the helicopter, and they were only headed to the state park to check in with the park rangers and see what they knew about AlliCroc.

12

The green minivan turned into the entrance of Clearview State Park and made its way to the ranger station. The parking lot was virtually empty except for three ranger jeeps parked near the front door of the building. Johnny picked a spot around the side of the building to park and thought it would be a good idea to stay in the vehicle while Don went inside to get some information.

"Hello, gentlemen," Don said as he stepped into the confined lobby.

It was obvious that the three park rangers had recently arrived for work. Two looked up and nodded, while the third replied, "Good morning, sir. Can I help you?"

"I certainly hope so. I heard there's a rather large alligator swimming around here and would like to know if anybody is hunting it," Don replied, not mincing his words.

The other two rangers sat up and turned their heads to Don. The ranger that greeted Don turned and met their stare, then turned back to Don, "There is a gator. It is being hunted by professionals, and that is all we know at this point."

Don closed his eyes and shook his head as if he knew about it. "Yes, I just wanted to confirm who they are and where they might be at the moment."

"Like I said, that's all we know. By the way, who are you?"

"I'm just a concerned parent," he shrugged, reaching for the door and stepping outside.

Don shut the door and wasted no time walking back to the minivan. With a quick glance back to make sure the park rangers didn't follow him out, he jumped into the van and told Johnny to step on it.

"Did you find out who's hunting AlliCroc?" asked Johnny, peeling out of the rocky drive.

"No, they said they didn't know."

The minivan was a quarter mile from the ranger station when they saw a low-flying helicopter descending. "Pull over," Don ordered.

They pulled off the road and watched the helicopter descend to a helipad behind the ranger station. The minivan took a U-turn and headed back before pulling off the road to where they could see the people get out of the helicopter. Waiting with anticipation, they were hoping to see the hunter or hunters that were hired to kill their reptile.

They watched through binoculars as it landed. When the door opened and the first man climbed out, Don's heart sank in his chest. "Bloodfoot!"

Virgil, Chuck, Bill and the man who threatened to kill him, Randy Taylor, followed close behind, and Johnny watched Don break out in a cold sweat.

"Friends of yours? You look like you're about to have a heart attack," said Johnny with a concerned look.

Don dropped the binoculars in his lap and leaned back in the seat, "Foes, not friends. Those are the same guys that wanted to kill me when they hunted the first AlliCroc."

Johnny couldn't believe it. How was it possible to have the same guys hunt their reptiles? Was Florida short on alligator hunters? It didn't make sense.

"What are we going to do now? I'm sure we won't be able to strike a deal with them."

"We will. We just have to be a little more creative."

"What do you have in mind?"

"Just drive. We've got to make an unscheduled stop in Fort Lauderdale."

"You're nuts! That's over five hours away!" replied Johnny, bewildered.

The Suwannee River Campground in Old Town was approximately five miles from Clearview State Park. The privately owned campground was so small the three adventurers didn't know it existed until they accidentally drove past it.

The sun was beginning its daily decent in the western sky as Angie, Ned and Jay put the last stake in their tent while Angie prepared a campfire so they could relax and contrive a plan to find the pertinent alligator.

After searching high and low at Clearview State Park for the reptile to no avail, they decided to search a new area where Ned thought it might be lurking. Amanda and Gina thought they were nuts and wondered what they would do if they actually found it. They had no intention of seeing the monster again and had decided to pack up and go home.

"There are one-hundred camp sites in this godforsaken area, and we had to choose the one with all the mosquitos," Jay complained, swatting his hands and legs for the umpteenth time since they arrived.

"I'll make this a smoky fire to chase off these little vampires," Angie smirked, adding dead leaves to the flames.

"Great idea," replied Ned, coughing through the smoke.

"Here, try some of this mosquito repellant," she replied, tossing him the can and trying not to laugh.

Jay wore a headband, and on his right eyelid was a red, puffy mosquito bite that made him look like he was in a fight with Rocky Balboa. It took all she had not to blurt out the name *Adrianne!* like in the scene from the movie.

"Don't say it," he said, catching the can.

Ned sat by the fire and pulled out a map of the area. "Okay, so this X on the map is where the alligator attacked," he said, pointing at the map. "Since we didn't see it in this area anymore, I figured it must have swum this way to where we are now," sliding his finger down the river. "If we quietly walk along the bank toward the State Park, we might spot it."

"Uh...yes, but that's over five miles we have to cover," Jay replied, raising his eyebrows, the right one lifting the massive red bite above his eye.

"I don't think anybody has seen it in days. Therefore, I'm thinking it could be around here," said Ned, drawing a circle on the map within a one-mile radius of where they sat.

Angie just sat and listened as the two plotted where they thought the reptile might have gone. As always, when they searched for the best fishing spot or anything else they were trying to find, they somehow always found it.

"Okay, hold that thought," Jay suddenly said. "These mosquitos are eating me alive...I'm going to take a hot shower and get this dirt off me, put on a fresh coat of repellant, and be right back." he continued, grabbing a fresh towel and clothing from the trunk of the car.

Angie and Ned watched with amusement as he walked off toward the bathroom/showers.

Angie left Ned sitting by the campfire and walked to the car. Reaching in, she withdrew a bag of marshmallows and three long sticks. Ned smiled as she returned and offered him the bag.

"Well, camping with an open fire is not fun without hot, burning marshmallows," she said, lightly poking his arm with a stick.

"And every time, wherever we are, we have fun every time," he replied.

"Time? Time isn't real."

Ned didn't reply, but he thought *Time isn't real? My girl's a nut.*

They sat in silence, watching the fire, when Angie finally cleared her throat and asked, "So, if we spot that monster, what are we going to do?"

Ned was prepared for the inevitable question, "We will call that police guy, Chief Clark, that we gave the statement to, and hope they catch or kill it before it attacks somebody else."

Angie gave him a look like she just bit into a lemon, "Really? You and Jay will just spot it and call the police."

"Yeah, that's right."

She returned her gaze toward the fire, "You better."

"That's all we can do. That thing is too big for us to mess with."

A full hour had passed before Jay returned to the camp. Ned and Angie were now standing by a grill preparing hamburgers.

"Cheese or no cheese?" Angie asked him.

"Cheese, please," Jay replied, strolling up with wet hair and a towel around his neck.

They sat at a picnic table and ate their cheeseburgers while trying to figure out what to do when they found the reptile. Angie just sat and shook her head. She knew they wanted to somehow catch the giant alligator.

All agreed that it was too big to catch, but both Ned and Jay were pretty sure they could get a rope around it and tie it to a tree so it would hopefully not get away until help could arrive and kill it.

The more she heard, the more she got frustrated, so Angie decided to take a stroll around the campground and let them figure it out. Deep down, she didn't think they'd ever see the monster again, and if they did, they'd probably set a speed record fleeing from it.

She followed a well-lit path that went through the campsites and then along the river.

Looking around, admiring the beauty, and for the first time, she noticed how deserted the area was. Goose bumps ran up the back of her neck as she walked over to a covered shelter by the edge of the river and took a seat on one of five picnic tables.

She sat looking around and wondered where the other campers were. *Who goes camping and just sits in their tent or camper?*

She decided to go to the boat ramp and see if anybody was fishing.

Deep in thought about what she would do if she came face to face with the monster again, she suddenly noticed a large wake in the corner of her eyes. Quickly turning her head, she gasped to see what looked like the wake of a thirty-to-forty-foot submarine.

"Oh, No?"

Running back to the picnic table, she stood on top and got a clear view of the form of a very large creature swimming just below the surface.

"Giant alligator heading for the boat ramp!" she yelled, looking around, hoping to find other witnesses.

AlliCroc leisurely swam close to the bank of the river with an imposing presence. The sound of a human shouting caused it to stop and slowly raise its gruesome head out of the water and look at the prospective prey with incarnate evil in its disconcerting eyes.

Her heart sank and she found it hard to take a breath when the vast reptile poked its head out of the water and glared at her. Never in her life did she get such a bad feeling while viewing a croc, gator, or whatever the hell she was staring at.

AlliCroc's genetically altered brain made the creature extremely intelligent. As it watched the human on the shoreline, its first thought was to attack the prey since it was so stunned that it probably couldn't move, but since witnesses got away at an earlier attack, it decided to stay low so that trackers wouldn't detect it.

Angie wanted to run away to warn other campers, but her legs wouldn't move. She almost felt hypnotized watching the hellish green eyes glaring at her, almost through her, as if raking down to her soul.

Finally, the massive head sank below the surface, and the diabolical creature vanished. Shaking her head and blinking her eyes, Angie snapped out of her nightmarish ordeal and sprinted to the campground office.

Within minutes, she frantically crashed through the front door and grabbed the counter, "Mister! There's a huge reptile swimming near the boat ramp! You've got to call the police and warn everybody to stay away!"

"Calm down, ma'am, keep your voice down and tell me what you saw," the elderly campground owner replied," looking at her sympathetically.

"Call the police! Get the park rangers! There's a giant alligator near the boat ramp!" she shouted hysterically. "It's the same one that attacked me and other visitors a few days ago!"

"Ma'am, I'll ask you one more time to keep your voice down!" the clerk replied in a sharper tone. "There're gators all over the place in these waters. What makes you think that is the one that attacked you?"

"Because I've seen it up close! It's huge!"

"Harry, can I see you for a moment?" the campground owner's wife called out from a small office behind the counter.

"Excuse me for a moment, please," Harry said, walking back to the office.

"If you don't shut that lady up, she will scare the campers away!"

Angie overheard the wife and figured she was pleading on deaf ears. She took a couple of deep breaths and tore out through the front door, sprinting back to her campsite.

She reached the campsite at the same time Ned was returning from the bathrooms.

"What happened, Angie? Are you alright?" he asked, catching her in his arms.

"Oh my god, Ned! I just saw it!

"Where?"

"It's swimming toward the boat ramp! We've got to call the authorities before it kills somebody!" she cried out, her entire body shaking.

Ned grabbed his phone from his pant pocket and cursed when it had no signal.

The three of them jumped in the car with Angie behind the wheel, and she sped off toward the campground office. The car came to a screeching halt at the front door of the office, and Ned jumped out and ran inside.

Henry's patience was wearing thin, "Sir, I advise you to take your wife back to your campground. I can't have her shouting and carrying on like this. Pretty soon, all the campers will be alarmed.

"She's my girlfriend, and you better call for help because there's a monster gator here!"

"Tell you what I'll do; at this hour, I still have two employees on duty. I will send them out around the boat ramp and have them search the area."

Ned stared at the man and shook his head, "I don't think you understand what I'm trying to tell you. There's a monster swimming out there that eats people! It's the same gator that attacked people in Clearview State Park!"

"No, son, I don't think you understand. There are big gators here all the time. What I can't have is you tourists running around like it's the end of the world. It's bad for business, and you will scare away our guests!"

Angie and Jay were leaning on the car, searching the river, when Ned walked out.

"Did you get through to that idiot?" asked Angie.

"Nope, he's a fucking idiot."

They piled back into the car and headed for the parking lot by the boat ramp. They decided to stand on the picnic tables where Angie sat earlier, where they could search the water and try to spot the reptile at a safe distance.

"Ok, looks like we found its new spot," Jay said excitedly.

"Great, now what?" replied Angie.

Ned stood on the table, staring at a wooded area near the water and answered, "It should stick around here for a while. It will see if it's a good spot to hide out and eat before moving on."

"Should we call that police guy?"

"I think if we call him now, he will come out here and talk to that campground idiot. They will both come down and take a look in the water and not see it, then tell us we're seeing things," replied Ned.

Jay laughed and said, "My thoughts exactly."

"Let's go back to the campsite and make a lasso with the rope and come back early tomorrow morning and set the trap over there," Ned said, pointing toward the wooded area near the river.

Angie didn't like the plan but knew she couldn't change their minds. She just shook her head and walked with them back to the car.

True to his word, Henry sent his two sons out to search along the ramp. He paid no mind about the alleged huge alligator the camper reported because he was sure she saw one, probably a ten-to-twelve-footer, which was not common in this area but had been seen from time to time.

Just before midnight, the two siblings returned. When asked if they spotted a monster alligator lurking around, they all broke out laughing.

Henry pat his boys on the back as they walked toward their living area in the back of the office, "If we find that gator tomorrow, it damn well better be a big monster, or I'm going to kick those campers out of the campground."

"Go easy, Dad, I'm sure they mean well."

"Well, we can't have no city slickers carrying on and scaring the other guests. Hell, this place is only half full already."

"That's probably because somebody got attacked at Clearview State Park the other day."

"I haven't heard. Somebody was probably feeding the damn gator."

Angie woke up in a sweaty mess. A beam of sunlight felt like it was burning a hole through her head when she checked her watch and saw it was just past seven.

It took a minute to gather her senses and remember that Ned and Jay returned to the boat ramp and stayed out all night trying to find the reptile.

"Wake up, Ned," she nudged his shoulder. "No luck, huh?"

Ned grunted and rolled over.

"Ned! We've got to warn people," she spoke louder, this time shaking his shoulder roughly.

Ned squinted his eyes and snorted loudly. Scratching his head and searching for the time, he sat up and looked around the tent as if he didn't know where he was.

"We just got back about an hour ago. It's gone. We couldn't find it anywhere. I'll get up and go back to the office and see what's going on," he replied casually.

"I can't believe I fell asleep with you guys out there," she whispered with a baffled look.

"It's okay. After we got back last night, you came to the tent here. Jay and I decided to leave you alone for a few minutes, you know, let you calm down a bit. After a half-hour, I poked my head in here to tell you we were going back to the ramp, and you were sound asleep...snoring."

"Yeah, but I woke up when you shook me and told me you guys were going to search for that monster."

"You were barely awake."

"And that manager never came by to tell us anything?"

"No, that's why I'm going back to the office."

Jay was already outside and rearing to go, "Alright, now that you sleepy heads are up, let's go search for that gator."

"Let's go back to the office and see if they saw it or called for help first," replied Ned.

"You go talk to the management; I'm searching for that gator. That guy doesn't believe a word of what you told him," Jay replied, swirling his arms around to shake the stiffness out.

"It will take a minute. We'll catch up with you at the boat ramp."

After a quick sausage and egg muffin from the campground's grocery store, Angie and Ned stepped into the office with an uneasy feeling at the sight of the woman behind the counter.

"Good morning. Can I please talk to Henry?"

Henry's wife stared at him for what seemed forever before looking down at the newspaper on the counter, "He's sleeping."

"I guess there was no luck in spotting the giant gator?"

"No luck," she replied, not taking her eyes off the paper.

Angie walked closer and leaned in with her elbows on the counter, eyes level with hers, "If you don't wake him up and tell him we want to talk, I will call the police and tell them you are concealing the fact that there is a large predator out there that can cause harm to your guests."

She looked up at her with slanted eyes as if deciding what to do.

"I'll get him," she hissed.

While they waited, Ned looked down at the paper and laughed to himself. *These backward idiots are reading a two-day-old newspaper.* The smirk on his face stayed until he flipped the paper around and read the headline: GROUP OF HIKERS ATTACKED BY THIRTY-EIGHT FOOT REPTILE.

The lump in his throat forced him to swallow hard as Henry resignedly entered the counter area.

"Good morning, you two. We did not find your reptile last night, and when I came to your campsite, you and your wife were snoring up a storm," he smiled warmly, trying to break the ice. "When I can spare a few workers," he checked his watch, "In about an hour or so, I'll have them continue searching."

With his eyes bulging down at the newspaper, Ned apparently didn't hear a word the manager said. When he was finished reading the story, he looked up and shoved the newspaper in Henry's face, "You knew about this attack? Why the hell are you letting campers go near the river?"

206

"Calm down, son, just calm down," Henry replied, moving his hands up and down as if trying to calm a bucking bronco. "You can't believe everything you read. Sure, those people were attacked by a big alligator…They're out in the wild for chrissakes! But there's no such thing as a thirty-eight-foot alligator. It was probably a ten- or twelve-footer. Big ones like that are indeed out there. But alligators are territorial. Those people are miles from here."

"Oh yeah, do you remember hearing about the monstrous hybrid reptile in South Florida a few years back?"

"Hybrid? Never heard about a hybrid," Henry replied, raising his eyebrows with a condescending look.

"It's out there!" he blurted and ran out the door.

"Damn city folks," Henry grumbled, picking up the phone to call his boys. He had to stop the two visitors before they scared away the other campers.

Ned and Angie sprinted down to the boat ramp. Two men with a couple of kids were standing on either side of a twenty-foot aluminum boat while a woman expertly backed a long-bed ford pickup down the ramp. They noticed Jay was having no luck trying to warn them of the danger that lurked below.

The kids were busy wrapping inflatable tubes around their waist as Angie slowly walked over to the closest man, "Excuse me, are you all planning on going out in this boat?" she asked, sounding like a fool.

The man was wearing a flannel shirt, jeans and a camouflage cap, and looked like he knew the river like the back of his hand. He spit dip out of his mouth as he turned slowly in her direction, "No, ma'am, it's too early. We're just gonna git the boat wet and pull her back out of the water."

The two kids, a boy and a girl about the age of nine, broke out in laughter and ran closer to the dock.

"Listen, mister, you don't have to be a smartass. Last night, I saw a gigantic alligator lurking around," she said, grabbing his arm with a serious tone in her voice.

The woman in the truck watched through the side mirror and stopped the truck instantly when she saw the pretty redhead grab her husband's arm.

Stepping out with a menacing look, she rolled up the sleeves of her camouflage shirt and proceeded to walk over, "Listen, honey, can you leave my man alone so I can drop this boat in the water? Go over and talk to my brother," she said, pointing at the other man as she walked back to the driver's door, "He's not married."

With an exasperating look, Angie looked at the redneck lady and put her hands on her hips, "I was just trying to warn him that I saw a gigantic alligator here last night. The same one that attacked my friend. I think it would be crazy for you people to go out in this boat, especially with these little kids."

The lady had one foot in the truck when she stopped and turned around. Adjusting her too-small bikini bottom, she strolled back over with a menacing look, "Well, you must be new around here," she smiled. "Me and these boys grew up here, and we saw gators all our lives."

"Well, this one is huge," she retorted, her voice trembling with anger.

The lady gave her a threatening look when she saw the kids stop smiling and slowly walk closer, "Thanks for your concern; we'll be careful. Now, back away so I don't run you over."

Angie shrugged her shoulders with a perplexed look as the woman crawled back in the truck and backed the boat down the ramp. She watched helplessly as the men grabbed the bow and stern lines as the boat plunged into the water.

They swung the boat to the side of the dock and held the lines as the kids stepped in. The mother parked the truck, hurried to the dock, smiled at Ned as she entered the boat and proceeded to put lifejackets on the kids.

"Please listen to me. It's an enormous alligator!" Ned insisted, trying to persuade them one last time not to go.

"Will you shut up with that crazy talk already? You're scaring the kids!" the mother retorted, glaring forebodingly.

Jay shrugged his shoulders and aggrievedly walked over and sat on a picnic table, "Fine…Can't say we didn't warn you."

Angie, Ned and Jay looked up and down the river, hoping the reptile was long gone, as the small boat motor cranked over, blue smoke pouring out of the exhaust as they set off down river.

As more people came to the boat ramp, waiting for their turn to drop their boat in the water, Angie began to doubt herself about what she saw or thought she saw the previous evening.

What with the twilight casting shadows in the water and ripples in the river, maybe the alligator really wasn't quite the size she had thought she had seen. She thought maybe she just imagined the huge gator since it was still fresh in her mind.

She smiled at the other campers scrambling on the dock and figured that all these people had probably been used to seeing big alligators swimming around this river. After all, the Suwannee River winds through the wilderness, and it's a fact that alligators have been around forever. Surely, these people are used to seeing them and won't try swimming in the river.

Angie stood up and stretched as she decided that she may have been wrong. After the shock of being right next to the monster when it attacked Amanda, she figured she might think she sees the reptile every time she's near a river. Funny how the mind plays tricks on you.

She swallowed hard and got her mind set on apologizing to the campground owners. She gathered Ned and Jay and sat with them on the picnic table, "I'm sorry, guys."

"Sorry for what?" replied Jay.

"Sorry that I think I made a mistake."

Ned stood up and crossed his arms while Jay stood with his hands on his hips.

"You think you did what?" asked Ned.

"I don't know. I think that maybe I didn't see it. Maybe it was just a regular alligator, and my mind went berserk."

Ned and Jay looked at each other and turned away.

"Well, after what you and Amanda went through, I'd be thinking the same thing. It's not your fault," Ned said reassuringly, rubbing her shoulders.

"I'm going back up to the office and apologize to the campground owners."

Ned followed Angie back to the office while Jay walked down a path near a more secluded wooded area down river to make sure the reptile wasn't hiding in the undergrowth.

Barely fifty yards up the dirt trail, he suddenly turned at the sound of a dog barking from the other side of the river. A large black dog was spotted running full speed through the marshes, bringing smiles to the people watching near the boat ramp. The smiles quickly vanished when they caught a glimpse of something massive chasing from about sixty-feet behind. Whatever it was was smashing through the thicket at break-neck speed and catching up to the frightened dog.

"Brody!" Henry called out as he busted through the door of the campground office.

The dog, hearing the familiar voice of its owner from across the river, stopped and poked through the brush. Whatever was chasing the dog also stopped and, by the looks of the tops of the grove, turned and scrambled into the water with a loud splash, just beyond a bend where it couldn't be seen.

AlliCroc was irate and ready to lash out at the fleeing prey. The speed at which it ran surprised the reptile, but it was rapidly gaining ground.

All at once, a now familiar human voice was heard, and the prey stopped running. AlliCroc also came to an abrupt stop in hopes of not being spotted.

As it sat unmoving in the thicket, hunger pangs fought with its newfound intelligence to remain elusive, once again agitating the fearful predator into a vicious frenzy.

Fighting off the urge to attack and risk a confrontation with the hunters, AlliCroc turned and headed for the safety of the river, where it could safely sit at the bottom and stay out of sight.

"What was that!" voices on the dock gasped as ripples from the wake could be seen.

Jay ran to the dock and joined Angie and Ned as they called out for Brody.

"Hold on, sir, I will get your dog," a man with a fourteen-foot aluminum boat said, cranking the motor and pushing off the dock.

"I will cover you," Henry replied, producing a shotgun as if by magic.

Henry's two sons scattered along the dock making sure there was no large gator ready to pounce as the boat quickly made it to the other side of the river.

The man aboard the boat threw the dog a live baitfish in hopes of getting him closer to the boat, but Brody had no qualms about jumping in the boat as he leaped in before the boat touched the muddy embankment.

The boat had barely made it to the dock when loud, horrific screams were heard downriver.

"What now?" Henry anxiously asked, trying to see around the bend. He quickly grabbed Brody, hugging him tight as the frightened dog licked his face. "Brody's been missing since last night," he related to a fellow camper.

"There's a family down river...two men, a woman and two kids that left the dock about a half-hour ago," Ned shouted.

"That would be the Sanford's. I lent them inner tubes for the two little ones," a worried lady shouted, running towards the boat ramp from her parked vehicle.

13

The helicopter flew low and slow through the mouth of the Suwannee River while the crew of the *Endurance* silently watched Bloodfoot searching the water and marshland through binoculars.

"How long until we reach Rattlesnake Jakes?" Bill asked the pilot through the headphones.

"E.T.A. in approximately ten minutes…Maybe a little longer if we keep sightseeing up this river, though," replied the pilot, suddenly regretting his last remark as he felt the wily pirate's eyes behind him burning through the back of his head.

"You have no idea what we're looking for, do you," Bloodfoot grumbled with an unbending grin.

Bill took a deep breath and noticed the crew anxiously watching the river down below. Seeing that everything looked under control, he leaned back in his seat and gazed out the window.

"Slow the chopper!" Chuck shouted suddenly, pointing toward some foliage on the riverbank. "Look at that bunch of bushes moving on the south side, near the water…about thirty degrees to starboard."

Bloodfoot took his eyes off the binoculars and glared at Chuck, "Just point!"

"Left side, ten-o-clock," Virgil cut in, focusing his binoculars and pointing at the disturbance down below.

Bloodfoot looked through his binoculars and focused on the commotion for a few seconds before sitting back and smiling, "That, my friend, is a family of wild boar. But I do admire your vigilance," he replied, through a deep baritone grumble.

Chuck dropped his binoculars and leaned back in his seat, his ego bruised.

The helicopter broke its pattern and crossed over a roadway when Randy set his binoculars aside and told the pilot to continue toward Rattlesnake Jake's Swamp Safari.

Minutes later, their destination came into view, and the pilot was looking for the area to set down as he prepared his descent. Randy was on the radio asking where the landing point would be when he unexpectedly saw the park rangers gathered around an open area.

Suddenly, a call came over the radio, and the pilot answered and held altitude. A minute later, the pilot flipped a switch in his mouthpiece so the crew could hear him speak, "Hey guys, your reptile may have been spotted near a campground about three miles from here on the Suwannee River."

"When?" asked Virgil.

216

"Less than an hour ago. A small boat was attacked, and I hear there are casualties."

"Let's check it out," replied Bloodfoot, not waiting for Randy's reply.

Virgil and Randy locked eyes and gave an affirmative nod as the pilot changed frequencies and notified the men on the ground about their situation. The chopper pulled up, did a one-hundred-and-eighty-degree turn and flew off.

"I believe those men down there were waiting to fill us in on the attacks," Randy chided.

"We received all the information we needed when we made the stop at Clearview," said Bloodfoot.

"I think you're just pissed because the mayor wasn't there," Randy refuted.

"I'll let you know when I give a rat's ass what you cops think."

AlliCroc played cat and mouse with an amusing animal for the past several hours. It had seen other dogs once or twice before, but they were much smaller and never ventured into the water.

Sensing its quirkiness and horrible skills for catching prey, the unfathomable reptile followed from beneath the surface as the spirited animal chased ducks. The reptile lost its diverted feelings when the dog jumped into the water. Fighting a ferocious appetite with its impeccable thinking pattern and desire not to be seen, AlliCroc became more and more agitated throughout the night.

While it was hardly enough to satisfy a fierce appetite, AlliCroc knew it would make an easy meal and not be able to send the humans to where it was trying to keep a low profile. The massive tail began to swim from side to side as the alert reptile moved in for the kill, its senses going off the scale when it suddenly detected fear in the animal.

When it was directly below the dog, AlliCroc quickly sprang from the bottom and snapped its humongous jaws when it breached the surface, but somehow, in fear for its life, the dog bolted and escaped the deadly jaws.

A loud splash ensued as AlliCroc turned its massive head to snare its prey, but the lucky dog made it to the mucky embankment and ran as fast as he could go with a surprised look on its terrified face.

Seconds later, AlliCroc burst through the marsh and gave chase. The flustered canine ran with all its might as the reptile sprinted from behind. Tree branches snapped, and the ground shook as if a freight train was barreling through the marshland.

Suddenly, the ferocious reptile sensed turmoil on the other side of the river. AlliCroc stopped and tried to conceal itself as it watched the melee across the way. It was people, humans shouting for the dog. Trying to remain camouflaged in the foliage, it watched patiently as its prey stopped and barked feverishly near the water's edge. When a small boat crossed over to pick up the animal, AlliCroc fought the urge to attack and became extremely agitated when it decided to remain undetected and splashed back into the water and dove to the bottom.

As it crawled on the bottom of the river, escaping the melee by the boat ramp, its incredible senses began to tingle feverishly. There was something or things in the water up ahead, splashing. The sound of laughter increased his appetite as it sprang from the bottom and swam around the bend of the river.

Slowly, it breached the surface and saw a boat with two humans in it. Its long muscular tail increased its side-to-side movement when it felt the vibrations of three more objects splashing in the water.

Two of the prey were small and not enough to fill the reptile's vigorous appetite, so it decided to eat one of the larger targets first. After that, AlliCroc would attack the boat and, lastly, finish its meal with the two smaller prey.

"Hey Albert! Are you sure it's safe to swim around here?" the woman shouted, floating on her back with a close eye on the kids.

"Sure it is. When was the last time somebody got eatin' by a gator," he replied, popping the top off another can of Bush beer.

"A few days ago. Remember? A gator attack in the Clearview Springs...of all places," her voice trailed off.

"Well, why the hell do you think I'm standing here in the damn boat? I'm watchin' out for y'alls."

"Yeah, right...and drinkin' all my beer," she teased, dunking her head back under the water.

Albert's brother-in-law laughed and reached in the cooler for another beer, "You've got nothing to worry about, sis. Al and I will ..." his voice stopped suddenly when he stood and looked beyond his sister. His heart sank into the pit of his stomach, and he suddenly felt numb, as he couldn't believe what he was seeing.

Twenty yards and closing fast was the biggest alligator he had ever seen. Before his mind could comprehend the catastrophic event about to unfold, his sister let out a horrifying scream and disappeared.

A red trail streaked beneath the kids and continued under the boat. The horror on the man's face was unfathomable as the humongous reptile continued under the boat with his elder sister in its hideous jaws. A glimpse of her face as it struck the bottom of the boat was one of shock and terror, frozen in the grip of the tremendous jaws.

"NOooooo!" he screamed out, pointing at the submerged mammoth. Albert jumped up to see the red trail fade off the port side. A look of shock registered on his face as he quickly turned to the children, still floating on their inner tubes and screaming for their mom.

"Swim back to the boat!" he shouted anxiously.

"Where's mom?"

"She's on the other side, now hurry up, swim to the boat!"

The kids began splashing and kicking as they started swimming back to the boat. Albert turned his head to see his brother-in-law still pointing and gawking and began to worry, "Jerry…What is it? What did you see? Is Trish hurt? What's that red trail in the water?" he asked, turning back to the kids.

"A gator got her!" he screamed.

"KIDS, GET OUT OF THE WATER!" Jerry shouted, his heart pounding in his head.

It took seconds for Albert to realize his kids were in grave danger. Without thinking, he leapt into the water and swam out to get them. He quickly made it to the kids, put an arm through the inner tubes and pulled them toward the boat, all the while hyperventilating with eyes locked on Jerry.

"Jerry! Throw me a line or something, man. We gotta get these kids out of the water and find Trish!"

Jerry sat in the boat with his back to Albert, sitting with his hands wrapped around his head as shock swiftly set in.

"Jerry! Goddamnit! We need a little help!"

Too numb to stand, Jerry turned to see Albert pulling his kids toward the boat. He fought the urge to vomit and found the strength to untie the dock line and coiled it up in order to throw.

221

Suddenly, without notice, the gigantic reptile leapt into the boat and clamped onto Jerry with tremendous force. The aluminum boat crushed like a beer can as Jerry let out a blood-curdling scream before being swallowed hole.

Albert and the kids lost the contents of their breakfast, as the scene seemed to play out like a slow-motion horror film. There was no way in hell that he was going to lose his kids to this reptile, so Albert summoned all his strength and pushed the inner tubes toward shore.

It felt like a hard bottom, but he was still twenty feet from the shore. He pushed off with the inner tubes still wrapped around his arm when he thought he and the kids would make it out alive until the ground moved upward. Startled, he slid off the ascending mass, tearing his feet and legs on the sharp armour-like plates.

The entire length of AlliCroc breached the surface when the kids screamed out with terror. Albert had a lump in his throat the size of a football and his chest tightened as the creature turned its massive head and stared him in the eyes. The repulsive look in its eyes was paralyzing, but as it turned and drifted ahead, he saw that it was truly relishing the terror flowing from its prey.

His last act was to push the inner tubes closer to the embankment, but he pushed too hard and caused the kids to slip sideways and fall out. The malicious reptile hissed loudly and opened its jaws, slowly swimming closer and leisurely clamping down on its prey.

Albert let out a chilling scream as the lower jaw compressed between his legs while the upper jaw clamped down on his head, slowly closing as the reptile submerged.

The horrific thoughts going through Albert's mind were unbearable as the monster descended to the depths. The malicious reptile began to swim faster and the flow of water behind Albert caused his back to arch while the jaws continued to compress. Suddenly, a loud snap confirmed that his back was broken.

AlliCroc preferred to let its prey float to the surface where the terrorized victim would drive it into a feeding frenzy, but it was smart enough to know that the humans upriver heard the screams and would be on their way over. It couldn't afford to have any witnesses to identify it and lead hunters on his trail.

It became extremely agitated by these uncommon thoughts and opted to bite down hard, killing its prey instantly and swallowing it whole. Chunks of flesh and sinew cascaded out its quivering jaws as it sank to the bottom and remained undetected. It would have to leave the little humans for another day.

The helicopter pilot radioed the Suwannee River Campground and requested permission to land. Henry was reluctant to let them land until Randy intervened and told him the situation.

Minutes later, the pilot spotted the campground and the people standing around the boat ramp. A path had been cleared in the parking lot, and the chopper descended.

Bloodfoot jumped out before the pontoons hit the asphalt and proceeded to walk toward Henry and his sons.

Startled by the sight of the hulking pirate heading their way, Henry chambered a round in his shotgun and shouted for him to stop. Bloodfoot stopped and shook his head with disappointment and lit a cigar, waiting to see what would happen next.

"What the hell is wrong with that man?" Randy said as he leapt from the helicopter and ran over to the men with his badge in hand. "He's with us. Lower your shotgun. I'm Randy Taylor from Fort Lauderdale PD, and we're hunting a massive reptile," he quickly said before a riot ensued.

The pilot shut down the engine and the winding blades began to slow as Virgil and his crew stepped out and walked over. Virgil stopped next to the burly pirate with a slight grin as he lit a camel non-filtered cigarette, "Looks like your reputation precedes you."

"Can't believe this candy ass. I bet that if I kept walking, they'd have wet their pants."

Virgil was about to reply and say they'd probably just shoot him, but he figured there was no point, so he blew cigarette smoke out of his nostrils and headed toward the boat ramp.

"Are you the men that reported a large reptile in the area?" Randy asked flatly.

"Yes, I called about less than an hour ago, and you are the only ones that showed," replied Henry, a bit agitated.

"Well, like I said, we're hunting a very large predator that nobody wants to tangle with. Can we get a boat to take us around the bend to where you heard the screaming?"

"It will take a couple minutes, but we can climb in that one," he replied, pointing to a twenty-five-foot pontoon boat tied near the end of the dock.

"Meet me out there," Bloodfoot grunted as he walked down the boat ramp and jumped off the end of the dock and onto the muddy bank.

Virgil flicked his cigarette butt into the water and walked back to the helicopter, twirling his finger above his head. The helicopter pilot acknowledged and started the engine as Virgil and his crew climbed in.

"Take her up and around the bend over there," Virgil pointed. "Keep a lookout for Bloodfoot."

"Where the hell is he," Bill asked, hanging his head out the bay door.

"The crazy bastard is running down the edge of the water," Chuck pointed.

Bloodfoot was the first to round the bend and see the mangled boat barely afloat on the river. A sudden cry startled him as he looked over toward the other side of the river and spotted two kids floating in the undergrowth. Without a thought for his own safety, he quickly withdrew his hunting knife from its sheath and dove in, Swimming like Tarzan in a scene from the old movies.

"Are you kids hurt?" he grumbled when he reached the other side, scooping them up in his massive arms.

The kids were in shock and so frightened that they were shaking as Bloodfoot ploughed through the mucky bottom and carefully set them ashore. He heard the pontoon boat coming around the bend and instructed the kids to stay put. Standing on guard, he stood between the river and the kids with nothing more than his deadly hunting knife gripped in one hand.

Henry and his sons zoomed into view with Randy aboard and hastily landed the boat on the embankment while Randy jumped out to help.

"I need your radio," Bloodfoot shouted, snatching it from Randy's belt.

The helicopter rounded the bend and hovered over the boat wreckage as Bloodfoot spoke to the pilot over the radio, "Any sign of the reptile?"

"I do not have a visual... but it doesn't mean it's not around," the pilot reported. "Looks like the water runs deep, and it's too brackish to see the bottom."

"Affirmative, stay close and watch for it while we get these kids to safety."

"Ten-Four."

Bloodfoot and Randy watched the river while Henry and his sons helped the kids in the boat and prepared to head back to the boat ramp. When the boat looked clear of the danger and rounded the bend, Bloodfoot called for the helicopter to sweep down and pick Randy and himself up.

Minutes later, the crew were staring out of the open bay door as the chopper circled about one-hundred feet above the boat ramp. Finally, a fire rescue truck, followed by two deputy sheriff vehicles, were on the scene. The helicopter pilot radioed Henry and notified him they were leaving as the chopper continued searching down river, looking for any sign that AlliCroc was lurking somewhere down below.

It was a fact that the hybrid reptile possessed an intelligent brain, and they were well aware of the fact that it could out fox them and remain undetected if it chose to. Their only chance of finding it would be to outsmart it and find a way to get one step ahead of its thinking process.

Finally, Bloodfoot reached over and tapped the pilot on the shoulder, "Veer away from the river and take us back to the salvage tug."

All eyes were on him as he leaned back in his seat and closed his eyes. He felt the eyes of the crew as they watched him, expecting him to say something. Virgil and Randy locked eyes and shrugged as they leaned back in their seat.

"Damn thing's probably long gone by now," Virgil spoke, lighting a cigarette, to the chagrin of the pilot.

"It's down there," Bloodfoot grunted, opening one eye with an arduous gaze.

"You saw it?" Randy asked.

"Where?" Virgil added, coughing up smoke.

Bloodfoot shifted his weight and sat up, "Our reptile is heading back to the mouth of the river."

"What gives you that idea? That brackish water is as thick as pea soup. It could sit there for days without being detected," Chuck added.

"It already attacked and ate in this area. I believe it will flee to the safety of another locale since it knows it will be hunted. I directed the chopper away from the river so it determines we're not searching overhead."

14

The helicopter did a circular pattern around the *Endurance* and descended until the pontoons splashed on the calm Gulf waters. Ian could be seen at the back of the salvage tug reeling in fishing lines as Christie untied the skiff and motored out to the helicopter.

Minutes later, the crew was in the galley talking about what had happened at the campground and where Bloodfoot thought their reptilian monster was heading. They sat in silence afterwards, reflecting on the tragedy.

Ian was busy at the stove preparing his surprise masterpiece of fresh fish tacos and laid it out on the table, "Eat up, gents, fresh grouper tacos and ice-cold beer for lunch," he said cheerfully, trying to change the solemn mood.

"Whoa, that smells great," said Virgil, grabbing a cold Heineken and pouring it into a non-chilled glass.

"Who caught this?" asked Bill, reaching a taco and taking a giant bite.

"We both did," replied Ian, walking up behind Christie and massaging her tanned shoulders.

"It took both of you?" Bloodfoot mumbled, watching Ian from the corner of his eyes as he poured a glass of rum and swallowed the contents in one gulp.

Ian sat down at the table and took a taco, "Christie hooked the fish on her line and fought like a pro...until it wrapped around a propeller under the tug."

"The darn fish snagged it pretty good," Christie chimed in, smiling.

Bill laughed and spoke, "Yep...been there. One time, I had a huge tarpon wrap the prop on my small motorboat. I had to jump in to untangle the line, and to my surprise, it was still hooked."

"Christie was so frustrated and tired, she put the rod back in the holder and sat down, drinking her rum and coke," Ian added.

"So?" Bloodfoot grunted, waiting to hear how Ian became involved.

"So I grabbed my mask and jumped over the side to untangle the line. It's only been out of the water for about forty-five minutes. These fish tacos can't get any fresher," Ian finished proudly.

"Good to see Captain Virgil didn't just bring you aboard for ballast," Bloodfoot responded wryly, looking at Christie out of the corner of his eyes with a shade of envy.

Christie's smile fell away, "Wow, you sound jealous."

Bloodfoot stood and retrieved another bottle of rum from the cabinet before replying, "I don't get jealous."

Ian didn't take too lightly where the conversation ended. He stood watching Bloodfoot through venomous eyes, "You think I'm here for ballast, big boy?"

Bloodfoot had his back toward him and smiled to himself. The smile faded as he turned to face the greenhorn, "And if I do?" he asked in a testy tone.

"Then maybe I will just have to knock your teeth through that big, ugly skull of yours," he retorted, his fists balled up and ready for action.

Bloodfoot stared at him for what seemed forever, then smiled and patted him on the back, "By all means, muscles…I'd hate to see that," he broke out laughing and grabbed Ian around the neck with one arm and ruffled his hair with the other. "I wanted to see what you're made of. I like it! Anybody brave enough to say that to me is just the man we need out here."

Virgil let out a deep breath and rolled his eyes as the rest of the crew relaxed and thanked the good Lord that their new deckhand wouldn't be slaughtered.

Finally, when things cooled down, and they finished lunch, Captain Virgil gestured for Bloodfoot to follow him to the bridge.

The crew cleared the table and spread out a map of the area while Bloodfoot followed the captain up to the wheelhouse. Once inside, Virgil shut the door and gave Bloodfoot a withering look,

"What the hell was that all about? We're out here chasing a monster, and you're harassing the crew."

Bloodfoot knew Virgil wouldn't care much for his tactic and replied, "Just testing the kid, had to see where his head's at. I wanted to see what he's made of before I lay my life on the line with him."

"Don't do it again," he replied, lighting a cigarette and looking the pirate in the eye.

Bloodfoot didn't argue as he knew the captain wasn't going to like his way of testing out new men for this deadly adventure. Deep down, he knew Captain Virgil would have no man aboard that he wouldn't trust with his life, but still...he had to find out for himself.

Virgil walked back to the galley and took a seat at the table, joining the rest of the crew as they pondered the map and pinpointed where the attack at the campground was in relation to where the *Endurance* lay anchored.

Bloodfoot entered the galley and sat next to Ian, giving him a wink before pouring another glass of rum.

"Alright, everybody, let's figure out our plan of attack," Virgil stated, lighting a cigarette. Closing his eyes and inhaling a long drag from his camel cigarette, he waited patiently for Bloodfoot to break the silence. Blowing a large cloud of blue smoke over the table, he opened his eyes and looked to see all eyes were on him. "Ok, Bloodfoot, you've got the floor," he said wryly.

Bloodfoot watched Virgil as he took another gulp from his glass and set it firmly down on the table, "The latest attack was right here," he said, pointing his thick finger ten miles upriver. My instinct tells me the reptile will be swimming out of the Suwannee River and head back to this Chassahowitzka National Wildlife Refuge to the south of us, where I believe it's been staying since it escaped the Everglades."

"Why do you think it's doing that?Ian chimed in.

Bloodfoot chose to ignore the man who just came into the picture but figured he might as well include him with the team and replied, "Like I said, it's my gut instinct...and I've had a lot of experience with hunting predators."

"Why else do you think it's headed back there," Randy asked.

Bloodfoot scratched his bearded chin and pointed further up the map, "It's been wreaking havoc over here for the last few weeks," he continued, pointing at Clearview State Park. "Then it swam into the Santa Fe River, turned back, probably because it was seen, and entered the Suwannee River and swam all the way up to the campground, where it attacked the family in the boat," he ended, sliding his finger down the map.

"So if that's the route AlliCroc is taking, it will pass by us very soon," Bill asserted.

"That is my assumption."

"What's the game plan?" asked Virgil, flicking his cigarette butt out the porthole.

233

"I want to stretch a net across the river about a quarter mile from the inlet. Three of us will be on the north bank, while the other three will be on the south bank. With luck, the reptile becomes tangled in the net, and we blast it with those three canons that Randy acquired," Bloodfoot assured.

"Do you think that net will stop it?" Chuck asked, with a lack of confidence.

"No, but I hope it will slow the reptile long enough for us to put some.905 caliber slugs into its head."

"Remember, that reptile's skin is covered with armor-plated scales that are practically impenetrable, so we're going to have to take every shot at the head, shoot out the eyes, snout and jaws," Bloodfoot added, remembering their encounter with the first AlliCroc.

Virgil looked at his watch and announced, "Ok, it's almost four-O-clock, so we better get moving."

"I think we have enough time to load up and get the Zodiac upriver in about an hour. It shouldn't take long to set up the net and get in our places before it passes through," replied Bloodfoot. "Since that reptile has a brain capable of forming ideas to stay undetected all these years, I believe it will stay at the scene of its latest attack until dusk when it can swim undetected."

"So, how long do you reckon we've got?" asked Chuck.

"I think we can safely say two…maybe three hours.

Bill and Ian unhooked the clasps that held a twenty-foot ribbed Zodiac with a center console secured to a platform behind the smokestack of the salvage tug. Chuck operated a winch and expertly lowered the boat into the water. As it sat floating beside the tug, the crew began to load the craft with six shotguns, a crate full of hand grenades and the huge net that they intended to stretch across the river. When finished, Randy disappeared into the bridge and, after a minute or two, struggled out the door carrying two heavy cases.

"Can one of you get the other case," Randy asked as he propped the cases on the gunwale and waited for Bloodfoot to load them into the boat.

"Ah yes, we can't forget the .905 caliber rifles. I sure as hell hope they do their job," said Bloodfoot, pulling the cases onto the boat.

"They will. They don't call them shoulder canons for nothing. Those twenty-five-hundred grain bullets traveling twenty-one-hundred feet per second will pulverize that damn reptile," replied Randy.

"Can you guys lift those things high enough to aim? I mean...didn't you say they weigh one-hundred pounds?" Christie added.

"One-hundred and ten pounds," Randy corrected.

Virgil was leaning on the tug's gunwale with his arms crossed, looking at the darkening clouds building fast in the western sky.

"Ian, while you're up there, grab those raincoats," he shouted as the deckhand was about to walk down the stairs with the other rifle.

While the crew waited for Ian, they joined the captain and watched the brewing storm, "Damn thing's coming this way," said Chuck.

"Count on it," Bloodfoot grumbled.

"Lucky for you and your crew to have raincoats," Randy quipped to Virgil, pulling the shirt collar up as a cool breeze began to blow.

"Don't worry; we have one for everybody."

"I'm only counting five, Captain," Ian said, stowing the raincoats in the center console.

Virgil lit a cigarette. The suspicious look on Randy's face made him smile as he replied, "Bloodfoot doesn't use a raincoat. It restricts his movement. I believe he informed us of that on Socotra Island if I remember correctly."

Bloodfoot was the last to climb into the packed boat and gave Christie a walkie-talkie, "I'm going to check in with you every half-hour. If I don't and you can't get in contact with us, something has gone wrong. Contact Stu and tell him to fly the chopper straight in for a hot evacuation."

"Where is he? I haven't seen him since we finished lunch," she replied with a concerned look.

236

"He's sleeping in the helicopter," added Randy, throwing a small weight from a fishing rod at the helicopter and making a direct hit on the window. "He said he wants no part of this hunt, and I couldn't pay him enough if I tried to get him to change his mind."

"Don't you think we should wake him up so he can be alert?" she asked.

Randy smirked and pointed to the chopper, "He's awake, see...he's got his arm out the door and giving me the bird."

Bloodfoot put a hand on her shoulder and squeezed, "He's got a radio and will be at the ready if we get into trouble."

"Maybe if Stu and I get the helicopter to hover high above where you guys are spreading the net, I can watch through binoculars and let you know if I see that monster."

Bloodfoot smiled, "Great minds think alike."

"You thought about it?"

"No, Captain Virgil suggested it. I had to reject the idea because this reptile has a thought pattern that very well may be smarter than us. It will sense the chopper up there. Those mad scientists who created it injected it with something that made it capable of planning out its moves. The first one was intelligent, and I'm afraid that this one has had more time to develop its thinking skills."

237

Bill cranked the Yamaha four-stroke motor and waited for the rest of the crew to board before pushing the throttle forward at a slow speed. When clear of the tug, he pushed the throttle to the max and sped off toward the mouth of the river.

A light drizzle fell as they slowed and entered the river. Ian reached for the raincoats and passed them out.

Virgil took the one extra raincoat and stuffed it in Randy's hand, "This one's for you."

"Give it to Bloodfoot."

"He doesn't wear one, watch...Hey Bloodfoot! Take this raincoat!" he shouted over the din of the motor.

Bloodfoot was holding the bowline as he stood at the bow, surveying the river, "Keep it! I don't wear them!"

Virgil smiled at Randy and shook his head, "The man is an animal."

Ian turned to see the sky behind him, "Wow, check it out," he said, pointing to where the salvage tug was anchored.

The crew turned just in time to see a grey curtain of rain envelop the tug and helicopter as it barreled in their direction.

"Just our luck," Virgil said to no one, reaching into his shirt pocket and retrieving his pack of cigarettes.

"It's going to be a wet one," added Chuck.

By the time they reached a quarter-mile upriver, sheets of rain were hammering the boat. Bloodfoot, still standing on the bow, pointed to a sandy clearing on the right bank as Bill acknowledged by reducing speed and turning in that direction, cutting the motor as the bow slid up into the sand.

"Randy and Ian…Grab two of the big guns and keep a lookout while the rest of us feed the net out to Bloodfoot," Virgil ordered, following the plan they made in the galley.

Bloodfoot was already out of the boat and pulling the net out. After taking a quick look around, he put the iron ring attached to the end of the net through a six-foot iron spike and began hammering it into the ground with a sledgehammer.

Chuck had a concerned look on his face as he helped feed the net out of the boat, thinking the ground might be too soft to stop the reptile.

"I hope the sand isn't too soft to hold that stake in place," he said.

"It's ok if it doesn't hold. When the reptile hits the net, and we begin blasting at it, it will get tangled, and we will blow it to smithereens before it can escape," replied Virgil.

It only took Bloodfoot a few swings of the hammer to drive the stake firmly in the sand. He pulled the net to make sure the spike would hold before returning to the boat.

As planned, Ian jumped out of the boat, put the destructive rifle over his shoulder and ran upriver about thirty yards.

Bloodfoot looked pleased to see the new guy carrying the heavy rifle like a seasoned pro; few people could run in the sand with a rifle weighing over one-hundred pounds.

Lightning struck a tree about one-hundred yards away, and Ian instinctively dove to the ground for safety. He got up covered in mud and looked like a comical swamp monster as he looked back with an unpleasant look, then trotted off and eventually found a tree stump to secure the heavy gun and wait for action. To the chagrin of the others, Bloodfoot couldn't hide the sound of his loud, deep laugh.

Randy remained close to the boat and found a tree that branched off into the water, making a perfect cross-section to situate the cannon on.

"Don't fire until I tell you to!" Bloodfoot roared through the noisy downpour.

Ian and Randy acknowledged with a wave of their hand as they watched the boat shove off and move at idle speed across the river. The rain was coming down in sheets, and they could barely make out the silhouettes of the crew as they carefully fed the net across the water.

"If that monster shows up in this downpour, we'll never see it coming!" Randy shouted.

"Just be ready!" Ian shouted anxiously.

The water's edge on the other side had no spot to land the boat. Coral rock surrounded the shoreline, so Chuck dropped two fenders over the starboard side while Virgil expertly docked against the rocks, careful not to puncture the zodiac.

Again, Bloodfoot jumped out and pulled the net to the best spot he could find while Bill and Chuck took up the slack. This time, Bloodfoot hammered the stake directly into the coral rock.

When the net was secure, Virgil handed Bloodfoot the third shoulder canon and a backpack filled with .905 caliber slugs. With shotguns slung over their shoulders, Virgil and Chuck climbed out of the boat and bid farewell to Bill as he returned with the boat to the other side.

They watched Bill return to the sandy bank and lift the motor's lower unit out of the water.

Randy radioed when Bill distributed the hand grenades, set up next to Ian and hunkered down in wait for the ambush. They grinned and jested when they looked across the river to see a cloud of grayish, blue smoke drifting through the rain-soaked air above Virgil, Chuck and Bloodfoot.

Ian followed suite and reached into his watertight pocket cigar case, retrieving one of three Cuaba Salomones cigars. Bill declined his offer to smoke one as Ian bit off the end of his cigar and lit it with his trustworthy torch lighter. Bill's thoughts were confirmed as to why they brought oversized cowboy hats with them. The masterminds brought them to keep their smokes lit in case of rain.

Securing his oversized hat to make sure the cigar would stay dry, he just lit the flavorful stick when the walkie-talkie crackled to life, "Put out that cigar, Ian. Looks like a forest fire over there," Bloodfoot's low, monotone voice rumbled. "I expect our monster will be swimming through shortly, and we can't risk that vile reptile sensing we're here. The smoke will give us away in a heartbeat."

The incredulous look on Ian's face was priceless. Randy and Bill grinned from ear to ear as they turned their attention to the other side of the river to confirm the cloud of smoke had vanished.

Without a word, Ian took three mighty puffs and extinguished his cigar, "I swear that pirate is really starting to piss me off."

The rain slowed to a slight drizzle as the rain-soaked hunters waited in the undergrowth. The cloud cover moved further inland, and the light of a half-moon slowly appeared, its reflection eerily dancing across the water.

Bloodfoot stood like a statue at the water's edge, taking in the surroundings, listening to the frogs and crickets as they made their presence known. Virgil got a kick out of watching the way he focused on everything that twitched and every ripple in the river but made no mistake about speculating if the cunning swashbuckler knew what he was doing.

The more time Ian had to think, the more he became aware that the surroundings looked nothing less than a scary movie setting and he began to wonder why he ever signed up for such a nerve-racking adventure.

Suddenly, he felt a slight vibration under his feet and looked over to Bill and Randy, "Did you guys feel that?"

They both nodded that they did and readjusted their stance as they pondered what could have caused it.

"Could be anything," Bill finally whispered. "Maybe a family of wild boar walking around or something."

"It could be a big truck passing by. Who knows, there's probably a road nearby," Randy added, immediately regretting his suggestion when he knew he didn't hear an engine.

"Hey fellas…Did you just feel the ground vibrate slightly?" Randy asked over the walkie-talkie.

"Negative," replied Bloodfoot in a deep, low tone. "Did the three of you feel it?"

"Yes."

"So, it's not your imagination running wild. Keep your eyes peeled; it could be our reptile. The water's not too deep around here, and the vibration could be from its enormous bulk pushing near the shoreline, causing the vibration in that loose sand you guys are standing on."

Bloodfoot waited for a reply, but there was none. He grabbed the binoculars from around his neck and looked to see the three men take a couple of steps back and focus their weapons on the water.

"Get ready," he said to Virgil and Chuck. "I think our monster is close. Keep an eye on the opposite bank. The others just felt a vibration under their feet."

Virgil and Chuck heard what transpired over the radio and focused their attention across the river. Virgil readjusted the .905 caliber rifle that Bloodfoot relinquished and secured it on a coral rock. When it seemed secure, he double-checked the chambered bullet while Chuck wished he had one of the same instead of the shotgun.

Thirty minutes later, there was no sign of the reptile. It was a cause for concern to Bloodfoot. He walked until he was knee-deep in the water and pulled his trusty hunting knife out of its sheath.

"What are your thoughts?" whispered Virgil.

I don't think it was here. It either sensed our presence and turned around or passed by us undetected," Bloodfoot replied in a loud, thunderous voice. He took off his shirt and tossed the walkie-talkie to Virgil as the captain walked out from his cover with the giant rifle resting on his shoulder.

"And you're going to swim after it?" Virgil asked sarcastically, catching the radio.

"Just going to make sure it's gone," Bloodfoot replied, jumping in the river.

The crew watched with amazement as their fearless friend put his hunting knife between his teeth and scaled the outside of the net until reaching the center of the river.

Ian shouted for the wily hunter to get the hell out of the water until Bill put a hand on his shoulder to quiet him, "This is what Bloodfoot does. He knows what he's doing…and he's good at it."

"He's nuts."

"No, he does it all the time. I witnessed him gut a huge great white off the coast of Socotra Island a couple years back with nothing but a facemask and his hunting knife."

"The guy's suicidal!"

"No…Crazy? Yes… Suicidal? No."

They watched silently as the insatiable hunter splashed around. When there was no sign of the reptile, Bloodfoot swam over to the boat and shouted for Bill, Randy and Ian to abort their post and climb aboard.

Bill pushed the boat off the sand and climbed in while Bloodfoot lowered the motor's lower unit into the river and cranked the motor. He angrily pushed the throttle forward and sped across to the other side, where Virgil and Chuck waited to board.

"Now what?" asked Virgil, lighting a camel non-filtered cigarette.

"We've been outwitted," growled Bloodfoot, turning off the motor. "The reptile is extremely smart, which makes it extremely dangerous, twice as dangerous as the first time we hunted it's genealogical other."

"So, you think it sensed our presence and turned around and swam upriver?" asked Randy, goose bumps rising from the back of his neck.

Bloodfoot took a minute to reply as he pondered the situation, "No. I believe the damn think crawled out of the water and went around us, then slipped back into the river."

"You can't be serious," said Ian, with a look of fear on his face as he looked around the area.

"When you felt the ground shake…It was the reptile," Virgil added, his eyes looking downriver as if waiting to see it swimming away.

"Let's take the boat upriver to see if we can find where it climbed out of the water," Bloodfoot said, putting the boat in gear.

They cruised upriver only forty yards when Bloodfoot cut the motor and drifted to the sand.

"Sure enough, there's where it climbed out," Randy said, pointing at the massive claw prints deep in the sand.

They sat silently in the boat, lost in thought, when the walkie-talkie crackled to life, "Christie to Bloodfoot…Come in, over."

Virgil tossed him the radio and checked his watch; the call-in was ten minutes late.

"Sorry, Christie," replied Bloodfoot, "We were caught up in a little situation."

"No worries, big guy, I'm just glad to see you guys are alright and heading back. I will have some cocktails waiting when you get here, over."

"Good idea, out."

Bloodfoot returned the walkie-talkie to his waistband and moved aside to let Bill at the controls when he suddenly froze.

"Thoughts?" Virgil asked, seeing the desperate look on his face.

"What made Christie think we are on our way back?"

Before anybody had a chance to reply, he grabbed the walkie-talkie and shouted, "Christie, come back!"

The radio was dead on the other end. He tried several more times before she replied, "What's wrong? I put the walkie-talkie back on the charger...Is everything alright?"

"Listen! What made you think we're on our way back?"

Christie smiled and rolled her eyes, "As you can see, the clouds are gone, and the moon is reflecting like a dream across the water. I can clearly see you guys heading back. Well, I can't actually see the zodiac, but I see the glistening wake. Why don't you pick it up a notch, you slow pokes," she replied nonchalantly, popping a green olive in her mouth.

247

"Christie! It's not us...It's the reptile! Get in the galley and lock the hatches. We're on our way!"

Her eyes opened to the size of golf balls as she choked on the olive and leaped out of the galley, straining her eyes to see the approaching wake.

It was gone, and the water was smooth as silk when the sound of Stu's voice lazily bellowed in the walkie-talkie, "Hey Christie, its Stu. Sorry, I dozed off and woke up when I heard the crew's heading back. I'm jumping in the raft and heading over, out."

Her heart sank when she heard Stu's voice, she completely forgot about the helicopter pilot. "Stu! The monster is heading toward us, and you've got to get aboard quick!"

"Where the hell is it!" his frantic voice exploded.

"I saw its wake about a quarter mile away a few minutes ago. Now it's gone."

There was no answer. She quickly ran into the galley and grabbed a flashlight. Waiting for a moment to collect her thoughts, she realized it was too risky to go back out on deck. Again, she tried to contact Stu, but there was still no answer. She knew the crew couldn't hear her since they were heading back at full speed, and the whine of the outboard motor would drown out the radio.

Finally, she took a deep breath and opened the portside hatch. Since the reptile was coming from the starboard side, she figured this would be a bit safer. "Stu, can you hear me? I don't know where the monster is," she spoke into the radio, the flashlight beam searching the water.

She jumped when his voice replied in a deathly, slow whisper, "It's here."

Christie swallowed hard and crept toward the stern, flashing the beam of light toward the helicopter sitting peacefully twenty yards behind the tug. Aiming the light on Stu, she noticed he was pressed against the side of the cockpit, staring into the water on the other side. She dreaded what she knew she would see as she slowly moved the beam of light where he was looking.

Christie gasped at the gigantic reptilian head that methodically turned to stare back at her. The gargantuan head was the size of the helicopter's cockpit. The malicious green eyes stared up at her with menacing evil, and the teeth were like something out of a science fiction monster movie. Unlike alligators that she had the unwitting pleasure of seeing up close, these conical-shaped teeth were at least six inches long and jagged near the jaws.

The dark greenish-black head slowly turned from Christie back to Stu. He held his breath and tried not to move, hoping the evil creature would swim away. To his dismay, the creature's eyes were locked on him, it knew he was there, and he sensed that it savored the sense of injecting fear in its prey, almost as if it could taste it.

"Hang on, Stu! I've got some grenades; I'll throw one past the reptile, and hopefully, it will swim away!" Christie shouted, reaching into a big steel box welded to the stern.

Stu heard her but couldn't take his eyes off the creature.

Bill pushed the Zodiac at full throttle, hydroplaning through the small swells as they hurried back to the salvage tug.

Ian had a hand-held spotlight and could just make out the sight of Christie standing at the stern and watching the chopper. Bloodfoot put his head down and muttered in disgust. He knew the only reason she would be back there was because Stu was still in the chopper.

The small boat approached guardedly and came around to the salvage tug's bow. All eyes were on the reptile as Bill put the motor in neutral, and the crew scurried aboard with the big guns in hand.

Suddenly, a loud explosion echoed as they looked to see a torrent of water shoot up behind the helicopter.

Bloodfoot was the first to reach Christie. He grabbed her by the waist, pulling her back, "Stay clear! That reptile can leap on deck before you blink an eye!"

"The grenade did nothing!" she cried out in frustration. "It's like throwing a ping-pong ball at a rhino!"

Agitated and ready to pounce, AlliCroc suddenly lurched forward and engulfed the entire cockpit in its jaws. Stu gasped in horror as the fierce head of the reptile shook violently until it shattered the windshield and creased the cabin. Randy and the rest of the crew watched helplessly as the reptile rolled over the helicopter and swam to the depths with the twisted machine firmly in its jaws.

Terrified and on the verge of drowning in his crumpled seat, Stu turned and struggled to climb into the cargo area, where he sucked in a lung full of air trapped in the corner. Searching for a way out, he was momentarily relieved to see the bottom was not more than about thirty feet. The tethered line was still attached, and the helicopter was sitting freely on the bottom after being spat out of the repulsive jaws.

The crew scrambled to aim the shoulder canons as the reptile swam to the surface. Christie let out an ear-splitting scream as they watched the monster's full body swim slowly toward the tugboat.

"That…thing…is…huge!" a slack-jawed Ian stated, pointing the spotlight beam up and down the creature and suddenly feeling helpless.

Virgil, Randy and Bloodfoot wasted no time planting their feet firmly on deck and firing the .905 caliber rifles. The recoil from the shoulder canons knocked Virgil and Randy back as Bloodfoot quickly reloaded. The reptile was gone.

"Did we get it?" asked Virgil, rubbing his shoulder.

"One bullet hit and blew off a chunk of meat behind its head. The other two ricocheted off its Hyde," Bloodfoot replied, pointing a spotlight toward the bottom and looking intensely at the outline of the chopper lying peacefully on the bottom.

"What's the helicopter pilots name?" Bloodfoot asked.

"It was Stu," said Randy.

"He's still alive, trapped in the cargo area," continued Bloodfoot.

"How do you reckon?" Chuck asked.

"I see bubbles. Cover me while I get him out of there," Bloodfoot shouted as he grabbed his hunting knife from its scabbard and dove into the water.

"Bloodfoot!" Christie screamed.

Captain Virgil handed Bill his rifle and ran up the ladder and into the wheelhouse. Bill watched as Virgil clicked on the massive spotlight attached to the roof and focused the light down toward the helicopter.

"Won't that monster be able to see Bloodfoot with that spotlight?" Christie asked, clearly panicking.

"The monster can see just fine in the dark. This light is for Bloodfoot and us," replied Virgil, reaching into his breast pocket for another non-filtered camel cigarette.

Bloodfoot swam underwater with the hunting knife between his teeth as the startled crew kept a lookout for the reptile's return.

With the spotlight beaming through the clear water, they could see Bloodfoot enter the helicopter.

What seemed like a lifetime was only seconds when they could see Bloodfoot come out of the helicopter and swim to the surface with Stu in his arms.

Randy and Ian hastily reloaded the rifles and joined Bill, who was already aiming his rifle at the gunwale as Christie threw a lifeline. When Bloodfoot handed Stu's inert body to Chuck, Virgil announced the return of the reptile, thirty yards and closing fast.

The rifles were aimed at the hellion as it lazily circled below without attempting an attack, "What the hell is it doing?" Ian asked, frustrated.

Bloodfoot climbed aboard and spat out saltwater, "It's smart. It doesn't want to come back up and get shot again.It also wants to keep our fearful juices flowing."

Bloodfoot leaned against the gunwale with his hands on his knees, catching his breath as he watched Chuck and Christie try to revive the helicopter pilot.

Chuck gave him mouth-to-mouth while Christie compressed his chest, which gave Bloodfoot a confused look. Stu finally coughed a lung full of water and opened his eyes.

Bloodfoot gave a slight grin and turned his attention to the three standing near the stern with rifles pointed into the water. He walked over and peered over the side.

"Look at it, the damn thing is just sitting there, watching us," Ian whispered.

"Wait to see if it swims up a little closer so we can blast it," Randy answered.

Virgil relaxed and put the pin back in his hand grenade, "It won't come up. The damn reptile is looking straight up at us. It knows we're out of range to cause damage."

Bloodfoot shook his head in agreement, "We've got a real problem here. That hybrid is incredibly smart and knows how to use that brain."

They watched the massive creature as it leisurely circled the tug twenty feet below, as if taunting the crew. Finally, after ten minutes, the malicious reptile disappeared.

"I'll bring the Zodiac around so we can hoist it out of the water before the reptile comes back and tries to eat it," said Bill, heading toward the bow and preparing to untie the line.

"No, I will do it," Bloodfoot countered. "You guys get those shoulder canons ready. I'm going to jump in the boat and start the motor. If I were that reptile, I'd attack the moment I knew there'd be prey in the boat."

"You want to use yourself for bait?" Christie gasped.

"That's the plan. Hopefully, we can blast that thing to hell when it comes up," the pirate-looking hulk replied flatly.

"But those bullets ricochet off that monster!" she protested.

"Two did…One blew a chunk of meat from its hide," retorted Bloodfoot, grabbing the line and following it onto the zodiac, untying the line from the boat's cleat while keeping a firm grip.

Bill thought it strange that he untied the line from the zodiac instead of where it was tied on the tug.

Bloodfoot stood on the bow as if waiting for impact, as the big rifles were aimed under the zodiac. Christie and Chuck aimed their hand-held spotlights on the small boat as Virgil searched the waters with the mounted floodlight.

This time, Bill, Randy and Ian were able to position the rifles on the bow for better support against the recoil. When they were set, Bloodfoot grabbed his hunting knife and moved to the controls, still holding the line. The crew watched with a questioning look, speculating if he really thought the knife would help him kill the predator or if it was just in his hand as a sort of crutch.

The attack came seconds after he cranked the motor. It was rising from the bottom like a silo missile; the reptile rammed the bottom of the boat like a runaway train, shattering the fiberglass bottom as it flew through the air. The rifles came to life the second the crew saw its dark form emerge from the water.

Somehow, Bloodfoot looked like he knew it was coming and was ready for the brunt of force. He sprang from the deck upon impact. The line wrapped around his hand saved him from falling into the water with AlliCroc and the splintered boat, but he landed hard in front of the bow of the salvage tug with his legs dangling below his knees.

The agitated reptile spotted the dangling prey and quickly swam in for the kill. The .905 caliber rifles quickly reloaded and blasted the violent monster once again.

Still clinging to the line, Bloodfoot pulled himself up and turned just in time to see the reptile shudder from the bullets and dive below the tug.

He quickly turned and pulled himself over the bow, where Bill grabbed the back of his pants and yanked him onto the deck.

Bloodfoot gave him a painful look as he slowly stood up and shook splinters out of his wild, unkept hair, "Thanks for the wedgey, Bill," he grumbled in a low baritone voice, stuffing his knife back into its scabbard.

Bill looked at him with amazement as the wily hunter walked down the starboard side of the tug and entered the galley, "And that's the thanks I get?"

Chuck and Christie carefully walked around the tug with their spotlights shining in the water while Bill, Randy and Ian rolled over on their backs, exhausted from the recoil of the rifles.

"Where's Bloodfoot?" asked Virgil, flicking the floodlight off and lighting a cigarette.

"He walked into the galley," replied Bill, fuming.

Ian lifted his head and smiled, "You gave him a wedgey?"

256

Bloodfoot was seated at the table, drinking from a bottle of rum, when Virgil entered the galley and took a seat across from the befuddled pirate. "Close call," he confirmed, reaching for his bottle of apricot brandy.

"Too close," replied Bloodfoot, Virgil noticing for the first time that his worldly hunter friend was a bit unhinged.

"AlliCroc is nowhere to be seen, we scanned all sides of the tug," Chuck said, following the others in.

Bloodfoot looked up to see all eyes on him. He gulped another mouthful from the bottle and cleared his throat, "I think it's as surprised as we are that the shoulder cannons blew a chunk out of it."

"So let's track it and finish it off," Christie spoke up, noticing the distraught look on everybody's face.

"We won't find it tonight. I believe that the monster is heading for the Wildlife Refuge. It is probably crawling along the bottom to stay undetected. When it reaches the sanctuary, it will be hell trying to find it."

"What sanctuary?" asked Randy.

Bloodfoot picked up the atlas and scanned down the coast, "This one right here," he said, pointing a finger at the Chassahowitzka National Wildlife Sanctuary. It's going to be tough, but we will find it in there."

"It looks to be pretty far south of here. Why do you think it's heading there," Ian asked.

"This reptile is not territorial. It travels to stay undetected," replied Bloodfoot. "I think it wants to go back to where it has lived the past few years. How or why it left is questionable, but if I was AlliCroc, that's where I'd be heading," he continued.

Chuck watched as the intrepid hunter spoke and saw something in him that caused concern. For the first time since they met, he saw fear or maybe a well-deserved touch of anxiety. "Maybe we should try to get some help for this particular hunt," he finally said.

Randy stood up and glared at Chuck, "Who did you have in mind? The National Guard tried to find it and had no luck. Granted, most of them were probably barely in their twenties and would most likely get killed trying to hunt it. Special Forces would be a good idea, but I can't imagine their commanders would think hunting a reptile is their problem. Nobody knows the extent of damage AlliCroc can do. I bet we'd be hard-pressed to get anybody crazy enough to believe what we're hunting. I mean, who's going to believe there's a thirty-to-forty-foot hybrid reptile that's capable of having thought patterns like a human? Let alone having armored plating, making it practically impossible to kill. We're the only hope of killing that damn monster unless the

258

higher-ups can see what we're up against. But as it turns out, AlliCroc knows how to remain elusive."

"I'll kill it," Bloodfoot spat.

"We'll kill it," Virgil corrected, taking a shot of brandy.

15

Don Henderson and Johnny Lee made it to Fort Lauderdale in good time. It was mid-afternoon and Don was nervous about acting out his plan. They checked into a small hotel to get some much-needed sleep, and it also gave him time to change his mind because if he did go through with kidnapping the woman, he'd known for the better part of his life.. He knew the consequence would be life-changing, Especially because she was married to his childhood friend, Virgil.

Finally, when they checked out of the hotel the next morning and cruised aimlessly down A1A, Don decided to carry out his plan. It was the only way to get the hunters to capture and not kill AlliCroc.

Don filled his partner in on his plan to hold Virgil's wife Jeanne hostage until he agreed to capture AlliCroc instead of killing it.

When Johnny learned that Don and Virgil grew up together in Kansas and were practically best friends until they clashed with the first AlliCroc, he wondered what would happen to him if he didn't cooperate with Don on this event.

"So, you're telling me that you were good friends with Virgil and his wife, and now you're going over there to hold her hostage?"

"In so many words, yes."

On the trip down, Don rebuked Johnny's questions on why they were going to South Florida when the reptile was in the central part of the state, but now that he was told of the plan, he wanted no part of it.

"I'm out. You have gone too far with this AlliCroc scheme," Johnny said, pulling off the road near a shopping center. "I've been called a lot of things, but I'm not a kidnapper! Get out of my car!" Johnny demanded, fuming.

Don was not surprised. It's exactly how he thought his partner would react, which is why he reframed from telling him the plan until they got into town.

"You don't have to be a part of the hostage thing. Drop me off at the house and go back up and make sure they tranquilize AlliCroc. You can leave the tranquilizers somewhere that Virgil will find them. I'm not going to hurt Jeanne, but I need leverage. That's all."

"And if I don't?"

Don looked at him and gave an evil smile, "I know where you and your lovely wife live, too."

Johnny hauled off and tried to punch him, but Don was too quick and grabbed his fist and twisted, "Simmer down, you skinny little prick. Do what I say, and nobody gets hurt!" Don ordered, smashing the man's fist into the steering wheel.

Johnny winced, put the minivan in gear and peeled off to the house. Figuring there was no chance of changing the deranged man's mind, all he wanted to do now was get Don to his destination and get him out of his van.

It was a little after nine a.m. when they pulled into Jeanne's driveway. Johnny left the engine running as Don opened the door to step out. Before he got out, he reminded Johnny to stay close to the hunters and make sure they received the tranquilizers. He was instructed to report back to him when he found the pickup spot for the serum so he could relay it to Virgil.

Jeanne was sitting on the couch in the living room watching television when she heard the van pull up and the van's door slam shut. Thinking it was one of the kids stopping by for a visit, she got up and peeked out the window.

Don smiled as he walked to the door and spotted Jeanne's surprised face watching from the window and waved.

Before he could knock on the door, it sprang open, and Jeanne stuck her head out, "What are you doing here?" she asked skeptically.

"Hi, Jeanne. Long time no see," he smiled.

"Virgil's not home, and I don't think he'd be happy to see you anyway."

"I know, I know. We're hunting another AlliCroc. I have some information for you to tell him," he said, pushing his way inside and closing the door.

"Get out of my house, Don," Jeanne demanded, her fists balled up and ready to strike.

"Is that any way to treat an old friend?"

"What do you want?"

"Sit down, and I will tell you," he said in a firm tone.

"I'll stand," she retorted.

Don took her arm and tried to push her onto the couch, but Jeanne acted fast and kicked him in the groin and slapped his ears with open hands before he crashed to the floor.

"I'm calling the police!" she shouted, stepping to her phone sitting on an end table.

"Sit down...Now!"

Jeanne froze when she heard the unmistakable sound of a gun chambering a bullet. She turned and saw Don lying in pain with a gun pointed at her.

"What do you want?" she demanded.

Don painfully rose and motioned for Jeanne to sit on the couch. He sat at the kitchen table and explained. "Virgil and his crew are hunting AlliCroc. It's the only one of its kind left on this entire planet. He won't listen to me about capturing it so we can make millions of dollars showcasing it, so now I'm desperate. If he thinks I'm holding you hostage, he will be forced to tranquilize AlliCroc, and I will take it from there. It's no big deal," he shrugged.

"Virgil is going to kill you for busting in here."

"Once he sees the big picture, I'm sure he will be onboard."

The Gulf waters were smooth and vibrant, and a light breeze was flowing from the south-east. The early morning sunlight glared from a porthole as Bloodfoot rose from his bunk and headed up to the bridge. He knocked twice at the door and entered to see Captain Virgil sitting with a cup of coffee in one hand and binoculars in the other.

"Spot anything?" he asked, peaking out the window and seeing the orange/red tint of the sky as the new day arrived.

"Nothing worth talking about," replied the captain, lowering the binoculars to look at Bloodfoot.

Virgil sipped his coffee as Bloodfoot lit a giant cigar. "After I grab some coffee, we can work out a plan to find the reptile.

"Great idea," replied Virgil, giving him a skewering look.

Bloodfoot shook his head and was about to leave when he suddenly stopped, "So what's biting you?" he grumbled.

"I don't like what I'm seeing," Virgil replied flatly.

"Specify what you mean."

"I think you are becoming unhinged. Jumping in the river and swimming in the middle was unsettling, but that's you. I'm ok with that. But last night, when you jumped in the water and swam to the helicopter, that was carelessness."

"Would you prefer Stu dead?"

"Nobody knew he was alive."

"I did."

Virgil sat quietly and considered his answer. Finally, "Ok, I can understand that. You've got a sixth sense or something. But when you jumped on the zodiac, knowing the monster would attack was just senseless."

"I know what I'm doing."

"I'm sure you do. The problem is, we have six other people aboard that can get caught in the crosshairs, and I will not have that," Virgil replied with a scolding tone.

Bloodfoot turned and faced Virgil, "Maybe I made a mistake asking you and your crew for help."

"I'm thinking the same," Virgil replied, returning the stare.

Bloodfoot took a deep breath and threw his cigar out the window. He sat on a stool and pulled it closer to Virgil.

"You got me. This creature is doing a number on me. The first one was big and bad, but we worked together like a team and killed it. This one is enormous! It thinks and plans out its attacks and knows how to quietly disappear."

"That's true, but you can't set yourself up as bait and hope that we can kill it when it eats you," replied Virgil, lighting a cigarette.

"I agree. I might have gone too far."

They sat quietly while Bloodfoot dug another cigar out of a waterproof case in his back pocket and lit it with a torch lighter.

"Where did you get that fancy lighter?" asked Virgil.

"I stole it from Ian."

They both laughed and blew smoke. They both knew that if they were miles away in a bar somewhere, they'd be having a cherry conversation.

Finally, Bloodfoot looked at the captain and said, "I made no mistake asking you men for help in finding this beast. I know I went too far, but I did not realize I put you all in danger. I'm sorry."

"Going too far is what you do. That's why you are the best at what you do," Virgil replied sincerely. "But when I see we're heading for a catastrophic ending, I have to put the brakes on."

"I agree and thank you for telling me. I will now request that we regroup, collect our thoughts and continue this hunt. I will reframe from pulling thoughtless stunts that can result in catastrophe."

Virgil gave the hulking pirate a stern look before replying, "Who else is going to kill this reptile? Let's do this."

Chuck, Bill and Randy were in the galley talking about the wild actions of the previous evening while the sun rose higher and promised another brutally hot day. Within the hour, Stu made his way down to the galley and sat at the table, holding his head.

"I have a splitting headache. I can't believe I'm alive. Who do I have to thank for getting me out of that helicopter?"

"Bloodfoot saved your ass," Randy answered, annoyed that his shoulder was throbbing from the rifle's recoil.

"Good morning, Cap," said Bill, with a concerned look on his unshaven face.

Virgil stepped into the galley, "Good morning, everybody, I trust you slept well," he replied, pouring another cup of coffee.

They talked loosely, keeping the conversation away from the attack the previous night. Finally, Virgil checked his watch and proceeded to step out of the galley, "It's half passed eight, I'll be right back."

A few minutes later, a loud horn blasted from the tug, followed by two short whistles. When Virgil returned to the galley, the entire crew was seated at the table, watching Ian at the stove, making breakfast.

"Okay, everybody, gather 'round so we can discuss today's plans," said Bloodfoot.

Ian turned off the stove and put a hefty portion of bacon and scrambled eggs on the table, "G'morning Cap," he said, taking a seat next to Chuck.

"Where's Stu?" Randy asked, wandering how he slipped out undetected.

"He's in the john. I went to check on him, and he seemed alright. He's just complaining about a bad headache," replied Christie, chewing on a piece of fatty bacon as if it were bubble gum.

"I think he wants to get the hell off this boat and go home," Randy added.

"Good idea. We'll take the tug as close as we can to the Wildlife Refuge and hire a small boat to come out and get us. Stu can rent a car and go home, and I'll head over to Clearview State Park and see what kind of help the Rangers can give us," Randy said, adding Worcestershire sauce to his eggs.

"While Randy's doing that, we'll continue tracking our reptile," Bloodfoot added.

They had just finished breakfast when a radio call blasted through a loudspeaker, "This is Sheriff Clark calling *Endurance*. Come back."

The call was repeated several times until Virgil made his way to the bridge and replied, "This is Captain Virgil of the *Endurance*."

"Good morning, Captain. I'm still looking forward to meeting you and your crew. Let's make it happen this morning, over."

"Are you able to come out here to meet?"

"I'd rather you take the chopper and meet me at the park, the same place you fellas almost landed yesterday," the Sheriff answered with a sarcastic tone.

"Sorry, Sheriff, that won't be possible. The helicopter is out of action."

There was a hesitation before the Sheriff replied, "Okay, I know you have a zodiac, so take it to the mouth of the Suwannee, and I'll meet you there."

"Negative, the zodiac is also out of action," Virgil smiled to himself.

This time there was a longer hesitation before the Sheriff replied, "Why do I get the feeling you hunters don't want to talk to me."

"It's nothing personal, I assure you. I'd rather not explain on the radio. Can you meet on my tug or not?"

The Sheriff sounded aggravated when he replied, "I'll be there within the hour."

"Roger that...By the way, what size boat will you be arriving in?" replied Virgil, rolling his eyes toward Chuck and Randy as they entered the bridge.

By now, the Sheriff was clearly agitated and retorted, "I have a twenty-footer and a twenty-eight-footer. Which do you prefer?"

Randy grimaced when he saw that Virgil was getting a kick out of aggravating the Sheriff, "For your safety, take the big one. *Endurance* standing by on seven-two, out."

Virgil let go of the mic as it dangled above the steering wheel and looked at Randy, "Your friend is on his way here."

"Uh...yes, I heard," Randy winced.

"Saves us a trip," smiled Virgil.

"I thought that went well," Chuck added, taking a seat by the window and looking out towards land.

By eight-thirty, the sun was blazing its way through the white, puffy clouds lazily drifting high above the mouth of the Suwannee River. The warm Gulf waters were smooth as a lake as the crew stood at the stern of the tug and looked thirty feet below at the remains of the helicopter.

"That twisted scrap metal down there doesn't even resemble a helicopter," Christie said.

"The Sheriff is going to have a fit when he sees it," added Ian, spitting a wad of Copenhagen dip.

"Well…at least the man won't think I was putting him on," Virgil replied, lighting a cigarette.

Bill walked over to the crew carrying a three-foot chunk of fiberglass and dropped it on the deck, "This is what's left of the Zodiac. I found it dangling over the bow with a heap of wires."

"That's it?" Ian asked.

"Nope, the motor and a piece of the transom it's attached to is visible on the bottom," answered Bill, hoping he wouldn't be asked to retrieve it.

"We'll have to retrieve it before we leave," said Virgil, to the chagrin of Bill.

Before the crew could figure out who was going to dive down to salvage the boat motor, Virgil withdrew binoculars from his eyes, let them dangle from his neck and announced, "Here comes the cavalry. Bloodfoot and Randy follow me to the bridge, and the rest of you can make sure the Sheriff doesn't get eaten while trying to board," he said, taking one last look at the approaching boat before heading to the bridge.

The crew stood dumbstruck as the twenty-eight-foot Zodiac slowed to an idle and docked alongside the salvage tug. Its twin 50 HP Yamaha 4-stroke outboard motors hummed quietly until the Sheriff shut them off and threw a line to Ian, who quickly tied it to a cleat.

"Permission to board!" he shouted toward the bridge.

"Granted," Virgil replied half-heartedly as he leaned out the window.

As the Sheriff climbed aboard the salvage tug and quickly shook hands with the crew while making his way up to the bridge, Captain Virgil, Bloodfoot, and Randy looked at each other, wondering what kind of a crackpot Sheriff would bring an inflatable boat where a large man-eating reptile was lurking.

"I suppose he doesn't realize what we're dealing with," Randy said, feeling the need to say something.

There were two knocks at the door before the Sheriff entered and took his hat off, "You must be Captain Virgil," he said, shaking Virgil's hand.

"I am," Virgil replied.

"And I'm Sergeant Randy Taylor, Fort Lauderdale PD," Randy said, not waiting. "When you hear what we're dealing with, you might not want to jump back in your spiffy new inflatable boat."

Before the Sheriff could reply, he turned and saw the huge pirate-looking man sitting on a stool behind him and made a move for his holstered gun.

"Easy, fella, I'm on their team," Bloodfoot growled, puffing on a cigar and blowing a cloud of smoke out of his mouth.

Startled and at a loss for words, the Sheriff recovered quickly and stood opposite Bloodfoot, "No offense, sir, but you look like you'd give Blackbeard the pirate a run for his money."

"I've heard that before," replied Bloodfoot with a low, menacing tone.

The Sheriff took a deep breath and ran a hand through his hair, "Ok, so let's get to the bottom of this. I'll tell you about the reports and sightings that I know about, then you fellas can tell me what you know."

"Fine, let's hear it," said Randy.

The Sheriff showed them the report from the kids who had been attacked at Clearview State Park and told them about the other attacks. He also said they had hired the local trapper and hadn't heard anything from him but found his boat.

"Tell you what. Let's take my helicopter pilot to shore so he can arrange to get back home, then look at the trapper's place and see if we can pick up the pieces," said Randy. "After that, maybe we can talk to the kids that were attacked. Are they available, or maybe they left a number?"

"Yes, us small-town peacekeepers actually made out a report. We can call them," the Sheriff replied, annoyance in his tone.

"Good. While you officers are doing that, we'll head to the wildlife refuge and start tracking that malicious reptile," Bloodfoot grunted.

"What refuge?" asked the Sheriff."

"Chassa-something National Wildlife Refuge," replied Bloodfoot, walking out the door and leaving a trail of cigar smoke behind.

"What makes you think your gator's in there?"

"He thinks it came from there before swimming up here," replied Randy indifferently, pointing at the massive man walking away.

The Sheriff took a long look at the door that Bloodfoot left wide open before replying, "That guy's not so friendly, is he?"

"He's not too fond of the cops," Virgil stated, lighting another non-filtered camel cigarette. "It takes time to know his idiosyncrasies."

It took another hour before the men left the bridge. After hearing the unbelievable story about the monster they were hunting, the Sheriff had a helicopter fly around the area to make sure they wouldn't be attacked on the way to shore.

When given the all-clear, Randy and Stu jumped into the inflatable, followed by the Sheriff, who shook Captain Virgil's hand and let him know that he saw the remnants of the small boat and sunken remains of the helicopter, "Thanks for having me aboard and make sure your crew cleans up that mess underwater."

"Will do," replied Virgil, pushing the inflatable away with his foot.

Sheriff Clark and Randy watched vigilantly as the inflatable cruised up the Suwannee River. Passing the area where the latest attack occurred, they just looked at each other, then back to the area where the attack occurred, both men trying to visualize the traumatic fate of the boating family. They cruised farther upriver and dropped Stu off at a park ranger sub-station.

A while later, they entered the Ichetucknee River and found their way to Jack Morgans' dock. The sheriff ran over a crab trap and wrapped a line around one of the propellers before swearing obscenities and ramming the dock.

Randy kept his thoughts to himself as he leaped to the dock and tied the lines, "Good job, Sheriff," he finally said, giving him a look to see if his words sounded sincere.

"It sure would have been nice if he didn't have that damn trap sitting out where nobody could see it," he spat.

Randy walked to the back door of the house and knocked. He watched as the sheriff looked around the disordered yard and made his way to the front. A duck landed on the dock and ruffled its feathers, distracting Randy as he turned to see the disheveled bird spread its wings and quack noisily. Since nobody answered the door and it looked like the house was empty, Randy walked back to the dock, "Where's your buddy?" he asked the duck.

"If you expect an answer from that Muscovy, I'd say you're about as crazy as the rest of that crew you're with," said the Sheriff, walking up beside him.

"Up yours," he replied, throwing a twig at his feathery friend. "She probably knows more than you'll ever know around here."

"She's a he. The female species is much smaller than that one," the Sheriff pointed out. The Muscovy is native to Central and South America. That guy weighs about twelve pounds while the female only gets to be about half that."

Randy turned to face him with his hands on his hips, "Okay, so you know your ducks."

"Sure do. I also know a lot about the animals and reptiles around here, and I damn well know there is no thirty-eight-foot gator swimming around in these waters," he replied with a stern tone.

"Listen, Sheriff, I don't give a rat's ass about what you think you know because I know what's out there. Hopefully, we can find this trapper John guy, and he can confirm what we've been saying so that you can call an army out here to get rid of it."

The Sheriff shook his head and sat on a piling, "If you don't mind me asking, how long have you known that big, burly, pirate-looking fella?"

Randy smiled as if he was waiting for him to ask, "Longer than I'd like to remember. Why do you ask?"

"Well, I sort of looked up his information and found he's a felon, I'm just wondering why an upstanding police officer is associating with a guy like that. I mean, the guy scares the hell out of me just standing there. I couldn't imagine trying to take that man down."

"Let's hope you never try," replied Randy, dead serious. "I'll tell you this: Bloodfoot, Captain Virgil and that entire crew are the toughest and most stand-up people you'll ever find."

"I just can't imagine why you guys think there's such a gigantic gator out there. I mean, you guys are grown men. How can you possibly believe there's a monster like that?"

"Let me tell you something, Sheriff. The mayor hired those men to find and kill an enormous reptile. No, it's no ordinary gator. If you took the time to read the report I sent you, you'd close the parks and keep everybody away from the water until our job is done," Randy replied, getting heated.

The Sheriff stared at him for a long moment and replied, "I read your report. I do agree that there's a large reptile swimming around out there. I took the threat seriously, and when we couldn't find it, we got the National Guard in on it. They searched high and low and couldn't find a damn thing until they were getting ready to call it quits. As they loaded their last boat on the trailer, one of the guards shot and killed a sixteen-footer, extremely rare but seen from time to time. I thought for sure that we killed the culprit...until the latest attack with those boaters."

277

"Well, your mayor seemed to believe in AlliCroc because he's the one who called Captain Bloodfoot and set a bounty on its head," Randy grunted as he looked around the boat dock. "Now we also have a missing trapper and an attack on those kids camping in the park. So, if you don't mind me saying, I hope you get your head out of the sand before this indescribable reptile attacks more people!"

The Sheriff glared at Randy as he jumped onto the boat, "Okay, Mr. Taylor, let's go to Clearview Springs and see what the drunk fisherman has to say. He's the guy who said the trapper and his fishing buddy were attacked and killed."

Randy took note that the Sheriff didn't call him sergeant or officer. If they couldn't find the drunk fisherman, which he was pretty sure they wouldn't, he was just wasting his time.

16

The *Endurance* picked up anchor and headed toward the Chassahowitzka Wildlife Refuge at twenty knots. All eyes were peeled toward the small islands around Cedar Key as they cruised a quarter mile offshore. Captain Virgil and Chuck stood in the wheelhouse watching Bloodfoot as he stood motionless on the bow.

"I don't know how the hell he thinks he's going to find that monster like this. I mean, look out there. All those little islands and marshes...it's like finding a needle in a haystack," said Chuck.

"He believes he knows how that reptile thinks. He's doing what he would do if he were AlliCroc," Virgil replied nonchalantly.

"But the attacks weren't near the refuge."

"He thinks the creature is going back to where it's been hiding out since it escaped the Everglades. Believe me, I saw his homework. He's got the stories from the last seven years of manatee parts washing ashore looking like they had been torn off, people mysteriously disappearing, porpoises half eaten, all kinds of things, and they all lead to the Wildlife Refuge."

Virgil lit a cigarette as Chuck poured another cup of coffee. When they looked up, they were surprised to see that Bloodfoot had left his perch.

Before they could say anything, the door opened and slammed shut behind them, and Bloodfoot stood with a malicious grin, "Virgil's right; I did my homework. We are on the right track," he winked at Chuck, lighting a giant cigar. "Stay the course and keep your binoculars engrossed on the marshes."

Virgil and Chuck were dumbfounded as Bloodfoot returned to the bow and continued his quest.

"How the hell does he do that?" Chuck asked.

"Great ears, I assume. He's not the best at what he does by following his prey, he becomes it, knows what it would do before it does," Virgil whispered.

A couple of hours later, and with no AlliCroc sighting, the salvage tug drew as close as it could to the mouth of the Wildlife Preserve. Captain Virgil put the salvage tug in neutral and drifted just outside of the entrance while the crew searched for abnormalities in the surrounding area.

He dug in his shirt pocket for his pack of cigarettes when his cellphone rang. It was his home phone number.

"Good morning, honey. How's it going on the home front?" Virgil asked.

"Not so good, Virge. You'll never guess…"

Virgil stopped smiling when his wife's sentence was cut short, and a familiar voice continued.

"Hello Virgil, this is your 'ol buddy Don Henderson."

"What the hell are you doing in my home?" Virgil barked like a rabid dog.

"I'll cut to the chase. You have something I want, and I have something you want."

"Put Jeanne on the phone NOW!"

"Not until you hear me out," Don insisted.

"I should have killed you the last time I saw you," Virgil replied.

By now, the entire crew was standing under the bridge, looking up at the captain shouting into the phone.

"Jeanne is fine. I will not hurt her, and we will not even leave this house…unless you fail to do what I ask and, of course, if you call the cops over here," Don replied nervously.

"Leave Jeanne alone and get out of the house now. Run and hide somewhere that I will never find you because I'm coming for you, and I'm going to kill you. I can make it quick or drag it out. It depends on when you leave," Virgil assured him.

"Damn, that's not the offer I had in mind. I have a better offer. One that can make us millions, and who knows?... Maybe we will be friends again."

Virgil paced back and forth as he listened to Don. It was no surprise that he wanted to keep AlliCroc alive. It was never confirmed from the last hunt, but now he was sure that it was Don who hired a hitman to try to kill them. Fortunately, he was killed by AlliCroc.

Don finished telling Virgil how he expected his plan to work and passed the phone to Jeanne.

"Don't worry Virge, I'm ok. I'm sure Donald will be a gentleman, and we'll just sit and talk about old times until this is over," she said.

"I'm not worried. Don should be worried."

"He is," Jeanne replied.

"He should be. I'm going to kill him."

"oh, before I forget, our green minivan is out for repair."

The phone abruptly went dead, and Virgil knew it was Don who disconnected.

Virgil put the phone in his pocket and shouted for Bill to drop anchor and then for everybody to meet in the galley. He continued pacing in the wheelhouse while the crew filed into the galley, thinking about his wife being held against her will in her own home. Don crossed the line big time, and now he will suffer the consequences.

The crew sat with concerned looks when Virgil stepped into the galley.

"What's going on, Virgil?" Chuck asked.

Virgil stood at the entranceway, reached into his pocket for his cigarettes and lit one before answering, "Don Henderson is holding Jeanne hostage at the house. If we don't tranquilize AlliCroc so that he can take it back to the Everglades Sanctuary so he can display it and make millions of dollars, he said he would hurt her." Virgil said flatly.

"Let's go get that son of a bitch!" Chuck replied with a vengeance.

The others agreed and looked more disgusted than Virgil.

"Jeanne's going to be fine. We have a gun in the bedroom closet that she is going to get and reverse the situation. Believe me, she knows how to use it," Virgil said, surprising the crew.

"Look, Virgil, I know how hard this must be for you. We can get a car and be at the house in…"

Virgil held up a hand to cut Bill's sentence, "Don won't lay a finger on her. He thinks he can get us to catch his reptile this way. I know he won't touch her."

"Ok, Virgil, what do you want to do?" Bloodfoot asked, keeping his anger in check.

"We will carry on as planned. Don has an accomplice who will contact us and tell us where to pick up the tranquilizers. I'm sure he's going to stick around and make sure we pick them up, and then he will relay it back to Don."

"It's going to be hard to find him. I'm sure he'll be well hidden," said Chuck.

"We'll be looking for a green minivan. Jeanne told me the minivan is in the shop, but we don't own one. I take it that she told me what to look for before the phone went dead."

Bill smiled and replied, "That wife of yours is something else, eh?"

Bloodfoot sat quietly and took in the conversation. He, too, like Virgil, knew Don was not going to hurt Jeanne but offered another option. "We can make it to the house in a few hours and get that idiot."

Virgil nodded in appreciation but said, "No thanks. The less people that know about this, the better."

"What do you mean by that?"

"When this is over, I'm going to kill him," Virgil replied.

It swam lethargically along the bottom, its menacing tail gliding from side to side with purpose. A small, steady stream of blood flowed along the keratin and bony plates on its back from the twelve-inch chunk of meat blown off from the rifle blast.

Swimming a half-mile offshore to evade exposure, it suddenly stopped and sat motionless on the sandy bottom, sensing a predator circling just beyond the grey wall of visibility. The agitated creature detected the vibrations, slowly opened its horrific jaws and prepared for the attack.

The twelve-foot bull shark was rather large for its species and swam up and down the gulf coast like a predator at the top of the food chain. Its six-hundred-ninety-five-pound submarine-shaped body swam effortlessly toward the scent of blood. It slowly circled above what looked like a small reef and followed the blood source in.

Agitated from hunger pangs and the fact it knew it was being hunted by the humans on the salvage tug, it wanted to spring up and ravish the shark the second it was in reach, but the water was too shallow, and AlliCroc did not want to stir the surface and bring the hunters in. It waited patiently.

The shark made one last pass over the seeping blood, its jaws quivering as the blood flowed through its gills. Suddenly, as it turned to attack, it was met with brute force with a blow to the side, driving the shark through the water sideways.

Before the startled predator could return the attack, a large pressure sensation whiffed through its body as AlliCroc's massive jaws clamped down and bit the shark in two.

With wild abandonment, the elusive reptile shook its massive head and rolled its body, shredding meat and cartilage as it threw caution to the wind and burst through the surface of the water like a ravaging brute. The shark exploded through the crimson-colored air like a fireworks display.

"Whoa! Check it out!" Ian shouted, pointing at the disturbance further offshore and behind the tug.

The crew gasped at the site of the carnage while Captain Virgil engaged the throttles and turned the tugboat toward the melee at full speed, "Get those big-ass guns ready! Christie! Get up here in the wheelhouse and brace yourself!"

"We got it, Virge," Bill whispered to himself as he ran with Bloodfoot and Ian into the galley to collect the powerful rifles. Ian met his glare and grinned, knowing he hated it when the captain shouted orders to the crew like a tyrant.

Five minutes after the assault, the tugboat was drifting through the bloody pieces of the shark. Knowing what the insidious reptile was capable of, Chuck stood inside the wheelhouse with a shotgun and surveyed the area with Virgil and Christie. At the same time, Bloodfoot, Bill and Ian quietly walked along the deck with the .905 rifles at the ready.

"Pretty quick attack," Virgil stated, lighting a camel non-filtered cigarette, watching the dissipating blood disperse.

"Lightning quick," Bloodfoot replied, standing on his perch at the bow. "Just keep 'er steady… that reptile is down there… and it knows we're here."

The tug continued drifting as the current took it slowly to the North. Bloodfoot caught the attention of Bill and Ian and motioned toward the safety lever on the rifles. In unison, the two rolled their eyes at each other as if questioning who the hell the pirate thought he was schooling, rookies?

Before they could launch a verbal attack, two clicks could be heard as they disengaged the safety. Bloodfoot didn't even turn with a knowing look. He just stood at the bow, shaking his head.

Christie spotted it first. The tugboat lazily drifted twenty feet above grassy spots and reef patches. She clearly saw the immense shape of AlliCroc twisted in a U-shaped pattern, "There it is!" she pointed.

Ian carefully poked his head over the side and found it difficult to see the monster, "Are you sure it's down there? I can barely see the bottom."

"It's easier to see from up here," Christie continued, her heartbeat pounding in her ears.

Bloodfoot ran up to the bridge where he could get a clear look at the reptile. The tugboat had drifted a bit since it was sighted, but he caught the vague outline, "Okay, the damn thing is sitting down there watching us.

"Got any suggestions? We're going to have to get it to come up to the surface somehow," replied Captain Virgil.

"Reverse the engines slightly to stop the drift. Keep the tug where we can see the reptile," Bloodfoot said, lost in his thoughts.

Virgil waited to reply as he noticed Bloodfoot pacing back and forth, scheming up a plan.

"I hope you're not planning to jump in and shoot a spear in its ass."

Bloodfoot looked at the captain with a quirky look and replied, "Something like that."

"I was really hoping you had a better plan. I know you're the best at what you do, but I'd like to remind you that it would be like poking a stick at a Sherman tank," Virgil stated with concern. "I think if we chum the water with something enticing, we can blast it when it surfaces."

"We tried that. The first couple rounds will hit the armor plates, and it will retreat."

"Diving down to it is suicide," Virgil continued.

"If we can connect a line to the cable winch, I can swim down there and shoot it somewhere with a speargun that will penetrate. Probably the underbelly. When the spear penetrates, its guttural reaction would be to go into the death roll. We can free spool the tow line and wrap the reptile tight and poll it up where we can blast

288

it to pieces with the big-ass caliber rifles," he declared, standing up straight and smacking his big fists together.

"Do you think our thickest tow line will be enough to hold that creature? Bill added.

"Well, it worked on Moby Dick," retorted Bloodfoot, giving Bill a wry look as he lit a cigar.

Virgil and Bill frowned at each other when they realized the man probably didn't know how that story ended.

Twenty minutes later, Virgil stood watch from the bridge as he lit a cigarette and gave the crew the thumbs-up signal to let them know the reptile was still sitting below.

Gathered at the stern, the crew handed Bloodfoot a spear gun with thirty-foot of slack line attached. Fastened to the other end of the line was the thick towline on the winch attached to the stern. If Bloodfoot was successful, the spear would penetrate the reptile, causing it to become extremely agitated and go into a death roll, wrapping itself up and becoming entangled in the cable, enabling the crew to haul it up and kill it.

"Ok, here it goes," Bloodfoot said, taking a few deep breaths before cautiously lowering himself into the water. When he was fully in, he looked at Virgil, who gave him the thumbs up, ensuring the reptile did not stir.

"I know you know, but I'll say it anyway," Ian said, handing him the spear gun. "AlliCroc can sense you in the water."

"I know. I plan to stay on the surface until I'm behind the reptile, then swim down and find a spot to shoot it. Once I shoot it, I will get the hell out of the way."

"That thing will know exactly what you're doing. I'll jump in and cause a diversion. You'll be more successful if it is focused on me instead of you," Ian piped up, sounding like he was surprised at what he had said.

"Good idea, but I…"

"It's moving! I see it turning toward you and looking up with that giant, hideous head!" Christie shouted, cutting off their conversation.

Bill and Chuck pulled Bloodfoot out of the water in a flash. They watched as Virgil kept a sharp eye on the reptile and waited.

"It's still down there. It moved to face Bloodfoot, and now it's just sitting there," Virgil said, edging the tug toward the opposite direction the reptile was now facing.

Bloodfoot sat on the deck with his mask and fins still attached. Lifting the mask off his face, he continued, "As I was saying, good idea, but you're too big. I need somebody smaller so the crew can haul her back into the tug in a split second."

"Her?"

"Christie, switch places with Ian. She's going to be the bait," said Bloodfoot.

Christie had a lump in her throat that made her feel like she couldn't breathe. She made her way down to the deck and joined the crew as they quickly made a makeshift harness to secure her in.

"I…I don't think I can do this," she mumbled.

"Of course, you can. If that monster decides to attack from down there, these guys will pull you aboard in plenty of time," Bloodfoot replied, giving her a wink.

His soothing smile seemed to calm her nerves as she took her clothes off, revealing a bright red bikini. Ian fought back the urge to suggest that he'd eat her if the creature didn't when he felt the menacing glare from Bloodfoot.

"Put this harness around you, and we'll lower you over the side," Bill said. "Don't worry. If that reptile so much as twitches, we'll have you back on the tug before it makes a move."

"Hope so…my life depends on it," she replied, checking to make sure the knots were tight.

"You'll be fine. Just make sure you splash around so AlliCroc pays you some attention," smiled Bloodfoot. "If I thought you would be in any danger, I wouldn't ask you to do this."

That, coming from a man who kills great white sharks with a hunting knife, offered no comfort, but deep down, she knew she was in good hands.

"Okay, let's do this," Bloodfoot said, putting his mask on.

"What's the monster doing, Captain?" Christie shouted.

Virgil stood on the bridge with his head out the window, staring through the water down below, "It's still sitting down there! It hasn't moved a muscle!"

"Once Christie is in the water, AlliCroc will sense her presence and follow her movements. I will slip in from the bow while she's splashing around," Bloodfoot said.

We will be standing by with the cannons ready," said Chuck.

Minutes later, Christie jumped over the side. Before her head came to the surface, she felt the urge to scream and climb back on the tug, but when she cleared her eyes, she saw Bill standing on the gunwale with a firm grip on the line. Their eyes met, and he gave her a reassuring nod that seemed to calm her nerves.

"Don't worry about a thing. If that reptile moves an inch, I'll have you in the boat," he guaranteed.

She nodded in agreement and floated on her back, her eyes not leaving his.

Once again, Bloodfoot slowly slipped into the water and tried to slow his heartbeat. It was working. AlliCroc was watching Christie and paid no attention to him but probably knew he was there. Bloodfoot took a couple of deep breaths before disappearing below the surface.

He systematically swam down toward a group of rocks, impulsively holding his hunting knife with one hand while the other held the spear gun. Hoping the reptile was focusing its attention on Christie, he concentrated his rhythm to be smooth and easy.

He suddenly froze when he spotted the hideous creature staring at him with its mouth half open.

"Splash around more! The damn reptile is about thirty feet from Bloodfoot and looking straight at him!" Virgil shouted from his perch, where he could clearly see the imminent danger.

Christie was so scared she hadn't noticed that she stopped splashing. Her throat was so dry she couldn't swallow, but she knew Bloodfoot would be in grave danger if she stopped being a decoy.

She took a deep breath and splashed wildly with her arms and legs, shouting at the top of her lungs, "I'm over here, you overgrown piece of meat! Come and get me!"

Her attempt to be a decoy startled everybody on board the tug but failed miserably at distracting AlliCroc. In fact, the hideous reptile sprang from the bottom and shot forward toward Bloodfoot at breakneck speed. He barely had time to raise the spear gun as he swam out of the way of the beartrap-like jaws as they snapped inches above his coiled legs.

Bloodfoot quickly turned only to see the colossal tail disappear through the gray curtain of darkness. Without hesitation, he swam with all his might to the surface, where Ian and Chuck swiftly pulled him out of the water.

On the other end of the tug, they heard an eerie screech and saw Bill pulling Christie's lifeline. Wasting no time, they ran over to the starboard side and saw Christie screaming as she was being pulled to safety. Before she had two feet on deck, a humungous torpedo blast shot straight up out of the water and hung in the air for what felt like a lifetime before landing flat out on the stern deck.

"Get inside and close the hatches!" shouted Virgil, reaching for the shotgun.

Christie, Bill, Chuck and Ian ran to the port side while Bloodfoot ran up the stairs and stood at the railing on the starboard side surrounding the bridge.

The reptile was gigantic. The tug leaned nearly forty-five degrees to starboard as half of the monster's body was on deck with only its hind legs and long tail hanging over the side.

Ian, Bill and Chuck opened portals from the galley and fired the .905 shotguns at the reptile's head, careful not to blow holes in the deck.

"That damn thing won't die!" Virgil shouted, watching the slugs bounce off its hide. At the same instant, Ian shot a round into the back of the behemoth where the open wound was, and the agitated reptile roared feverishly and scrambled to return to the water. Christie was in the galley where she thought she found safety, only to poke her head out and see the hideous reptile thrashing wildly.

Bloodfoot, seeing the head was stuck between the winch and gunwale, took the opportunity to jump on its back and drive his hunting knife deep inside the wound behind its head.

Feeling the full effect of the blade, AlliCroc roared out in agony and freed itself. Bloodfoot was on its back when it attempted a death roll, but there wasn't enough room and the two rolled over the gunwale and into the water.

Bloodfoot held tight as the reptile plunged toward the bottom. Never in his life did he feel he would die like he did now, and he knew if he let go, he wouldn't stand a chance.

The armor-plated scutes tore into his arms and legs as he held tight. The hideous reptile reached the bottom with a flurry of sand and silt, giving Bloodfoot a chance to pull the knife out and plunge it deeper into the wound. AlliCroc rolled and spun several times, kicking up a mass of blinding sand as Bloodfoot sprang clear of the melee. With his lungs screaming for air and awaiting the inevitable attack, he turned to face his adversary and was baffled to see the tail disappear into the darkness. Bloodfoot knew it would come charging back and prepared for an attack from the opposite flank.

He looked up to see the bottom of the tug twenty feet above and swam for it.

"He's coming up! Bloodfoot's coming up!" Christie screamed out, her head over the side while pointing down into the water.

"Stay clear! Get back into the galley and shut the door!" Virgil shouted, watching the large torpedo-shaped menace swimming just below the surface and heading for Bloodfoot.

Ian saw it and braced himself on the ranking that led to the wheelhouse with the rifle pointing at the enormous object. Chuck aimed, his immense rifle securely resting on the gunwale while Bill loaded the large twenty-five-hundred-grain bullet.

"Bill! Help me get Bloodfoot in the boat!" Virgil shouted, running out to the railing and jumping to the deck below.

Ian took a deep breath and focused his attention like a seasoned sniper. His intent was to shoot AlliCroc between the eyes with a bullet that was literally the same size as his hand and be done with it. Hitting the monster at such a close distance was guaranteed to blow its head off, or so he thought.

At the same instant that Bloodfoot burst through the surface, the .905 caliber rifles blasted their single shots in unison when AlliCroc was in striking distance. The impact made the reptile shudder, which gave Bloodfoot an extra second to grasp Virgil's outstretched arm and hoist himself on deck.

The hideous jaws scraped the side of the tug, missing Bloodfoot by inches. With no time to spare reloading the single-shot cannons, the crew used shotguns to try to shoot its eyes out or blow its head off, but the prevailing creature once again retreated to the bottom and disappeared.

Bloodfoot was disappointed and angry; the reptile got away but turned and gave Christie a pat on the shoulder, "Great job."

She tried to repay the compliment but instead passed out in Bill's arms.

Chuck thought he blew his arm out of its socket but dusted himself off and stepped into the galley, "I'm fine."

"Those cannons didn't do what I hoped they would," Bloodfoot grunted, out of breath and sprawled flat out on deck.

"We need to aim for the head. The body is too tough with those armored-looking plates, we nailed that damn thing, and nothing happened," Ian replied resignedly, holding his bruised shoulder while extending his hand to help Bloodfoot to his feet.

Virgil gave the order for Bill to drop anchor and Chuck to shut down the twin diesel engines. When completed, they assembled with the rest of the crew in the galley to gather their thoughts.

"Ok, boys, we've got AlliCroc on the run again. I was able to plunge my knife deeper into its open wound, and it was in a lot of pain. This reptile is much smarter, bigger and deadlier than its sibling we hunted last time," Bloodfoot professed, pouring his second glass of Sailor Jerry.

"I don't know if we can do this alone. Why won't the local authorities help?" Christie asked, shaking like a nervous wreck.

Virgil eyed the weary crew and lit a cigarette, "The National Guard tried but couldn't find it. Like Bloodfoot said, this monster is a lot smarter…and bigger. It knows we're hunting it. Maybe Sherriff Clark and Randy can influence the mayor to call out the military. Especially after what just happened."

"It's hurt. It's hurting really bad. I think one of you guys blew its eye out," Bloodfoot revealed.

"I also managed to put a slug in its open wound," Ian replied, taking credit for both.

It was mid-afternoon when the Sheriff and Randy Taylor docked at the Ranger Station at Clearview State Park. As they jumped to the dock, they were met by the lead Ranger and his partner, "Welcome, gentlemen. Follow me to my office, and we'll have a talk."

They followed the Ranger up the rickety dock and stepped into the back door of the building. The Ranger offered them chairs as he slid behind a large oak desk and sat down, "Sergeant Taylor, please tell us about this mutant reptile you believe is lurking in the water at our park," he asked, leaving the niceties outside.

"First of all, I damn-well know it lurking around out there because I saw it," Randy cut to the chase, realizing they didn't want to believe it, "I fought and killed the first one a couple years back, and I saw the other one last night…and it's bigger and nastier."

The Ranger put up his hand, gesturing for the visiting police sergeant to keep his voice down, "I understand. Let me tell you what we have here, and maybe you can fill in the blanks."

"I'm listening," Randy shot back, leaning back in the chair and crossing his arms on his chest, concluding they don't believe AlliCroc exists and that it is most likely a big alligator.

"A couple months ago, some people started mysteriously disappearing. Somebody reported a large alligator, and we figured we had a large gator to deal with. Then I got an e-mail from the higher-ups telling me the National Guard was coming to search for the gator. Now, large gators are rare but not uncommon in these parts, so I asked to keep the hunt on the down low so there wouldn't be a panic. For the life of me, I never heard of the National Guard hunting large predators, so I figure somebody, maybe you caught the mayor's ear and he believed in your mutant reptile story."

"Did you happen to read the report I sent up here? We had the same type of reptile stalking our waters in South Florida. We even spoke with the man who created them. There were three, and we killed one, and another was killed in the Everglades. The third reptile that they named AlliCroc, escaped and went north. We were assured it would never be a threat because it would remain in the wild and keep away from areas known to man. Now we figure the one here is the one that got away."

"I read your report," the Ranger interjected, looking up at the Sheriff with skeptical eyes. "I also read the newspapers from down there. It seems they were saying it was a large gator. They said nothing about a mutant hybrid reptile."

"Like your mayor, our mayor wanted to keep it quiet."

"And what does your good mayor think now?"

Before Randy answered, the Sheriff dropped his head and put a hand over his face. Evidently, the Ranger hadn't heard.

"I'm sure he'd believe it now, seeing AlliCroc ate him and his family," Randy retorted.

The Ranger closed his eyes and shook his head. Looking up, he cleared his throat, "You want to look at the files from the latest attacks? Here they are," he said, pushing the files over to Randy. "We have an attack on some kids camping here in the park, another one in the park, but it's not clear if we can take it seriously. Seems two guys were fishing when they were attacked. One guy made it to shore and watched his friend get eaten or drown, but this guy is a known drinker, always telling stories."

"Well…did his buddy ever show up?" Randy asked incredulously.

"No."

"Here's one where a diver and his wife disappeared."

"Who reported it?"

"Family members who tried to come up here and surprise them. They found their car in the park, but the divers never showed up. Finally, when the park closed, they filed a missing person's report with us. They said they went to dive into the springs. We searched and found a dive fin with a foot in it," he continued, his breathing becoming heavy.

Randy was beside himself. He got up and paced the floor while the Ranger read a couple more reports, then walked to the window.

Looking out, he saw an old, white Jeep Cherokee pull into the parking lot. A redhead in her early twenties sprang from the back seat and strolled toward the station, followed by a young man standing well over six feet.

"Well, well, speak of the devil. Here comes that red-head. I think her name is Angie," a ranger said, peeking out the window. He barely made it back to his seat when the front door burst open, and the pretty redhead walked through. The door slammed behind the big guy as they walked to the front counter like gangbusters.

"Hello folks, how can we help you?" the ranger asked.

"I talked to you a couple weeks ago. My name is Angie, and you took the report we made about a very large alligator," she responded with a serious, no-nonsense tone.

The ranger took a deep breath and let it out slowly, "Yes, I remember. I have the report sitting right here and we are keeping an eye out."

"Look, sir, it sounds to me like you guys are doing nothing. Angie brought a picture so you can see what she's talking about," Ned added.

The ranger looked at the young man and casually asked, "And who might you be? I don't recall you as being one of the campers at the scene?"

"I remember him," Sheriff Clark confirmed. "Angie and Ned also gave me a statement after Angie and her friend attacked."

Angie and Ned were surprised they didn't recognize the Sheriff when they walked in, "Oh, Sheriff Clark. Sorry, we didn't recognize you with your hair messed up like that," Angie smiled.

"I was out on the water all morning. It tends to make me look a little haggard," the Sheriff replied.

"Well Angie, I think I told you I'd give you a call if we needed more information, and as of yet, we have nothing," the ranger cut in.

"Well, I have something for you," she replied, reaching into her purse and retrieving a Go-Pro camera. "I took a picture of Amanda when she was on that branch, but my camera fell in the water when the huge alligator attacked. It took a while for me to retrieve it, but now I'm here to show you the picture," she said, connecting the camera to her cell phone. "Here you go," she continued, passing the phone to the men behind the counter.

Randy watched as the first ranger's eyes bulged when he viewed the picture. The same happened to the next ranger he passed it to.

"Let me have a look," Randy said, reaching for the phone.

The picture was somewhat out of focus, but he clearly saw the humungous head as it appeared to strike the tree branch that the terrified girl was sitting on.

"You mean you dove down in that water after seeing that giant gator?" the Ranger asked skeptically.

"No way. I forgot about it until I tried to find it the other night. We were at that other campground where the same gator killed that family on their boat. I told Ned where I thought I lost it, and he and his friend Jay went back and found it."

"That took a lot of nerve. You weren't afraid of getting attacked?" Randy asked.

"I dive with a spear gun all the time in the keys and have been face to face with some pretty big sharks, but believe me, if I knew how big this reptile is, I would never have gone in that water," replied Ned.

Angie retold her story about the attack so Randy could hear it as Ned watched attentively at the look in the rangers' eyes. He also watched the guy named Randy, who seemed to know exactly what she was talking about.

When she was finished talking, Ned asked what they planned to do about the reptile.

"Well Ned, Sergeant Randy Taylor is working with some men that are trying to find this reptile as we speak. Angie, thanks for showing us the picture and we'll let you know if or when we capture it. Until then, please do us a favor and stay out of the water."

"Shouldn't you close the park?" Ned asked, unimpressed.

"Leave that to us son. Thanks for coming," the ranger replied, hustling them out the door.

Before they were literally tossed out the door, Ned stopped and turned to Randy, "You are Sergeant Randy Taylor from Fort Lauderdale? You work at the station in Port Everglades, right?"

Randy cleared his throat, "Yes sir, I am."

Ned smiled and continued, "I fish in the port. You guys stopped me so many times to check my boat. I knew I recognized you when I stepped in the door."

Randy smiled and patted him on the back, "Small world."

"I also know that you were one of the guys that hunted that big ass gator a couple years ago."

Randy's smile vanished, "That's true, and from what you and I both know, I think there's another one here."

Ned wanted to talk more, but Randy told him he had business with the Sheriff and park rangers. Before he closed the door, he gave him his card and told him to give him a call.

The door shut, and the lead ranger barely made it back to his chair before his subordinate claimed, "We've got a real problem on our hands."

"Well, there's a start. I'm glad that picture snapped your attention," quipped Randy.

"Our hands are tied," the ranger rallied. "I'm sure as hell not hunting that monster, and I'm sure the mayor won't close the park."

"You good 'ol boys won't even close the park!" Randy spat, shaking his head in disgust.

"The men I'm with will find and kill that hideous reptile. If you guys don't want more people missing, you'll stake out locations and keep a keen eye out for that thing!" continued Randy, storming out of the building.

"Randy, wait!" the ranger said, following Randy out the door. "I spoke to the mayor. He said he hired a well-known hunter to catch and kill this gator. He doesn't want to cause a panic, so he wants to keep it on the down low."

Randy was about to reply when his radio chimed in. It was Captain Bloodfoot relaying what had happened while Randy was out and was reminded to stay vigil on the way back with the Sheriff.

When the transmission was completed, Randy secured the radio back on his belt and looked around to see the stunned look on the Sheriff and Ranger's faces.

"That was the hunter that your mayor hired. Looks like the problem is getting bigger," Randy spat out.

305

"What the hell is a mutant reptile? The bewildered Sheriff asked.

"Sheriff, you have got to talk to the mayor. We need to close Clearview Springs and the entire area around it," the lead ranger said.

"That's a good start," replied Randy, finally getting their attention.

17

The ride back to the *Endurance* was quiet and uneventful. Randy had to take an uber to a Ranger station on Cedar Key since the latest adventure took the *Endurance* too far south and out of jurisdiction for the Sheriff to bring him back, or so he wanted Randy to believe.

Randy was met at the dock by a deputy with a twenty-five-foot Whaler. Still seething from the lack of cooperation from the authorities at Clearview State Park, he noticed his transporter kept a worried, watchful eye on the surrounding water.

"Look, Sergeant Taylor, I know you think we're a bunch of cowards, but there's nothing we can do. None of us are trained to hunt alligators, especially the one you guys are after," he shouted above the roar of the engine.

"I'm not asking you, people, to hunt. I'm simply asking to close the area until we kill the reptile," Randy chided.

The deputy shrugged his shoulders, "The mayor has his own problems."

"The mayor is the one who called Captain Bloodfoot, so I know damn well that he knows what's going on."

The deputy remained silent as he spotted the *Endurance* and steered towards it.

He reached for the radio, "This is Deputy Ryan Davies calling the *Endurance. C*ome back."

"This is the *Endurance*; go ahead, deputy," Captain Virgil's voice returned.

"I'm approximately a half-mile away and heading over to drop off Sergeant Taylor. Is it safe to rendezvous? Over."

"I can't guarantee that it's safe, but I appreciate you bringing the sergeant back in one piece over."

Bloodfoot was sitting with Virgil on the bridge and smiled at the way he spoke bluntly on the radio, just enough to keep everybody on their toes.

Randy noticed the concerned look on the deputy's face when Virgil replied. Reducing speed, he slowed to an idle and came up alongside the tug.

Ian stood on the starboard side and received the line thrown over by Randy as he jumped onto the tug and headed straight to the wheelhouse, where Virgil, Bloodfoot and Chuck watched.

"Permission to come aboard?" the deputy requested as he prepared to take the leap.

"Denied!" shouted Virgil, flicking a cigarette butt out the window.

The startled deputy nearly tripped and fell overboard as he stopped midstride and looked up to see the grim look on the captain's face staring back at him.

"You need to get back to shore, deputy. It's dangerous out here. That monster could be anywhere. Go back to shore, and I will stay in radio contact with you until you reach the dock," Virgil said.

Without a word, Ian untied the line and tossed it in the boat. Cranking the engine, the deputy put the boat in gear and made a beeline back toward shore.

"Looks like you pissed him off," Chuck said.

"Randy said the deputy's a dumb ass. I'll take him at his word. Besides, he has no business here. He should be chatting with his superiors and get them to close the area before more people get killed," Vigil responded.

"I concur," Bloodfoot growled, not a big fan of the sheriff deputies.

Virgil stepped toward the back of the bridge where his cabin was located and retrieved a fresh pack of Camel non-filtered cigarettes when his phone rang. It was an unfamiliar number, which usually resulted in him ignoring it, but since Jeanne was held captive, he picked it up.

"Speak," he imposed.

"Virgil Goodman?"

"Tell me where I can find the tranquilizers."

"You sound like a very mean man."

"You're holding my wife hostage; I'm hunting a monster reptile, and I'm talking to a soon-to-be-dead man. Mean doesn't describe how I am."

"First of all, I want it to be clear that I have nothing to do with the hostage part of this ordeal. We need to capture AlliCroc instead of..."

"Save it, punk! Where am I to pick up the serum?" Virgil cut him off.

Johnny was nervous and taken aback by the stern tone in Virgil's voice. He cleared his throat and replied.

"I see you're anchored just offshore at the entrance of Chassahowitzka preserve. I'm sure you are going hunting in there, so take your boat upriver for a quarter mile. On the left bank, you will see a red rag tied to a tree branch. Pull your boat over to it, and the serum will be in a leather satchel resting under the tree."

"I will be there in one hour," Virgil replied and ended the call.

"Everybody in the galley! Pronto!" Virgil shouted to the crew, taking a quick look with his binoculars toward the thicket on shore, hoping to catch a glimpse of the man on the phone. He knew he was out there somewhere, but he couldn't spot him.

Virgil stepped into the galley and joined the crew at the table. He gave a slight smile when he noticed the crew must have heard the phone conversation and looked like they were all set to go.

"I just spoke with the idiot that will supply us with the tranquilizers. He's dropping them off a quarter mile upriver at a boat ramp. Let's gather our gear and go get him," Virgil said.

"The other zodiac is inflated, tied over the side and loaded with shotguns and the three big rifles. We're ready when you are," Ian replied, dripping sweat from his forehead.

Virgil looked at him and noticed his sweaty t-shirt, "You look like you just ran a marathon."

"When we heard you talking on the phone, we helped Bill get the zodiac prepared while Bloodfoot loaded the guns."

"I think you guys just set a new record," Virgil replied, noticing for the first time that everybody was drenched.

"Bill already had the zodiac on deck and filled with air. We just tossed it over the side and attached the motor," Chuck added.

"Bloodfoot, Randy and Christie hold down the fort. We'll be back soon," Virgil said, getting up from the table.

"Like hell, Captain, we're coming along," Bloodfoot grumbled.

Virgil stood and lit a cigarette, "This is my problem. I told the man I would be there in one hour. If we leave now, we can be there in a half hour. We may surprise him and catch him while he's still there."

"Great idea, but we're coming with you. Like Ian always reminds us, *in for a penny, in for a pound*," Bloodfoot replied, giving Ian a wink.

Virgil couldn't argue. He didn't want to ask Bloodfoot and Randy to come along because he figured it wasn't their problem. Deep down, he was happy they insisted.

"Ok. Now, let's jump in the boat and go get him."

As before, Christie was to watch from the bridge as the crew departed. If AlliCroc returned to attack the *Endurance,* she would call them on the radio and retreat to Virgil's cabin until they returned.

She waved goodbye as the twenty-foot zodiac was unleashed from the salvage tug, and Virgil pushed the throttles to their max and sped off toward the inlet.

Johnny Lee watched from a safe distance as the zodiac neared the inlet. He knew the captain would take less than an hour to retrieve the serum and try to catch him in the act.

He ducked down behind bushes as the zodiac zoomed past, careful not to be seen. When he was clear, he quickly ran back to his minivan parked on the side of an isolated road and headed toward the drop zone. Stopping the van fifty yards behind a thicket, Johnny got out and hid behind some foliage, adjusting his binoculars on the red rag tied to the tree. Once they completed the pickup of the serum, he was to call Don to confirm the exchange.

Just after motoring inside the inlet, Virgil reduced the throttle to a slow idle and pulled over to the embankment.

"You stopped too soon, Virgil. I don't see the red tag," said Ian, looking ahead.

"I'm getting out here. I'm going to find that guy, and we'll meet at the drop zone," Virgil replied, stepping out with a loaded shotgun.

"You'll never find him in these woods. It will be like finding a needle in a haystack," Chuck stated.

"I'll be looking for the green minivan."

"Oh yeah, I forgot Jeanne revealed that. I must be losing my mind."

Bloodfoot smiled and shook his head, "When this is over, I have to meet that woman."

Randy jumped out behind Virgil, "I'm coming with you."

Virgil turned with a distasteful look, "You probably won't like what you see when I find him."

"That's why I'm going with you. When we find him, I want to make sure you don't kill him."

Bill tossed him a shotgun as Randy kicked the zodiac off the sand and watched them continue upriver. When he turned, Virgil was already twenty yards up, near a deserted stretch of a rocky roadway.

"Wait up, Virge," he whispered as loud as possible.

Virgil waited and watched as the police officer stumbled and tripped on every vine and pothole in his path. When he finally reached him, Virgil was smirking and said, "Jeez, Randall. Don't they teach you how to walk in the wilderness at boot camp?"

"No," he replied curtly, smacking a mosquito off his forehead.

The zodiac slowly cruised upriver when Bloodfoot pointed at the red tag on the tree branch. Chuck slowly pulled the boat over and cut the engine.

"Should we wait for Virgil?" Bill asked.

"No, jump out and grab the serum. If the guy is watching, we have got to make it look smooth," replied Bloodfoot.

Chuck agreed and jumped out of the boat and walked over to the tree. The satchel sat where it was supposed to be, and he picked it up, looked around and went back to the boat.

"Bill, pull the cover off the motor and act like you're working on it," chuck whispered.

"Great idea. This should stall some time," Bill replied, unlatching the cover.

Virgil and Randy quietly followed on either side of the rocky path, searching for a green minivan or the occupant. They searched up in the trees and in the heavy thicket, knowing he had to be out there somewhere, making sure they picked up the serum.

Randy was the first to spot the minivan, hidden off the road behind a clump of bushes.

"PSSST," he sounded off.

Virgil heard his call and ducked low. Looking over, he saw Randy pointing up ahead at the hidden minivan. They both knew the man was not inside because there was no view of the red tag from that point.

He watched as Randy pointed two fingers at his eyes, then pointed ahead at the surrounding area. They crept ahead for another fifty feet when Virgil spotted the man behind a tree, watching the zodiac through binoculars.

To get Randy's attention, Virgil thought he'd use Randy's way of calling, "PSS..."

It was cut short when Virgil interrupted with a hacking cough. Johnny quickly turned to see the two men sneaking up on him. He

315

recovered from the surprise and tried to run before two shotgun blasts stopped him in his tracks.

"Hold it right there!" Virgil shouted, aiming the shotgun at Johnny.

Before Johnny could do anything, Randy came running over and tackled him to the ground.

"You have the right to remain silent and bogity bibbidy bop," said Randy, getting up and mashing the guy's face in the dirt for support.

"What the hell?" a black-faced Johnny asked when he plucked his face out of the dirt.

"I'm a cop and I just read you your rights," Randy smiled, brushing the dirt off his clothes.

Virgil walked up with the shotgun still pointed at Johnny's head. "Holding my wife hostage was not such a good idea."

"Now, wait a minute. Just wait a minute!" Johnny pleaded on his knees with his arms waving.

"Sure, I've got a minute," replied Virgil, with the shotgun resting on Johnny's forehead.

Randy checked his watch and winked at Virgil, "It's getting late. I don't know if we have a minute."

"Holding your wife hostage was Don Henderson's idea. I have nothing to do with that. I didn't even know he was going to do it until I dropped him off at your house," Johnny pleaded.

"Who are you?" Virgil grumbled, pressing the barrel harder on his forehead.

"My name is Johnny Lee. I am one of the biochemists Don talked into creating the AlliCrocs."

Randy's eyes grew the size of golf balls as he blindsided the man with a punch to the face, knocking him back off his knees.

Taken by surprise, Virgil quickly recovered and grabbed Randy, "Easy now, we don't want to beat Johnny to death."

Randy looked like a wild man. His fists were balled up, and he wanted to hit the man again, "This man is responsible for the countless deaths of innocent people. If it weren't for him, your old deckhand Skip would still be alive!"

"We have plenty of time for revenge, but first, we have questions that need to be answered," replied Virgil, picking Johnny up off the ground.

Bill and Chuck heard the commotion and came running, "Is that our boy?" Chuck asked.

"Sure is," replied Virgil. "You two take him back to the boat. Randy and I will follow behind in a minute."

"Where's Bloodfoot?" asked Randy.

"He's standing guard in the boat. He wants to make sure AlliCroc doesn't slip by," replied Ian, walking over and grabbing Johnny by the collar.

The three men made sure Virgil and Randy were ok before whisking Johnny off to the zodiac.

Virgil and Randy lagged behind with grins on their faces.

"Good cop, bad cop, eh?" Virgil smiled, reaching into his shirt pocket for a cigarette.

"It was quick thinking. I'm surprised you caught on and went along with it."

"I used to watch Starsky and Hutch. They did it all the time," Virgil lied.

"Oh, by the way, can't you say "Pssst" without coughing up a lung?"

Virgil looked at his cigarette and replied, "Evidently not."

It was dusk, and the fading sun just dipped under the horizon as AlliCroc swam undetected through the mouth of the Chassahowitzka National Wildlife Refuge. Its hunger pangs were sidelined only by the immense pain from the gash on its back, which was now more painful than ever due to the deep penetration of the knife wounds.

It also had to adjust to the painful side effects of the recent blast that penetrated its armor-plated hide and continued through its belly.

The agitated creature swam upriver, looking for a spot to mend and recuperate without being detected.

Suddenly, it stopped swimming and sank to the bottom. Its acute senses were tingling as it picked up strange vibrations a half-mile away. The insidious hunger pangs were winning the battle to remain hidden as AlliCroc swam slowly ahead until he came to the area of the vibrations. It was slowly surfacing until its one remaining eye poked through the surface of the water, where it recognized a small boat entering the river.

"Let's go, let's go! Drop it in already," a voice shouted from the boat.

"Take it easy! I don't want my truck to slide into the damn water!" replied a second voice inside the pickup truck.

Low tide and a slippery ramp made for a risky combination that Taylor Wilson knew all too well. When she was in her pre-teens, she and her father lost the boat, trailer and vehicle when it slid down a slippery ramp at low tide.

A native of Cooper city, the twenty-seven-year-old took the four-hour drive late in the day to purchase the airboat. Her father already had a nice custom airboat back home, but she wanted to surprise him with one of her own.

A small problem with a flat tire on the trailer was the cause of the late launch, but it had to be done so she could test out what she was purchasing.

"Slow and easy, that's how you do it, slow and easy," said a third voice standing on the dock.

Scott and Ted weren't the best of friends but worked together as busboys at a local restaurant called Trapper's Grill. Ted recently purchased the airboat that looked like it had been sitting in somebodies back yard for decades, but after months of working to refurbish it, he was pleased to see it looked attractive enough to sell and double his investment.

Another co-worker, a dish washer named Freddy, also came along for no other reason than to try to get lucky with the woman interested in the airboat.

While Scott and Ted were carefully guiding the boat into the water, Freddie stood impatiently on the dock, clicking his flashlight on and off to make sure it worked.

"You guys sure you don't want to wait until tomorrow? The sun's gone down, and it's dark out here. I can barely see the other side of this smelly river.

"No, we're doing this now."

"I can take Taylor out for dinner and drinks, and we can come back here bright and early tomorrow morning," Freddy pleaded.

Taylor sat patiently in her truck, shaking her head. At this point, she reached under her seat and retrieved her small Smith & Wesson, slipping it into her back pocket just in case the little redneck on the dock tried anything.

320

"Taylor wants to get back home tonight. She's not going to stick around another day. The boat's got running lights, and we'll be done soon," replied Ted, anxiously licking his lips as the airboat dipped into the water.

"She can stay with me tonight. I'm getting eaten alive by mosquitos, and it's going to be blacker than black out here," he continued, drawing the light to the other side of the river and into the marsh, back and forth in a frenzy.

Taylor rolled her eyes and looked at the two guys in the boat from her rearview mirror. *Not a chance, lover boy*, she thought.

Freddy was striking out faster than a blind man playing baseball. He shrugged his shoulders when it was evident the lady had no interest in staying another day and continued playing with the flashlight.

 He turned the light to the left, the beam of light caressing the brackish water. When he ran the beam to the right, he was startled to see a large, glowing eye staring back at him less than thirty yards away. His arm jerked away for a split second, and when he tried to locate the devilish eye again, it was gone.

"Hey guys! Let's get out of here and come back tomorrow when it's light!" he pleaded dreadfully.

Ted turned and gave a nasty glare as the airboat slid off the trailer and into the water, "Are you nuts? We're going now," he replied, shaking his head as he tied the line to a cleat on the dock.

"I don't think it's a good idea. I just saw a big eye staring at me from over there," said Freddie, walking slowly backward and away from the dock, his flashlight scanning the surface.

"Really? One eye, like a one-eyed monster?" Replied Scott, snickering.

"I'm not joking. I saw one eye and the silhouette of a gigantic gator head."

"Let's get this over with so we can get out of here," Taylor shouted as she pulled the green chevy pickup truck and trailer out of the ramp and headed off to the nearest parking space.

"Freddie, we're going to let her test this boat out. We're just going upriver about a mile and coming back. Stay on the dock and wait for us," Scott said as he leaned over the bow and untied the line.

"Look, daylight is gone, and I saw giant eyes staring at us. No joke, there's something big out there."

"Eyes? I thought you saw one eye?" Taylor laughed as she walked down the dock.

"Look, guys, I'm not kidding. There's a gator or something in the water about the size of a dinosaur!" Freddie retorted, losing his patience.

"Look, Freddie, why don't you stay here with me and wait for them? There are only two seats on the airboat anyway. They're just going to cruise upriver about a mile and come back. Ted wants to make sure Taylor is satisfied with the way it runs before she buys it," Mike said, putting his hand on Freddie's shoulder.

"If I go, Taylor will have to sit on my lap," Freddy smiled.

"Get lost, loser," said Taylor, finally having enough of him.

Freddie felt heartbroken and turned off the flashlight and crossed his arms, "Fine, I'll wait here and I'm keeping the flashlight with me," he said, kicking a coconut into the water.

Taylor pushed the airboat off the dock and jumped in, "If we get attacked by a monster gator, I'm going to kick your ass," she informed Ted.

"Oh, ok. *Idle threat,*" Ted replied under his breath.

The airboat cranked up like a well-tuned spectacle and slowly backed away from the dock when it suddenly thumped into something under water. Ted cut the motor as the airboat shuddered, and the two occupants nearly fell out of their seats.

"What the hell was that? Freddie, shine the light in the water behind the airboat!" a panicked Ted shouted.

Freddie wasted no time and already had the light shining behind the boat. Silt from the bottom floated up with some bubbles before dispersing back down.

"I think I just backed over a boulder or something," said Ted, as he gestured for Taylor to put her two-way radio headphones back on and cranked the motor back to life.

The hair on the back of Scott's neck stood straight up as he crouched down on the dock and replied, "Yeah, or something. What if something hit the boat?"

In the shroud of darkness, AlliCroc sat at the bottom of the river after unsuccessfully creeping up to lightly nudge the airboat, testing the density of the vessel until it suddenly backed over and struck its quivering jaws. It could have easily attacked and savagely eaten its prey but took great pleasure in detecting the escalating fear, ensuring a tastier meal.

Freddie and Scott watched as the two gathered their nerves and cruised upriver. He watched as it sped up on a slow plane and disappeared around a bend. The sound of the new 6.2L Gen V Airpac engine thundered stridently as it echoed through the marshland.

Turning the flashlight back to the water, Freddie searched for the glowing eye and luckily didn't find it. He decided to wait in Taylor's truck for the airboat to return but cursed his luck when he found the truck was locked.

Looking around, he suddenly realized the fact that he and Scott were all alone in the middle of the wildlife refuge. As that sank in, he became aware of all the sounds around him.

Frogs were croaking, crickets were making their irritating screeching sound, and he swore he heard a wild boar snorting nearby.

A half-hour went by, and the airboat was nowhere in sight. He decided to walk vigilantly to the end of the dock where Scott was resting his head against a dock post and flashed the light upriver to see if the boat was in view, hopefully not broken down.

The night air was hot and muggy, and the dock was already feeling moist as he strolled to the end. Leaning on a dock post, listening for the whining sound of the propeller, he became painfully aware of how quiet it had suddenly gotten.

Crickets sounded off sporadically, but the croaking of frogs had stopped completely. His heart skipped a beat when he turned toward the small parking lot and thought he saw a large mass out of the corner of his eye.

His fears were confirmed as he quickly showed the flashlight down on the boat ramp, illuminating the biggest reptile he'd ever seen.

His knees buckled as he watched the enormous head slowly turn and direct its attention toward him. A huge glowing, green eye stared at him with a hypnotic look, the look of pure evil, intentionally instilling fear in its prey. The reason the monster was missing the other eye was because there was a gaping hole where the socket used to be.

Freddie could barely muster a sound to wake up Mike, and they both stood in awe, too frightened to move.

Scott grabbed the flashlight and aimed it down the length of the hideous beast, only to find the back legs and tail were still deep under water.

Quickly scanning the light back up to the head at the top of the ramp, he figured the creature was well over thirty-five feet long.

Paralyzed with fear, their legs refused to move as they watched the menacing reptile crawl ever so slowly out of the water, without a sound or ripple of trickling water behind, its eyes never leaving its prey. The disturbing thought they couldn't get out of their minds was the fact of how it seemed to take exceptional liking to the distress it instilled.

Pressure building in the back of his head and on the brink of a heart attack, Freddie suddenly heard the airboat returning and tried to scream for help, but nothing came out.

Scott watched in horror as the reptile gave a low, disturbing hiss and stood up, clearly agitated by the intruders. They watched as it opened its jaws unbearably wide, snapped them shut with a loud, muffled sound, and slid back into the river.

AlliCroc was incensed by the airboat's return, particularly when the scent of fear was literally pouring off its prey, and the timing was perfect for the attack.

Blinded by pure rage, the agitated creature swam at full speed toward the incoming vessel. Its intention was to quickly obliterate the airboat and shred the occupants for the attempt to come between its prey at the dock.

"Hey Ted, what the hell is that?" Taylor asked, pointing to the large wake heading in their direction.

The half-moon was not fully out yet, but it cast enough light on the river to see the parting water.

Ted took a deep breath and swallowed, "Looks like somebody fired off a torpedo."

"With a tail!" Taylor cried out, pointing, clearly eyeing the back-and-forth movement of an unbelievably huge tail.

"Hang on!"

Ted suddenly turned the airboat to the right when it looked like a collision was eminent, hoping the torpedo object would miss and pass on their port side. They held on for dear life and braced for impact when the wake weakened, then disappeared.

"Jeeezzz! What the hell was that!" Ted shouted from the top of his lungs.

"It's that big-ass gator that Freddie saw!"

"That's no gator! I've never seen anything like it! It's huge!"

"Let's get the hell out of here!"

"I'm going as fast as I can!"

Ted steered the airboat as fast as he could through the darkness while Taylor faced the stern, futilely watching the pitch-black water behind them, hoping not to find something giving chase.

Freddie and Scott heard the airboat speeding down river and slowly crept to the end of the dock and turned the flashlight on and off, signaling S.O.S.

Ted and Taylor saw the flashing light at the dock but were too terrified to realize their friend was signaling for help. Within minutes, they reduced speed and recklessly rammed the dock while Taylor jumped out, nervously securing a line around a cleat.

"That was the scariest landing I've ever seen," Freddie screeched as his heart rate pulsed through his neck.

Ignoring the remark, Ted took a deep breath and tried to put the incident in perspective. Sure, it was a large gator, but then again, it was dark, and it was probably chasing something. What with the darkness and spooked by what they hit when they launched the boat, their imaginations must have just gone wild, he assured himself.

Taylor grabbed her keys out of her pocket and looked at Ted, "Ok, I'm going to back the truck down the ramp as far as I can, and you can drive the airboat straight up on the trailer."

"It won't work. It's still low tide," he retorted, trying to sound poised.

"If the truck starts to slip, gun the throttle, and the airboat engine should be able to help the truck up the ramp, Taylor replied, not wanting to hang around for the tide to rise."

"Why don't we leave it and come back tomorrow?" asked Freddie, relieved they were finally leaving. If that monster comes back, we're dead!"

"What the hell are you talking about?" said Ted.

"Don't give me that crap! I watched you guys swerve out of the way when that thing was coming straight at you!" Freddy replied hysterically.

"Yeah, yeah. We saw your alligator, and it's a big one," replied Taylor, wasting no time as she trotted toward her truck.

"We swerved out of the way so we wouldn't hit the damn thing," Ted replied feebly.

"I saw it slither up the ramp. It's a big one," said Scott, untying the line and pushing the boat off the dock.

"Damn thing had a wake like a submarine," Ted continued, steering the boat to the middle of the river and lining it up with the oncoming trailer.

Freddie became quiet and physically turned pale as he quickly stepped away from the dock, "Why don't we just secure the boat and come back tomorrow to pick it up?"

"Don't be a wimp. This'll just take a minute," Scott replied, nervously looking upriver.

The truck backed down the ramp as far as it could go without slipping, as the tide was now at its lowest point. Ted put the boat in gear and prepared to meet the trailer when a loud thud stopped the boat in its tracks.

"Damnit! I can't see out here! Freddie, flash your light in front of the boat. I think I hit bottom again."

Freddie fumbled with the flashlight and dropped it before scooping it up and shining the light in front of the boat, "Oh no..." he said in a low tone, his heart sinking.

Ted drifted a few feet and saw the gigantic head and menacing green eye glaring up at him. Fighting the urge to cry out in horror, he threw the throttle forward and tried to swerve around the predator and make it back to the dock.

This time, the reptile slammed the airboat broadside and clammed down on the aluminum hull, crushing it like a candy wrapper.

Taylor screamed at the top of her lungs as she watched through the rearview mirror of the truck. She quickly pulled the trailer away from the ramp, got out of the truck, and ran to the dock, "Ted! Floor the throttle and steer it straight up the ramp!"

AlliCroc was quivering from the fear it sensed from the prey in the airboat. It could have easily sunk the boat and eaten the quarry, but as proven time and time again, the longer it instilled fear, the better the prey would taste.

Scott and Freddie watched helplessly from the dock at the way the reptile seemed to taunt Ted. Finally, it opened its vast jaws and clamped down on another section of the airboat, driving it to a crumbling wreck on the embankment of the other side of the river.

"Run, Ted! Get out of the water and run like hell!" Freddie screamed out as they watched Ted jump out and scramble through the undergrowth.

Like a horrific nightmare, they stood dumbfounded as the creature scurried up the bank and gave chase. The immense size of the reptile was beyond belief.

Too scared to move, they stood silently on the dock, listening to their friend's screams as he tried to get away. Suddenly, everything went silent, the screams, the rustling thicket, everything.

"We've got to get outta here," Freddie squeaked out, wrestling the vomit in his throat.

"We can't leave Ted," Scott cried.

"We'll wait a while to see if Ted made it. If we see any sign of that monster coming this way, we'll jump in the truck and get out of here," Taylor said, surprised she was able to speak.

"Why don't you give me the keys, and I will get help while you wait here," Freddie sobbed.

Scott took in a deep, thin, wavering breath, "Let's give him a couple minutes. If we don't hear anything, we'll do what Taylor said and jump in the truck and get the hell out of here."

They waited for a half-hour. They listened for their friend while watching every ripple in the water, making sure the monster wouldn't creep up on them. Taylor sat in her truck with the keys in the ignition and doors open, trying to get a signal on her cellphone.

After not hearing anything from the other side of the river, Freddie and Scott looked at each other and nodded. Too overwhelmed to speak, they headed for the truck. Freddie focused the flashlight on the truck as they walked. The numbness in their legs made them feel like lead weights.

As he waited for Scott to get in and sit in the middle, Freddie turned and flashed the light to the other side of the bank one last time, just in case Ted would be standing there waving for them to wait. No luck. He traced the light across the water and back on the boat ramp, "Noooo!" he screamed.

Startled, Taylor fumbled with the key and snapped it in half. "I broke the key! I can't believe I broke the key!"

The repulsive creature crawled up the ramp, opening its gigantic jaws and revealing blood-soaked teeth. When spotted by its prey, AlliCroc let out a deep, guttural hiss and picked up the pace toward them.

"Get in!" screamed Freddie, paralyzed with fear and unable to move the flashlight away from the monster.

Scott jumped in the truck and instinctively slammed the door behind him, leaving Freddie outside.

"Scott!! Open the door! Freddie shrieked."

332

To their dismay, Scott slammed the door and locked it before he knew what happened. They sat speechless, staring at Freddie's twisted face outside the truck a second before they were slammed by what felt like the impact of a freight train.

Dazed, they quickly recovered and heard a gut-wrenching scream, followed by what sounded like bones crunching.

Peering through the cracked window, they heaved the contents in their stomachs at the sight of what was left of Freddie being torn apart and swallowed by the creature.

Taylor closed her eyes and shook off the urge to give up, "Scott! Scott, listen to me! Snap out of it!" she shouted, turning her head to keep from seeing the gruesome seen outside. "Reach in the glove box and hand me the pliers!"

Scott was almost in a state of shock, but to his best ability, he opened the glove box and retrieved the pliers. He passed them to Taylor with his mouth open and a wary look but was unable to speak.

"There's a little piece of the key sticking out of the ignition. I'm going to try to grab it with these pliers and crank the motor!" she shouted to deaf ears as Scott was in a daze and turned back to watch the carnage.

On the fourth try to squeeze the key and turn the ignition, the roar of the engine came to life.

All at once, the gigantic head of the reptile smashed through the passenger door window, missing Scott by inches as he saw it coming and leaned forward until his head touched his knees.

Taylor screamed as the snout was only inches away from her shoulder. The reptile was stuck and couldn't go any farther. Agitated, it shook its head from side to side, snapping its jaws.

She screamed out for Scott to make sure he was alive when she saw he was compressed under the monster.

His back felt like it was about to break, but Scott managed to stick his arm out and grab Taylor's leg.

Taylor cautiously reached for the gearbox and put the truck in drive, enabling the vehicle to move forward a few feet before the reptile pressed more weight against the side and crushed the engine compartment with a powerful swipe of the tail.

All hopes for escaping had failed. Instead of giving up, Taylor got mad and stared the creature in the eye. It made her sick to see the hideous eye glaring down on her, its nostrils flaring, sniffing the alluring smell of fear.

Suddenly, as if provoked by an unseen nemesis, AlliCroc dragged its head out of the cab and slammed the truck again with its massive tail, causing the truck to roll over on its side.

Scott could hardly catch his breath as he was flung to the upright position when another hit from the tail sent the truck upside down. His head was bleeding and dazed from slamming the back of his head against the rear window. He found it odd that the only thing that came to mind was how happy he was that he wasn't wearing a seatbelt. Now, all he had to do was jump out and hide behind the trees, he thought.

"Snap out of it! You're dazed and probably have a concussion!" Taylor screeched when she saw Scott smiling into space and blood dripping from his nose and ears.

He absentmindedly rolled over and got to his hands and knees, then gauchely crawled out of the truck and stood up. Trying to focus through blurry eyes, he suddenly realized he was standing beside the truck. Quickly turning to see where the creature was, he found himself staring down the throat of the menacing creature.

Scott didn't have time to scream as AlliCroc's jaws clamped shut, ravaging its prey in a single gulp.

Taylor saw there was no hope for Scott. The minute he smiled and crawled out into the open, she planned her escape. Her only chance was to run and run fast.

She waited patiently for the attack. Part of her wanted to call out to Scott and try to get him back in the truck, but she knew he'd never make it in time since the reptile was just feet away.

The attack came quickly, and she fought the urge to scream when she rolled out on the driver's side and took off running into the dense woods. She thought for sure the reptile wouldn't leave a meal to chase another and luckily, she was right.

Fifteen minutes of running like an Olympic gold medalist, she came out on a paved road and collapsed. Out of breath and completely soaked from sweat, she sat up and listened carefully to make sure the monster didn't give chase.

It was only then that she realized she was soaked with blood. For a second, she thought the creature may have attacked her. But she quickly realized that she was cut from the branches and sticks while running through the woods blindly in the dark.

18

It was nearly midnight, and the crew was sitting in the galley sipping brandy with their coffee, contemplating their next move. Johnny Lee was also sitting in the galley after he proved to be less of a threat than expected.

Once he was cogently brought aboard the *Endurance* and surprisingly cooperated by making the call to Don, saying the serum had been successfully picked up, Virgil felt there was no need to hold him prisoner. He just wasn't free to go. The entire crew agreed and concluded that the biochemist was enticed by Don into believing they would make millions of dollars exhibiting the monster.

The conversation inevitably fell on the subject of what they were going to do when they found the reptile. Randy was thorough while drilling Johnny on the state of mind Don was in, and the crew determined Don was an unstable fanatic, willing to do anything to keep AlliCroc alive.

"Jeannes in trouble. Don will kill her if he knows we killed his reptile," Virgil stated.

"You really think he would go that far? I mean, you grew up with the guy and were best friends since you were teenagers?" Chuck asked.

"Let's not forget a couple years ago when we hunted the other reptile; the deranged sociopath hired a hitman to kill us," Randy interjected.

"It's a five-hour drive. I'm going down there and rescue my wife," Virgil decided. "Don't worry, Randy, I will try not to kill Don," he added, seeing the concerned look on the officer's face.

"That won't work. By now, Don will have the perimeter wired. If he sees the police or anybody trying to sneak inside the house, he will kill her," Johnny said.

"I can't believe it," Bill added, shaking his head.

Johnny swallowed hard and looked at Virgil, "I truly believe the man is insane. I'm sure he would have killed me if I refused to go along with his plan. Believe me, he's not the same man you once knew."

Bloodfoot heard enough. He stood up and walked over to Johnny, placing a foot on his chair.

"I say we continue the hunt as planned. When we kill the reptile, we'll send Johnny back to tell Don the mission was a success, and Don can let your wife go and come up here and collect his AlliCroc. That's when we can catch him."

"There are a couple of elite officers I had already contacted," Randy confessed. "These guys are friends of mine and are watching the house as we speak. If Don attempts to do harm to Jeanne, he'll be dead before he hits the floor."

Virgil gave him a scornful look, "When the hell were you planning on telling me?"

"I just now received the text. I had to wait until they assured me that they were in position."

Virgil stared at Randy for a long minute before replying, "Thanks. Coming from you, I believe they're the best."

Randy returned a positive nod with his head, then asked, "Do you think we can blow that damn monster up with a case of dynamite?"

Bloodfoot looked at him with wonder, "Well, officer. I suppose we could figure something out...you know if we had a case of dynamite."

"I saw a case at the Ranger Station."

"I'm pretty sure they won't just hand it over in a gesture of good will," Ian replied, packing a dip between his cheek and gum.

"I don't even think dynamite can penetrate that armor-plated hide," Bill added, holding his bald head in his hands.

"No, but if we could get that thing to eat it, it just might blow its damn head off," replied Randy, pouring another shot of apricot brandy into his coffee.

339

"Any of you fellas ever fool around with dynamite?" asked Bloodfoot.

"I did. Years ago, when I was in the army," Virgil replied, taking a deep breath. "One thing I do remember is that the mixture of nitroglycerin can be pretty unstable in damp areas."

"So, what does that mean?" asked Ian.

"It means we'll have to watch our ass out here," Virgil snapped, figuring he wouldn't have to explain the dangers of being near the water fighting a monster with dynamite.

"So, we'll have to blow that reptile up on dry land," Chuck added.

"Ok, wait a minute. Let's not get ahead of ourselves," said Bloodfoot. "Let's get our hands on the dynamite before we figure out where to blow the reptile up at."

Christie made another pot of coffee as they sipped brandy and figured out how to get their hands on the dynamite. They finally reached the conclusion that they couldn't just waltz into the ranger station and politely ask for the explosives, so they planned to steal it.

"Ok, let's get the small black fourteen-foot zodiac ready for a midnight ride. Randy, Ian, and Christie, we're going to have you get ready to go steal some dynamite," Virgil said, swallowing the last of his brandy and heading out the hatch.

"I had no idea we had another Zodiac aboard," Ian whispered to Bill.

"It doesn't have a rigid bottom. We keep it folded up in a bag in the storage room. The air tank is hanging on the wall above it. It's no secret; we just rarely use it," Chuck winked.

"Uh, with all due respect, Cap, I think I should go in Christie's place," Bill announced.

"Not this time. We might need someone small to slip through a window. This is the perfect little jaunt for her to earn her keep," Virgil replied.

A half-hour later, the crew was ready. Chuck had the fourteen-foot Zodiac tied to the side of the salvage tug, and Bill was just finishing up attaching the motor and gas tank.

Christie, Ian, and Randy looked comical as they made their way to the small inflatable dressed in black, with Christie's black makeup smeared on their face.

"We'll be back in an hour," Randy whispered as he crawled into the Zodiac.

"Good luck, guys," Chuck whispered back, giving Christie a hand over the gunwale.

Ian started the motor and whispered, "Back soon," and put the boat in gear and sped off into the night.

As they watched the Zodiac disappear toward shore, Bloodfoot leaned into Virgil and smiled, "Why were they whispering?"

"It's got to be the black clothes, black face, special ops mode. You play the part you dress for. It's just like you, see," he pointed at Bloodfoot's attire. "You dress like a pirate and say aarrgh!" chuckled Virgil, walking up the stairs leading to the wheelhouse.

The Zodiac glided smoothly across the calm Gulf waters. The half-moon reflected across the water, and the stars were strikingly bright. Christie sat on the inflated gunwale with a slight smile, happy to be included in the task ahead. If not for their unnerving mission, it would be a lovers' dream to be out there, she mused.

The boat entered the inlet and cruised upriver. It slowed to hide the wake, in case anybody was on land, as Ian carefully crept up to the Ranger Station.

The place was lit up like a carnival in the middle of nowhere. When he got close enough, Ian cut the engine and skillfully guided the Zodiac toward the dock.

Four ranger boats were tied side by side to the dock, and one had the motor pulled up, exposing the stainless-steel propeller. Ian plowed into it with the inflatable.

"What the hell, Ian!? You trying to sink us?" Randy whispered loudly.

"Currents ripping. It's hard to be spot on with the motor turned off," replied Ian, spitting a wad of Copenhagen over the side.

Lucky for them, between the frogs croaking and crickets screeching like nature's symphony, nobody would have heard the bump if they were there.

Christie slithered off the inflatable and onto the dock like a ninja, tying off the bow line as Randy rolled off and tied the stern. Looking around, Ian waved them on, and they slowly crept up to the building. Randy had his back against the wall and slowly peeked into the window, only to find the blinds down.

"Blinds down, can't see inside," he whispered.

They listened for a minute or two to make sure nobody was inside before Randy smashed through the front door window with a fist-sized rock. Reaching in and unlocking the door, he stepped inside with the others closely following behind.

"Whew, nobody home," said Randy, making his way to the back corner of the room where he first saw the dynamite.

"It's not here."

Christie looked around and replied, "Maybe they stored it in the office over there in the back."

"Great, have you got a hair pin to open the lock?"

"We don't use hair pins like that anymore, Officer," Christie responded with a smile. "When was the last time you were with a woman who had a bobby pin?"

"Just turn the knob, it may be unlocked," said Ian.

Randy and Christie turned and looked at him as if he were an idiot.

"Who in their right mind…" he turned the doorknob, and it opened… "would leave a room with dynamite unlocked?"

"A back-woods, country hick, park ranger," Christie replied with a southern twang.

It took a minute or two, but they finally located the case of dynamite in a corner, covered with a decorative blanket and a glass lamp with seashells on top.

"How original," Randy sighed, removing the lamp and blanket.

Ian scooped the case up, hoisted it on his shoulder, and hustled out of the room while Randy and Christie replaced it with a smaller box they found in a closet, covered it with the blanket, and set the lamp on top.

"It's quite a bit smaller than the case of dynamite. Think they'll notice?" asked Christie.

"Nope."

Minutes later, the three amateur thieves were back in the boat and headed back to the *Endurance*.

"Here they come!" Bill announced, peering through binoculars and barely making out the frothy splashes splitting the water from the Zodiac.

"I hope they were successful," replied Bloodfoot, looking over to the captain with a concerned look.

Virgil was smoking a cigarette and lost in thought, considering the risky situation with the dynamite.

Nobody onboard had used it before, but him and that was in the army when he was only eighteen years old. One thing that kept coming back to him was the day they accidentally blew up a donkey while transporting the explosives. He was walking a quarter mile from the blast and remembered how the sergeant preached about the instability of dynamite.

"What's on your mind, Virgil?" asked Bloodfoot.

Virgil inhaled the last of his cigarette and flicked it out the window, "I'm thinking about the dynamite."

"It is one thing I have never used, and it's because of the same concerns that you have."

"Nitroglycerine is nothing to take lightly," Virgil added.

"It's your call. I will understand whatever decision you make. But one thing we know is that hand grenades and shotguns don't work. We've had some success with the big rifles. I think that if we can make that reptile eat dynamite, we'd blow its head clean off," Bloodfoot stated.

"I concur. Here's what we're going to do. The case of dynamite stays in the Zodiac. I don't want to accidentally blow up the *Endurance*. When they arrive, we will carefully inspect each stick," Virgil replied.

Bloodfoot and Bill nodded and prepared to meet the Zodiac.

19

It was four a.m. when Ian rolled out of his bunk and checked his watch. He glanced over and noticed Bloodfoot was gone as he quickly threw a t-shirt and jean shorts on and took a quick inventory of his cigar collection. One of Bloodfoot's favorites was missing.

The rest of the crew and Johnny were in the galley drinking coffee when Ian stepped in and poured a cup, "Good morning, all. Is Dr. Lee coming along for the ride or are we going to use him for bait?"

"Dr. Johnny Lee is coming with us. He might be of some help since he created AlliCroc," Bloodfoot responded, looking up at Ian, studying his face to see if he was miffed about the missing cigar.

Ian didn't bother responding as he helped Virgil load a backpack with the explosives. He carefully checked the dynamite and secured the five sets of four sticks taped together in separate pouches.

The plan was to load up the Zodiac before getting a few hours of sleep, then to get up early and cruise slowly upriver to hunt the reptile. They figured that four sticks of dynamite taped together would be enough to destroy AlliCroc, and they had five chances to accomplish the task.

The pickup truck turned into the long and winding gravel road that led to the secluded boat ramp. The sleepy driver was glad he got an early start and beat the locals to the ramp. In fact, he was the first one there.

Looking at the early morning light reflecting off the calm water made him smile until he turned his head toward the empty parking lot and saw the mangled truck lying upside down.

He stopped his truck and scanned the area, wondering what kind of people would fool around and drive so recklessly to flip their truck.

Looking around to see if anybody was lying hurt, he cautiously stepped out of his truck and walked toward the mangled vehicle. He thought it suspicious how there were no skid marks or anything unusual on the rocky lot. When he was closer to the overturned vehicle, he abruptly stopped short when he spotted a large pool of blood surrounding the accident.

Feeling nauseous at the sight of all the blood, he took a couple of steps back and fell to a knee. With his heart pumping so hard he could feel it in his ears, he tried to take a few deep breathes and stood, fishing in his front pocket for his cell phone. No signal.

He slipped the phone back into his pant pocket while jogging back to his truck, reached for his radio, and turned to 39.46 MHz to contact the local police.

"Break emergency! Break emergency, come back!"

It took four times of repeating the same message before the radio cracked back.

"I read you loud and clear. What's your emergency? Over."

"I'm at the Chassahowitzka National Wildlife Refuge boat ramp. There's an overturned vehicle in the parking lot with blood all over it!"

"Is anybody hurt?"

"I don't see anybody, but there's blood all over the place!" he replied, fighting to control his voice.

"My name is Doug Robbins; I am a park ranger. I'm approximately a mile from your location and en route. Please stay on the radio until I arrive."

"Will do," he replied, trying to relax in the front seat.

A rustle in the thicket shook him as he leaned out of his truck and searched the wooded area, hoping to find somebody in need of help. "Who's there?" he called out.

The bushes stopped moving as he came to realize that whatever was in there was large. He slowly stood erect and took a few steps toward the bushes, and they began to move again.

Whatever was in there was moving away. All at once, he felt the ground vibrate as the unknown entity took off, running in the opposite direction.

He shuttered when he caught a glimpse of the tail and muscular hind legs of what looked like a dinosaur running between gaps in the undergrowth.

Standing in disbelief, his hair stood up in the back of his neck as he realized he was all alone out there. He took another quick glance at the surroundings before jumping back into his truck and rolling up his windows.

After sitting behind the wheel and gathering his wits for a few minutes, two park ranger vehicles, a Sheriff's deputy car, and paramedics showed up and stopped near the crumbled vehicle.

The deputies and park rangers got out slowly and looked at the damaged truck as the paramedics searched in the cab, shaking their heads as they backtracked to the police car.

They stood huddled by the car, trying to figure out what had taken place, when one of the deputies noticed the disorientated man step from his truck and walk toward them.

"Hello, Sir. Are you the person who called in the emergency?"

He shook his head and stopped when he reached the group of responders. "Yes, sir, my name is Dan."

While Dan was telling the responders everything he knew, a small Zodiac pulled up to the dock with six men and what looked to be a pirate. They turned off the motor and focused their attention on the crumbled truck as Ian and Bill secured the boat to cleats on the dock.

"Hide the guns," Virgil said as he stepped onto the dock.

The six men walked toward the responders as they broke their conversation and watched them approach.

"Well, well, look what the cat dragged in," a deputy said, the same man who was denied permission to board the *Endurance*.

"That would have to be a pretty big cat," Virgil responded, stopping next to the police car. "Did you tell these good officers about AlliCroc?"

"Your so-called reptile did not do this damage," retorted the deputy, with hands on his hips and a not-so-welcoming stare.

Virgil shook his head and walked closer to the truck, "I disagree."

"What do you men know about what happened here?" the park ranger asked in a commanding tone.

Virgil ignored the question as he continued examining the vehicle and pointed his thumb toward Bloodfoot.

"I was hired by your mayor to come here and kill a thirty-eight-foot reptile. The reason you fellas don't know the details is because your mayor also thinks it's just a big gator and wants this taken care of quietly," Bloodfoot rumbled in his deep baritone voice.

351

The ranger raised his eyebrows and looked at his associates before replying, "Sounds like a relative of that huge man-eater in Africa...what's its name? Gustave, I believe," he smirked. "Although I know it is much smaller than thirty-eight-feet."

"Gustave was a pussy. This reptile is at least eighteen feet bigger and one hundred percent more aggressive," grumbled Bloodfoot.

Suppressing the urge to laugh, the ranger continued, "Was?"

"I killed it in 019."

Dead silence filled the air as the two stared each other down. Finally, the deputy cut in, "The alligator you guys are looking for is quite a few miles north of here, wouldn't you say? They're not known to attack an area and then swim for miles and attack another area. Believe me, your alligator did not attack a pickup truck. I see this all the time; these locals get drunk out here late at night and drive around like lunatics. Sometimes, they roll over, and people get hurt. By the looks of all that blood," he said, pointing, "Somebody got hurt pretty bad. When I wrap up this scene, I'm going to check the hospital and find them."

Before Bloodfoot could explain why they believed it traveled into the preserve, the ground shook like a small tremor, and AlliCroc broke through the dense thicket and charged toward the men.

"Take cover!" Bloodfoot shouted.

They scrambled for cover as the massive reptile ran faster than expected. Virgil and Chuck ran for the Zodiac while Bloodfoot grabbed the two paramedics and jumped into the back of the rescue vehicle. While the park rangers scrambled into their vehicles, the two deputies retrieved shotguns from their vehicles and crouched in a combat stance, firing relentlessly at the approaching monster.

Bloodfoot looked out of the window and caught a glimpse of the reptile as it tore through the flesh of a deputy. The blood-curdling scream was enough to paralyze the remaining deputy to make him collapse in the fetal position.

Bloodfoot was swift but not fast enough when he opened the rear door and jumped out to help. "Get up! Let's go, get in here!" he shouted.

The deputy did not respond, so Bloodfoot ran over and grabbed his arms, dragging him toward the vehicle. AlliCroc responded by stepping on the deputy's legs, crushing the bones like matchsticks, and then biting him in half from the waist down.

Still grasping the man's arms, Bloodfoot fell back and hit his head on the rescue vehicle, where the paramedics bravely reached out and dragged the husky pirate into the vehicle.

When he was able, Bloodfoot sat up and looked out of the window to see the reptile staring back at him, the lifeless remains of the deputy dangling from its closed jaws.

Bloodfoot's face became dark and menacing when his eyes connected with the creature, staring through the dark green eyes of the pure evil reptile, provoking him.

He quickly snapped out of it when a paramedic cried out, "What are we going to do?!"

Bloodfoot responded by sticking out his hand to silence the man and continued looking out the window. He saw the park rangers huddled in their pickups, peering over the dashboard. Searching the area for his five friends, he was surprised to see four of them crouched down on the dock near the small boat. Chuck, Randy, and Ian, with the .905 caliber rifles, trained on the reptile while Virgil held four sticks of dynamite taped together and a lit camel cigarette between his lips. His heart sank a bit when he didn't see Bill, but he finally spotted his bald head behind some bulwarks.

He focused his attention on Johnny, who slowly walked from behind the mangled truck, blowing a high-pitched whistle. AlliCroc heard the sound and backed off, staring and hissing at the biochemist as he slowly walked forward with outstretched arms. When he was within ten feet of the monster, AlliCroc turned and walked back into the thicket.

After twenty minutes of silence, Bloodfoot cautiously stepped out of the vehicle as Virgil and Chuck slowly walked toward him. Ian and Randy stayed in place, aiming the rifles in the reptile's direction. Bill could be heard running down the dock and retrieving a shotgun from the Zodiac.

"I was wondering why you guys ran for that tiny little boat," Bloodfoot grinned when he saw the weapons.

"Had to get the dynamite," Virgil replied with a somber tone. "I see the two deputies didn't make it."

"I shouted for them to take cover, but they just didn't know what they were up against," replied Bloodfoot.

"What's with the whistle?" Randy asked Johnny.

"We used this whistle to train the AlliCrocs."

"It seemed to work," replied Chuck. "How many have you got?"

"Just this one. It worked for a while until two AlliCrocs learned to disregard the sound and go about their business. I took a risk, hoping this is the one that still responded to it," he said nervously.

"Why are you shaking like that?" Ian asked.

"I had no idea how big that reptile is. It must be killed."

"That's the plan, Johnny," Virgil replied, lighting a cigarette.

"Where did you men get that dynamite?" asked one of the paramedics.

"It's better that you didn't know," replied Randy, blocking the view of the paramedic as he stared at Virgil's hand clutching the four sticks of dynamite taped together.

The lead park ranger called them over, as there was no way he was coming out of the truck. "The woods are so dense here, I don't think that monster escaped. We had better take cover or get the hell out of here because it's coming back; it's got nowhere else to go unless he takes the road out or returns to the water," he said evenly, trying to stay calm and collected. "As for the dynamite, we'll talk later."

"I think you're right. If it can't escape through the woods, it will return; that's a fact. That reptile does not like to be trapped," replied Bloodfoot, keeping a lookout. "We need to block the road with these vehicles so the only way it can escape is through the boat ramp."

They stood quiet as Bill walked up and asked, "Where's the guy with the pickup and boat? One minute, I see him hunkered down in his truck, and now it's gone."

"He's gone. The minute our reptile attacked, he cranked his engine and tore off," said Bloodfoot.

"Good for him. I was hoping he wasn't another casualty," Bill replied.

"Ok, let's take this little huddle over behind that concrete building," said Virgil, pointing toward the restrooms near the dock.

"Good spot to set up," replied Bloodfoot. "I'll get these guys on board with the plan and meet you there."

"Here, take this in case you need it," Virgil said, handing the bundle of dynamite to the pirate. "You want a cigarette, or do you have a stogie?"

"Now's not the time to enjoy a good smoke," a paramedic advised.

"The dynamite has a fuse, not a push button," Virgil scolded, walking away.

Bloodfoot lit a cigar that he stole from Ian's collection earlier and made it seem like he was about to ignite the fuse, "See, here's how we do it," he grumbled.

"I know, I know!" replied the paramedic, grabbing Bloodfoot's arm."

The two park rangers, along with the paramedics, listened to the wily pirate's plan to block the entrance road with their trucks.

They agreed that lining them up side by side on the road should successfully block the reptile's route of escape.

The one problem the paramedics had was that they didn't want to be near the scene if the hideous monster returned. They opted to leave the trucks once they made the barrier and walk to a gas station a mile up the main road.

Bloodfoot changed his mind and figured that he'd ride up the gravel road with them to secure the vehicles and walk back toward the restrooms. Hopefully, the reptile would attack, and he would blow its head off with the dynamite.

357

Knowing AlliCroc was most likely watching their movements, he decided to shout out to the crew instead of wasting time running to the dock to explain his plans.

"Change of plans, Virgil! I'm hitching a ride with these guys to help set the roadblock! I'm going to walk back to where you guys are! If our monster attacks, I will blow its head off with the dynamite!"

Calling out and replying that it would be a mistake was useless, so Virgil simply responded, "Good luck!"

The crew watched from the boat dock as the trucks made a U-turn and headed away.

"Ok, let's unload the weapons and split up the dynamite," Virgil said.

"I'm using one of these rifles. Who else wants one of these one-hundred pounders?" Randy said, setting his rifle on the dock.

"I thought you said they were one hundred and ten pounds?"

"Those two are; mine weighs fifty-two pounds if you want specifics."

"What?" Bill asked, giving Randy a weird look.

"I forgot to tell you guys. Mine is the prototype. It weighs less, but the kick is a lot harder than those. Once the makers figured it was too light, they made them heavier to absorb some recoil."

"That explains why it knocked you on your ass on the salvage tug," replied Chuck with a smirk.

"And why you held your shoulder all night like a girly boy," Ian added.

"Bill and Ian, all puns aside, can you handle them?" Virgil asked.

"I can manage," replied Bill.

"Me too."

"Good. One of you set up beside the restrooms, the other set up on the other side of the dock. Find a good spot for cover. Randy, maybe you can set up over there by the overturned pickup. Chuck and I will split up this dynamite and take cover on the rooftop and that boulder sitting over there," Virgil pointed.

"Which one do I get?" Chuck asked.

"You can take the roof."

Not for lack of a good reason, Johnny looked around like a frightened dog and asked, "What should I do, Captain Virgil?"

Responding as an afterthought, Virgil glanced at the biochemist and replied, "Hide at a safe distance and use your whistle as needed."

"I'd feel a little safer if I had a shotgun."

Virgil exhaled heavily and replied, "Don't get confused with my generosity. I didn't drag you out here in handcuffs or beat you to death for holding my wife hostage, but I can't trust you with a shotgun.

"I understand. If I were in your position, my thoughts would be the same," Johnny replied, turning and walking away to find cover.

Johnny was nearing the restroom building when Virgil called his name, "Johnny! Catch!" he tossed a shotgun. "Do you know how to use it?"

Without a word, Johnny chambered a round and nodded, then disappeared into the ladies' room.

"I hope that was a wise decision," Ian stated.

"He's not the bad guy. Don Henderson is," Virgil replied, lighting a cigarette.

20

With the entrance path blocked by the vehicles, the only path the creature could escape was to exit through the boat ramp.

Bloodfoot knew the perceptive reptile was close, hiding in the thicket, watching him as he raucously dragged his feet on the gravel as he walked back toward the boat ramp. The eerie silence was only broken by the annoying sound of crickets in the near distance.

All at once, the wily pirate spotted movement out of the corner of his eye. Bushes and tree branches shook as AlliCroc emerged from the wooded area up ahead about seventy yards.

"It's making its move!" Bloodfoot shouted, making sure his cigar was well-lit as he raced towards the monster.

The rest of the crew watched silently when the reptile edged slowly out of the foliage. Randy nearly had a heart attack as the monster crept up behind him since he was next to the overturned pickup and closest to the wooded area.

Only when he heard the loud explosion from Ian's .905 caliber rifle and the alarming sound of it hitting and ricocheting off the armor-plated scutes did he run for cover on the other side of the truck.

Bill took aim but waited until Randy was out of the way before he made his shot with the same results.

Virgil stepped from behind a boulder and shouted for the reptile. The cigarette dropped out of his gaping mouth when the reptile turned and growled and advanced in his direction.

Virgil quickly recovered his cigarette and lit the dynamite fuse. He waited until AlliCroc was close enough and threw the dynamite to where it would land on the ground beneath its head.

To the bewilderment of the crew, they watched as the reptile turned and ran back into the woods, effectively avoiding the explosion.

Bill and Ian walked over towards the overturned pickup with their rifles trained on the wooded area where Virgil and Randy were standing.

"Am I seeing things, or did that monster get out of the way of the dynamite?" Ian asked.

"It sure looked like it," replied Virgil.

"Thanks for shooting that thing before it could sneak up and attack me," Randy said to Ian.

"You owe me one," Ian winked.

"Close call. Any closer you could have nailed me," Randy continued.

"Like you said, close call. If we shouted for you to get out of the way, I'm afraid you'd be in the reptile's stomach right now. Shooting it was the best decision," Ian continued.

Bloodfoot finally came walking up the path, looking ominous, "Did you guys do some damage?"

"Ian nailed it in the side from thirty yards, but the slug bounced off," Randy replied.

"And get this, we think your reptile knows how harmful dynamite can be. I threw it where it would have landed under its head, and the damn thing retreated into the woods before it exploded," said Virgil.

Bloodfoot let out a heavy sigh and replied, "This means we will have to be closer than thirty yards in order to kill it with those rifles. I'm pretty sure it's also going to have to eat the dynamite for it to be effective. By the way, where's Chuck?"

The four of them didn't answer; they just turned and pointed at Chuck, standing on the roof of the restrooms like a statue. One hand held the dynamite while the other no doubt held a lighter. It would be the perfect time for one of them to make a wisecrack, but nobody did.

"How about Johnny? Where's he hiding?"

"I never saw him come out of the restrooms," said Bill.

Finally, Bloodfoot swallowed his pride and turned to face the crew, "This reptile is much more than I expected. I want to thank all of you for risking your lives and trying to hunt with me. But like I said, it's too much. From here on out, I will hunt this beast by myself."

"You're absolutely right. That reptile is much more than we expected. But if you plan to go it alone, you're a dead man," Virgil replied flatly.

"You are the boldest men I have ever had the pleasure to meet. But you can't tell me that every single one of you is not feeling like Chuck. He's broken. He's standing up there scared out of his mind, and I can't blame him."

"You're just as scared as we are. But we know this beast. We are the only ones that are willing and able to kill it. If we leave it for somebody else, they'll die and that reptile will go on its destructive path for fifty years."

"In for a penny, in for a pound," Ian added, spitting a wad of tobacco,

"Let me make it simple," Randy chimed in. If we quit, you won't stand a chance. It's true; you are the meanest, toughest son of a bitch I have ever seen. But AlliCroc is tougher. If we don't work together, we will go back to our lives and hear about the carnage this beast will leave in its wake. Finally, they will send some brave souls to try to blow it up, like we're doing now. If that doesn't work, maybe they will finally involve the armed forces to kill it. But how many people are going to die before all that happens? We're the only people that know this thing exists."

Bloodfoot crouched down and put his fist on his chin. Finally, after several minutes of thought, he stood with a different outlook, "Ok, fellas, I had to say what I said. Let's go kill that monster."

"That-a-boy," Virgil replied, patting the burly pirate on the back.

The group sprang for action when they heard a loud crash at the entranceway where the roadblock was set up. Horns were blaring as the sound of twisted metal scraped together.

Bloodfoot ran off while lighting another cigar and holding the dynamite like a running back in a pro game.

Virgil was inches behind while Randy, Bill and Ian could only jog with the heavy rifles.

Fifty yards up the road, they slowed and saw two of the vehicles still in place. The other two were tossed to the side of the road in a heap.

"Hold up," Bloodfoot whispered. They cautiously stepped off the road and took cover next to a cypress tree.

"I don't see any movement in those vehicles," said Ian.

"I do. There's a head peaking out of the window in the back of the emergency vehicle," replied Randy, completely out of breath from running with the heavy rifle.

"Is that blood running down the rangers' door?" Virgil spotted.

"Pretty sure," Bloodfoot growled, trying to whisper.

"It's watching us, waiting for us to walk up to the vehicles," Virgil said with trepidation, lighting another cigarette for the dynamite fuse.

"Are you ok toting that rifle?" Ian asked Randy.

"I'll manage," he replied, manipulating his shoulder.

Virgil looked over and noticed a hint of dread in the pirate's tone, "You ok?"

Bloodfoot reached into his pocket and pulled out an unfinished cigar. He lit it, took a couple hard puffs and replied, "I'm good. I just dropped my cigar back there."

"Well, that's good. We don't need you freakin' out with that dynamite in your hand," Virgil replied frivolously, making a bad attempt to calm their dire situation.

Bloodfoot squinted his eyes and glared at Virgil, "You think I'm afraid?"

"No, of course not. I just thought I detected a little quiver in your tone."

Bloodfoot took another long look at Virgil and realized nobody had ever said that to him before. And for some reason, his respect for the captain just went up another notch.

"I thought those guys were going to run off after the vehicles were situated," said Bill.

"I guess they were pretty sure AlliCroc would escape through the boat ramp and decided to stick around," replied Randy.

"One of us should slowly walk up to the vehicles. I know damn well that reptile is waiting out there, and this will draw it out. When it makes its move, we will blast its head off with these rifles," Bloodfoot stated.

Virgil raised his eyebrows and looked at Bloodfoot, "So, looks like I'm the guinea pig."

"I'll go if you're afraid," Bloodfoot smiled. "If that reptile attacks, those rifles should blow it to pieces from here."

"I thought you said they'd have to be closer than thirty yards," retorted Virgil.

"Ian's moved closer; he's within striking distance. He can handle that rifle pretty good," said Randy, before crawling off closer to the vehicles.

Bill brought up the rear and found a spot within fifteen yards of the mangled vehicles. Minutes later, the men were set up and ready for battle.

Virgil took a deep breath, lit another cigarette and stepped out onto the road, walking guardedly toward the smashed vehicles.

He was within talking distance from the surviving ranger when he noticed the wide-eyed man shaking his head and pointing into the thicket. Virgil stopped and looked over to where he was pointing.

The morning sun cast a misty shadow in the dense trees. Squinting his eyes, Virgil thought he could make out the silhouette of AlliCroc: big, nasty and facing his direction. He fought the urge to run and pointed his finger at the reptile for Bloodfoot and the others to see.A split second later, AlliCroc charged straight for him.

As Virgil raced to take cover under the truck, three canon blasts were heard from behind. AlliCroc rolled on its side as blood exploded from its mid-section. The provoked reptile hissed louder than a steaming locomotive, then gave a throaty growl that shook the ground.

Astonishingly, AlliCroc rolled over and got back on its legs. The right side of its gargantuan body was bleeding as it scrambled to run back into the thicket. The .905 caliber rifles were quickly reloaded, and another three blasts hit the creature's hindquarters but seemed to ricochet off the armor plates.

"It's getting away!" the ranger screamed, opening the door.

Bloodfoot scurried to light the fuse and threw the dynamite into the rustling thicket. The loud explosion made the reptile change course. "It's headed to the boat ramp!"

"Let go! "Spread out and take aim!" Randy shouted,

Bill and Ian were the first ones at the ramp and quickly reloaded their rifles and took their places on either side of the dock. Chuck was still on the rooftop but looked entirely in control as he prepared to throw dynamite. Randy took cover behind the mangled pickup truck and took aim.

Seconds later, Virgil and Bloodfoot could be seen carefully walking down either side of the wooded area. "It's over there!" Virgil shouted, pointing toward the dense trees. "Beware, it's going to charge out and head for the boat ramp and try to escape!"

"We got it covered, Virge," Bill shouted.

"I'm going to fire the shotgun towards the undergrowth and draw it out! Virgil stated, setting the dynamite at his feet while reaching for the shogun.

"Hold on, wait until I'm in the Zodiac," Bloodfoot shouted.

"What!" Virgil replied.

"I have a plan; just wait until I get in the Zodiac, then fire at will. Hopefully, it will flush out the beast, and it will head for the safety of the river."

That said, Bloodfoot took a long look at the bushes and flora in the woods. The reptile was kept out of sight, but every time it moved, the surroundings shook. He pinpointed where it was and looked in the other direction, at the dock and where he needed to go to get to the Zodiac.

He quickly found the best passage, which was straight through the gravel parking lot, then down a grassy area to the dock.

Bloodfoot took a deep breath and burst through the gravel. The crew watched in stunned silence as the burly pirate ran at a rate of speed that seemed impossible for a man that size.

369

The silence was broken when the flora rustled, and the immense reptile gave chase.

"Run! It's chasing you!!" Virgil shouted, running behind it, ready to throw dynamite if he found the right moment.

Randy, Bill and Ian were quick to fire off their .905 caliber rifles. Ian hit the front right leg and tore a chunk of flesh out, causing the creature to stumble and bury its snout in the gravel. Bill's shot hit the hind quarters which looked like it gashed off a few armor-plated scutes. Randy fired his shot from behind the creature and blew the left hind leg completely off.

The three massive shots effectively stopped the reptile, and seconds later, Chuck blasted it with dynamite thrown from his rooftop position. The bundle hit the ground and slid up to the creature before detonating.

The blast caused AlliCroc to roll over on its back and let out a painful roar, allowing Bloodfoot to safely reach the Zodiac.

Johnny's whistle was suddenly heard coming from the restrooms. The crew watched in stunned silence as Johnny appeared in the doorway and slowly walked out toward AlliCroc.

"Get the hell out of the way!" Bloodfoot roared.

"It's ok. The whistle should calm AlliCroc, and I will be able to plant the dynamite straight down its throat. Virgil, please trust me to do this and give me the dynamite," Johnny replied, holding his hand out toward Virgil while intermittently blowing the whistle.

Virgil made a quick decision and walked over and gave him the bundle of dynamite and his cigarette to light it with, "Do it quick and run like hell," he instructed before trotting away.

Johnny continued to walk forward, blowing the whistle as he was now standing inches from the reptile's snout. When he locked eyes with AlliCroc, he felt it recognized him. As he pocketed the whistle and put a hand on its snout, "Rest easy, AlliCroc. I had no intention of making you the monster you became," he whispered.

Johnny puffed on the cigarette to get it ready to light the fuse when AlliCroc abruptly rolled and got up on its three remaining legs. Johnny stood dumbfounded as its gaping jaws engulfed him and snapped shut in the blink of an eye.

Just as quickly, three more booming shots were fired, and dynamite exploded. When the smoke cleared, AlliCroc let out a thunderous growl as it was still standing with the repulsive remains of Johnny clutched in its jaws.

Chuck watched from his rooftop view as Bloodfoot quickly untied the boat line from the dock and formed a lasso.

Before they could reload the rifles, AlliCroc let out another guttural roar and headed toward the water. Bloodfoot took full advantage of its slow movement and jumped under the dock.

"Take cover!" Virgil shouted as he tossed the last bundle of dynamite at the reptile.

The dynamite exploded on its back, causing it to quicken its pace onto the wood dock, splintering it like matchsticks. As its enormous head left the dock, Bloodfoot leaped up from under the dock, looped the line around its closed jaws and pulled it tight before the dock caved in on him.

The reptile splashed into the water and headed straight for the bottom.

"Bloodfoot!" Ian shouted as he dove in to find him.

The rest of the crew ran up and searched the water. They didn't see Ian or Bloodfoot, but to their surprise, they spotted the Zodiac cruising upriver at top speed.

"What the hell?..." Bill said.

Just then, Ian splashed the surface with Bloodfoot in his arms, "Somebody give me a hand!"

Virgil jumped in and helped Ian drag the unconscious pirate and swim to safety. By the time they reached the ramp, Chuck and Randy were waiting to drag them out of the water while Bill kept a lookout in case the reptile returned.

Once on dry land, Virgil shook Bloodfoot until he opened his eyes.

"What the hell was that all about," was the first thing out of Virgil's mouth.

Bloodfoot sat up and felt the bump on his head. Looking to see that the Zodiac was gone, he gave a slight grin and answered, "Now we have a buoy attached to our reptile."

"Well, that was risky. You almost got killed when the dock and reptile collapsed on you," replied Virgil, sitting in the grass and lighting a camel non-filtered cigarette.

"A risky plan that worked," replied Bloodfoot, taking off his sleeveless shirt and wrapping it around his head to stop the blood flow.

"The first aid kit is in the boat," Ian added.

"It's just a flesh wound. I'm alright."

"What the hell was Johnny thinking?" asked Chuck.

"He thought he cold control his monster. What worked when he raised them didn't work today because he failed to realize how smart it had become. When he had that cigarette next to the bundle of dynamite, his little monster sprang into action," Bloodfoot replied with disappointment.

They sat in silence for a moment, reflecting on the carnage, then looked upriver.

"So, what's the game plan?" asked Chuck.

They all looked up to see a ranger's vehicle skid to a stop.

"Oh my god! Did you see the size of that thing? We've got to close the area! Nobody! And I mean, nobody can be near the water!" the shaken ranger sobbed.

"No shit," Randy replied. "Now, why don't you go do what we asked you people to do since we got here? Close the area!"

The flustered park ranger nervously looked at the crew and jumped back in his truck. They looked at each other with raised eyebrows as they heard him screaming into his radio as he sped away. "Let's reload those canons and go track that monster. We'll walk along the edge of the river until we find it," said Bloodfoot.

"I know it's hurting. I blew its leg off, and I see some bloody armor plates in the gravel," Randy added.

"It won't be able to walk on land so well, but it can still swim like hell," Bloodfoot stated.

"How much dynamite do we have?" Chuck asked.

"None," replied Virgil, tossing the empty satchel.

"Well, that's just fantastic!" Chuck shouted in a shocking display of anxiety.

"Easy, big boy. Those five bundles of dynamite did a good job. I think we can finish the job with these rifles," Ian replied, trying to reassure Chuck.

"I concur," said Bloodfoot, giving Chuck a foul look.

They sat and rested for a half-hour before getting up to continue the hunt. Randy, Bill and Ian reloaded the .905 caliber rifles and checked to see how many shells they had left. There were six, and they split them evenly, placing them in their backpacks. For what it was worth, they all still carried a shotgun strapped on their shoulders.

It was high tide when they started off upriver.

21

Ranger Doug Robbins was on the radio, talking hysterical about what took place at the boat ramp as he sped to the station. In all his ten years in the park service, he had never seen a reptile so giant.

To his surprise, his supervisor cut in on the radio and ordered him to stop jabbering and get to the station pronto.

As he turned off the main highway and sped down the path, he noticed a handful of police cars and fire rescue parked at the station's parking lot.

He urgently skidded to a stop and exited the truck. Peeking through the window before entering, he was glad to see the room was full.

"We've got trouble at the boat ramp!" he bellowed as he burst through the door.

Before he could answer the many questions from his concerned colleagues, his supervisor grabbed his arm, whisked him into his offices and slammed the door.

"Do you know what kind of panic you caused with your loudmouth over the radio?"

Ranger Robbins stood there and took a moment to calm down and gather his thoughts, then looked his supervisor in the eye and returned the foul glare, "You have no idea what kind of monster is lurking in that water…do you."

"As a matter of fact, I do. See that police car sitting there?" he said, pointing a finger through the window. There's a young lady in the back seat. She's so scared she can barely talk. Her name is Taylor. She and some friends were attacked last night at the boat ramp, and she's the only survivor."

Ranger Doug Robbins made his way to the window and peeked out, "When did they pick her up?"

"They picked her up about an hour ago, walking down the road dazed and confused with cuts and bruises all over her body. She said she's been hiding from that damn gator all night."

"She's lucky to survive. That monster is huge."

The supervisor shook his head agreeing, "I know, we heard the complete details."

"What are we going to do?"

"Law enforcement has blocked off every conceivable route so nobody can get near the water. All parks are closed until further notice, and I'm told the mayor hired an experienced hunter to kill that thing."

"I met him. His name is Captain Bloodfoot."

The supervisor looked up and smirked, "Captain Bloodfoot? Sounds like a pirate."

"Meanest looking pirate you'll ever meet. This guy looks like he'd rip your arms off if you looked at him wrong," Ranger Robbins replied flatly.

"Well, you seem impressed. I hope he comes through for us," shrugged the supervisor. "Anyway, I don't want you saying anything more about this alligator on the radio. We're not the only ones listening. Every redneck hunter from miles around might hear this and get the urge to hunt the alligator too. Before you know it, it will be a circus out here, and more people will be dying."

Captain Bloodfoot and the rest of the crew walked a quarter mile up the banks of the river when they spotted the partially deflated zodiac floating half sunken under a tree branch hanging over the water.

Bloodfoot was in the lead and suddenly stopped, holding up his arm with a balled fist so the others would stop. Pointing at the derelict boat, he squatted down as the others followed his lead.

"Do you think the boat broke free, or is our monster down there?" Virgil asked as he sidled up to Bloodfoot.

Bloodfoot was fixated on the slight tension where the line was tied to the bow and replied in a whisper, "It's down there. Sitting on the bottom, probing its wounds. It's hurting, hurting badly."

Virgil's eyebrows raised as he looked at the burly man, then turned to see Chuck and Randy with the same expression.

"Ok, doctor, how'd you come to that conclusion?" Ian whispered as the rest of the crew winced.

Bloodfoot didn't flinch. He turned his attention to Ian as a father would treat his unwitting son, "I see tension on the bowline. I attached it to the reptile. The tension means it's still attached. The Zodiac probably ruptured when it hit the tree branch with considerable force, meaning the reptile was retreating quickly. If it were strong and healthy, it would have plowed through without concern, but since it stopped and sat on the bottom, I believe it's in considerable pain."

Ian sat in stunned silence. Never before had the hair stood up in the back of his neck when spoken to. The others were just grateful that the pirate didn't just turn around and punch him in the nose.

"I agree, what's the game plan?" Virgil asked.

"I think we can shoot it when it comes up."

"How can we get it to the surface? If that monster is hurting so badly, it's going to be extremely pissed off, too," said Randy.

"Randy, Bill and Ian will be ready to fire three more slugs, hopefully hitting it in the head, while you and Chuck finish it off with the shotguns. I'm going to take a swim to the Zodiac. When it knows I'm in the water, it should come up and attack," replied Bloodfoot.

"That's your plan? Sounds like suicide," said Virgil, edgily lighting another cigarette.

"That's the plan. I'm going to swim over to the other side and get out at that clearing," Bloodfoot pointed. "That gives plenty of room for the big-ass rifles to find their mark. Three of those slugs in the head should do the trick."

"It's thirty yards across, too far away for the shotguns to do any damage," Virgil interjected.

"Save it in case it swims this way."

Randy, Bill and Ian set the .905 caliber rifles on bipods and took aim at where they thought the reptile would appear. Virgil and Chuck stood ready with the shotguns while Bloodfoot took his hunting knife out of its sheath and jumped in the river. He watched as the tension on the bowline slackened the minute he began to swim.

"Be ready, fellas. AlliCroc is on the move!" he bellowed.

"Get out of the water!" Chuck shouted in reply.

Bloodfoot waited until he saw the Zodiac move away from the branch and turn in his direction before he swam with all he had to make it to the other side of the river and up the embankment.

The wounded reptile showed no signs of falter as it breached the surface and continued swimming at an imposing speed towards Bloodfoot. Only when it reached the other side and climbed out of the water, they noticed it was floundering to one side.

Bloodfoot jumped to the ground when the roar of the canons echoed from the other side.

The blast was deafening as one round hit its target, blowing out a chunk of meat from its' armor-plated body while the other two ricocheted off. AlliCroc roared as it stopped dead in its pursuit and turned to face the other side of the river. Agitated and ferociously infuriated, the insidious creature gave an ear-splitting roar and charged back into the water toward the hunters, causing its pain.

Ian and Bill remained confident and calm as they reloaded another shell while the gigantic reptile raged their way. Randy's shoulder felt broken from the rifle's recoil, and remained on the ground holding his shoulder.

Ian lined up the crosshairs between the reptiles' eyes and pulled the trigger, effectively stopping the monster in its tracks. The recoil sent the rifle behind him twenty feet and into some water behind him. A second blast from Bill's rifle exploded through what was left of the reptile's head.

Virgil and Chuck cheered wildly as they ambled over to the riflemen, who were still lying on the ground. "Nice shooting," a clearly exhausted Virgil said, lighting a cigarette and helping Randy to his feet.

"I think I pulled my shoulder out of the socket," Randy winced in pain.

"Sure looks like it," Chuck replied, reaching into his backpack and pulling out a tee-shirt for a makeshift sling.

Bill smiled as he got up and stepped over to Ian, offering his hand; he asked with a grin, "So where's your rifle?"

"Behind me…in the water, that recoil kicked my ass."

Randy finally stumbled over shaking his head, "Those guys I borrowed the rifles from are not going to be happy."

Bloodfoot took a restful swim across the river and praised his friends as the sound of a loud helicopter came into view and hovered overhead before moving to a clearing where it landed.

Minutes later, a group of paramedics and a deputy walked over and joined the men as they surrounded the massive reptile and gawked at the size.

Bloodfoot took out his bowie knife and removed a tooth from the creature when Ian produced his own large hunting knife and walked past him.

"What the hell are you going to do with that?" Bloodfoot grumbled.

Ian walked to the rear of the reptile and plunged the knife into its tail, "Christie asked for us to bring back some gator tail."

Bloodfoot smiled to himself and glanced over to see a paramedic working on Randy. He pocketed the souvenir tooth and walked over, "What have we here?"

"Sir, it looks like a fractured arm. We will take him back in the chopper, and you men can pick him up at the hospital later," replied the paramedic.

Bloodfoot gave a slight smile and took a step back. When Randy nodded and said he'd be alright, he turned his back and proceeded to the helicopter with the medic. That's when Bloodfoot struck. Without warning, he grabbed Randy's hurt arm and slammed his flat hand on his shoulder.

Randy let out a painful cry as the paramedic looked on in shock, and a sheriff's deputy pulled his gun.

"What the hell are you doing?" the medic screeched.

Bloodfood grinned and replied, "I just healed my man. I popped his shoulder back in place."

They watched as Randy rotated his shoulder a few times before taking the sling off his arm. Turning to face them with a tear in his eye, he replied, "Thanks, next time warn me."

"No way. A warning would leave you tensed up. It wouldn't work," Bloodfoot replied with a thundering laugh.

The deputy and paramedics couldn't get away from the crazy hunters fast enough. They took pictures of the immense reptile and made sure everybody was safe, then promised a van was on the way to pick them up and disappeared into the sky.

22

Virgil Goodman and Randy Taylor were in a rented Ford Explorer headed South. Another hour on Highway 7, and they'd be at Virgil's house.

After the successful hunt for the last AlliCroc, Virgil had his crew take the *Endurance* back home to Port Everglades while he and Randy had some unfinished business to deal with. Since Bloodfoot was a captain, it was clear that he would steer the boat as long as he gave Ian some steering time as well.

The Ford Explorer pulled into the driveway at dusk with the high beams shining at the front door. Randy notified his elite police buddies surveilling the house to stand guard in case things went south.

Virgil honked the horn twice and stepped out of the vehicle. He saw the window drapes slide slightly to the side and knew Don was watching.

"It's over, Don. AlliCroc is dead, and so is Dr. Johnny Lee. Come out and face the music. If you hurt one hair on Jeanne's head, I will kill you," Virgil shouted.

At that point, Randy exited the vehicle with his gun drawn, "Don Henderson, I'm Sergeant Randy Taylor, Fort Lauderdale P.D. Come out with your hands up!"

After a brief moment the front door opened, and a remorseful Don Henderson walked out with his hands up. Randy stepped forward and handcuffed him as his fellow officers emerged.

Jeanne ran out of the house and landed in Virgil's open arms, "I'm so happy you made it back. Don told me stories about that alligator croc monster that made me shudder," she said, giving him a hug so tight it made him cough.

"I'm just happy our idiot friend here didn't hurt you," Virgil replied.

Jeanne looked over at their fallen friend and scoffed, "He's lucky I didn't hurt him."

Virgil and Jeanne walked over when they placed Don in the backseat of a police car that seemed to come out of nowhere. Randy stopped them before they reached Don.

"Look, Virgil, Don's in enough trouble. Please don't kill him."

Virgil looked surprised and answered, "Whatever do you mean, Officer Taylor?"

Virgil knew better than to cause a scene in front of his fellow officers. He casually reached into his shirt pocket, pulled out a pack of his camel non-filtered cigarettes and lit one. Puffing a long cloud of blue smoke, he walked up to the police car.

"Donald, you're lucky you're handcuffed in the backseat of this car because if you were standing here without these fine officers walking around, I'd beat you to death with my shoe."

"I'm sorry, Virgil. You know I wouldn't hurt Jeanne. If we could have kept AlliCroc alive, we'd be rich. I would have cut you guys in on it," he replied feebly.

"I know, I know. 'Nature said it couldn't be done, but man made it happen.' Now, look where you're going. I hope it was worth it," Virgil said flatly, wrapping an arm around Jeanne as they turned and walked away. Virgil's teeth ground as he fought the urge to kill his old friend.

Three days after the formidable hunt, the crew of the *Endurance* were celebrating at the Anchor Bar along with Captain Bloodfoot and Sergeant Randy Taylor.

A new bartender named Kelly was serving up another round at the crowded corner table when the men cheered as she finally dropped off bottles of apricot brandy, Sailor Jerry rum and Crown Royal and told them to help themselves, as she couldn't keep up.

"Thank you, my fair lady. This should save you quite a few steps," Bloodfoot said, smiling as he unscrewed the bottle of his favorite rum.

"I didn't know how much longer I could keep running back to this table," she replied, sliding a chair over from the next table and having a seat.

Ian was happy she sat with them and quickly got up and retrieved another shot glass from behind the bar, "This should knock the edge off," he said, filling the glasses with his bottle of Crown.

"Oh, I can't," she said halfheartedly.

"Drink it!" Ian replied as he and the others raised their glasses.

She thought about it for a fraction of a second, then raised her glass, "Cheers to my new friends!"

"By the way, where's my man Carlos?" Ian asked.

"He was fired. They caught him knee-deep in a liars' poker game at the bar," she replied, getting up to continue working. "While he was working!"

"Damn, we used to play the game all the time in here," Ian shrugged.

As the night wore on, Bloodfoot watched a tall young man enter with a pretty redhead lady, "Now there's a tall fella," he said, triggering everybody to turn their heads.

"What did you do now? I think they are coming this way," Virgil stated.

"They're probably looking for Ian. I think everybody in this bar knows him," Bloodfoot grunted.

"He probably owes them money from liars' poker," Bill snickered.

They watched as the two eyeballed their table and walked over, "Excuse me, are you the guys that killed that huge fucking reptile?"

"Watch your language, Ned," the lady said, jabbing him in the ribs with her elbow.

Bloodfoot smiled, "Word gets around quick. Yes, we are. We killed it far from here, up the West Coast, about five hours from here."

"My friends and I were attacked by that monster. We were camping near Clearview State Park," she explained.

"Then we searched for it and found it the day it attacked a family in a boat. We were there when you guys landed with a helicopter," Ned added.

"Small world," said Bloodfoot, waving a hand for them to join the table while the crew toasted their good health.

While the men at the table listened to Ned talk about the adventures they had searching for the reptile and the sad death of their friend Tommy, Taylor Wilson pulled into the parking lot and stepped out of her new Bronco. She was headed inside when she walked by Elaine and Marge and overheard one of them say, *"We will just stay long enough to thank those guys for killing that monster."*

She stopped in her tracks and asked, "Excuse me, I couldn't help but overhear what you just said. Were you two attacked by that gigantic reptile near the springs?"

They looked stunned, and Marge replied, "Yes, it ran after us; we were lucky to get away."

"Me too!" Taylor replied eagerly. "What are you two doing here? Wow, what a small world."

"We heard this is where the hunters that killed it hang out," replied Elaine.

"Me too!" Taylor repeated.

"Besides that, we just live down the street," Marge added.

"I live here too!" Taylor replied with a surprised look.

"Let's go meet those guys and tell them thank you," they said in unison, heading for the door.

They walked into the bar and found the table with no problem. It was the crowded one with smoke-filled cigar stench hanging above like a thundercloud.

They walked to the table to thank the men and were offered chairs so the men could hear their stories.

Hours later, the entire bar had listened to the wild tales of the reptile while Kelly stood on the bar and toasted the hunters and survivors of the thirty-eight-foot reptile they called AlliCroc.

Other Bruce Norris Books

2 - What Lurks Below

3 - Escape Socotra Island...

dead men still tell no tales

www.ingramcontent.com/pod-product-compliance
Lightning Source LLC
Chambersburg PA
CBHW051505120626
46551CB00012B/778